Education and Social Change

Themes in the History of American Schooling

Education and Social Change

Themes in the History of American Schooling

John L. Rury
DePaul University

2002

LAWRENCE ERLBAUM ASSOCIATES, PUBLISHERS
Mahwah, New Jersey   London

Lawrence Erlbaum Associates, Inc., Publishers
10 Industrial Avenue
Mahwah, NJ 07430

Cover design by Kathryn Houghtaling Lacey

Library of Congress Cataloging-in-Publication Data

Rury, John L., 1951–   .
Education and social change : themes in the history of American
schooling / John Rury.

   p.   cm. — (Social foundations in education)

Includes bibliographical references and index.
ISBN 0-8058-3339-0 (paper : alk. paper)
1. Education—United States—History. 2. Educational sociology—
United States. 3. Social change—United States. I. Title. II. Series.
LA205 .R67   2002
370'.973—dc21
2001056913
CIP

Printed in the United States of America
10 9 8 7 6 5 4 3 2

To Aida

Contents

Preface

Education and social change are facets of experience that sometimes affect our lives in dramatic fashion. As I was completing the final steps in preparing this book, the tragic September 11 attack on the World Trade Center in New York and the Pentagon in Washington shocked the nation. This was a singular event, in terms of both its savagery and its impact on the world. It also represented an unusually poignant moment, one that juxtaposed the mores and bearing of modern civilization against those wishing for a more traditional and illiberal society. The individuals and organizations that planned and executed this barbaric act imagined themselves fighting the forces of social change that they associated with the United States in particular, and with Western civilization in general. Even though it was not among the immediate targets, a part of what they objected to was the contemporary educational system and its role in perpetuating and extending modern society.

In some respects the connection between education and the September 11 tragedy was quite direct. Many commentators have observed the irony in these terrorists' use of current technology and sophisticated communication and coordination strategies to effect their deadly plans. They employed the instruments and the techniques of modern society to attack it, and to do this they required schooling. This included both technical training and more general education in the organization and execution of complex operations. The leaders of the attack were highly literate, sophisticated, and systematic. Although they saw themselves as battling the forces of modernity, these extremists were required to learn the critical, rationalistic, and calculating modalities that have come to characterize today's society, and to do so within institutions of formal instruction. Even in the case of this terrible tragedy born of conflict, it is possible to see education and social change as inextricably tied to one another.

The devastation of September 11 also revealed how we often have taken the conditions of modern life for granted. We fly in airplanes, work in skyscrapers, and communicate instantly across vast distances. We publicly object to discrimination, celebrate principles of equality, and cherish the idea of freedom. We also hold an extraordinary belief in the transforming power of education. These facets of contemporary American experience, however, have not existed since time immemorial. To one extent or another, each is the consequence of a vast and complex process of social change that has unfolded over a period of several hundred years. They also are the result of human sacrifice and anguish, conflict and struggle to achieve a better life. Such change represents a course of events that continues today, and one that has come to affect much of the rest of the world as well. This is partly what enraged the September 11 attackers, and yet their actions may have contributed to the perpetuation of these tendencies. Understanding this process of social conflict, transformation, and renewal is critical to deepening our appreciation of who we are, and how we can best contend with what lies ahead. It is to this end that this book is committed, focusing on the particular question of education as a condition and aspect of social change.

This also is a history book, one that addresses a broad and complicated topic. Its purpose is both analytic and descriptive, relating what has transpired and explaining why events have taken a particular path. Finding the proper balance between these different goals has often proved difficult for me as a historian. But I trust this book is a testimony to the importance of the goal. It is meant to be an aid for readers just beginning to think about these questions, although I hope that others also will find it interesting and useful. It is intended to help generate insights into the ways in which formal systems and practices of education have been related to social change. In this respect, it is an exercise in the history of education, a field of inquiry and explanation with a long and distinguished tradition of its own. Hopefully, the book will convey some of the power of this branch of scholarship as a means of comprehending the present and contemplating the future.

A final word about the events of September 11: Although the attackers may have intended to strike a blow against social change, the historical record suggests that they surely will not succeed in significantly altering it. This is partly the consequence of their own delimited comprehension of the problem they set out to address, a reflection of an educational process that was doubtlessly circumscribed and distorted. They appear to have believed that they were attacking a thing, an evil entity represented by the physical structures they destroyed. If history is a guide, however, it appears they were tragically mistaken. The process of social change is the consequence of human action, people making decisions every day, and struggling to transform their lives in countless ways. As a result of these shocking events security measures may increase, but otherwise the attacks are unlikely to have the intended effect. This is history in the making, of course, and it is hazardous to predict the outcome of recent events, but the course of social change is difficult to alter. Indeed, these attacks have only strengthened the resolve of many Americans, at the same time that people everywhere were awakened to certain issues they hitherto may have overlooked—such as worldwide inequity and intolerance. It is this quality of human agency that ultimately lies at the heart of social change: the ability to adapt to shifting historical circumstances and to devise imaginative and effectual responses to the problems that arise from them. To a very large extent, such agency is the focal point of this book, as reflected in the realm of education and related issues. Understanding this aspect of life, after all, may be our best hope for posterity.

ACKNOWLEDGMENTS

In writing a book an author incurs many debts. In the 2 years that I have been at work on this project, I have amassed a number of my own. The first is to Lane Akers, my editor at Lawrence Erlbaum Associates, who conceived of a book such as this, and asked me to write it—although I am not certain this is quite the book Lane had in mind. At the time I was a little astonished and somewhat doubtful, but I eventually warmed to the idea and finally came to relish it. I have learned a great deal in the interim, about both the history of education and writing for a general audience. I hope that the readers of this book find these lessons to have been advantageous.

It is a pleasure to note that the preparation of this volume was generously supported by the Spencer Foundation. This assistance did not take the form of a grant, Spencer's typical means of sustaining scholarship, but rather as "research days" afforded me while I worked as a program officer at the foundation. This enlightened policy, started by President Patricia Albjerg Graham and continued under her successor, Ellen Condliffe Lagemann, allowed me and other program-staff members to maintain a scholarly life while reading and considering the scholarship of others. Both Pat and Ellen were keen supporters of this particular project as well, and kindly offered their valuable time to read and comment on the book while it was in preparation. It has been a joy to work with two such experienced and accomplished historians while at Spencer, and each has been a source of inspiration and guidance. Of course, the Spencer Foundation itself provided a most stimulating and supportive environment for thinking about the issues discussed in the book, and my other colleagues there were unfailingly helpful and patient as I struggled with various questions related to this project. I should add the usual caveat that this work in no way expresses the opinion of the Spencer Foundation or any of its officers.

The preparation of this book has also benefited from the critical reading and advice of a number of other scholars. John Burton, Susan Dauber, Tim Reagan, and Wayne Urban commented on different portions of the manuscript, and B. Edward McLellan, Jeffrey Mirel, and Jennings Wagonner provided reactions to the entire book (along with Pat Graham and Ellen Lagemann). Each offered valuable observations for revising and improving the text. I have attempted to adopt their numerous suggestions, but many problems undoubtedly remain. Consequently, the customary academic aphorisms are especially applicable in this case: My friends should remain blameless for my own shortcomings as a historian, and responsibility for any errors and infelicities that remain is mine alone.

I also would like to acknowledge the support of DePaul University, particularly Executive Vice President Richard Meister and the School of Education, for granting me a leave to work at Spencer, and by extension on this book. A project such as this would be impossible without the advantages afforded by modern library resources, including technological capabilities. The staff members of DePaul University's libraries have been invariably helpful as I have requested books and other materials, many through interlibrary loan. DePaul's extensive array of electronic database resources has been invaluable as well, making it possible to locate an astonishing range of materials from the comfort of my office at home.

Finally, it is important to note the sustenance I received from my family. My teenage sons, Aaron and Derek, offered edification and perspective as I have watched them learn and grow over the years. With this project they endured yet another term of Dad's tying up household computer resources. They also exhibited remarkable good cheer in the face of all-too-frequent references to history and education. One can only hope that the cultivation of such forbearance ultimately will serve them well in life.

To close, I especially would like to acknowledge the support and assistance of my wife, Aida Alaka, who has been a steadfast and enthusiastic advocate of this project since its inception. Although not a historian herself, and engaged with her own demanding professional career, she has been unstinting in her willingness to endure a spouse's private fixation with obscure historical events and seemingly arcane social science concepts. She also is an excellent writer and an experienced editor, and although I would scarcely hazard her appraisal of the manuscript, she has been a discerning and persistent critic of my writing throughout the project. Beyond all that, she is a continuing inspiration and an endless source of encouragement—and it is for these reasons, among countless others, that I dedicate the book to her.

—*John L. Rury*
September 2001

Introduction: History, Social Change, and Education

This book is an introduction to the history of American education. It approaches the topic by considering ways in which education has been related to social change. Accordingly, it begins with a simple question: Do schools change society, or does society change the schools? Obviously, the answer is more complicated than this rather straightforward way of expressing the matter suggests. As one might guess, influences run in both directions. Education clearly affects the course of social development, and schools also invariably reflect the influence of their immediate social environment. Still, the question of fundamental relationships remains. Can schools function effectively as instruments of social change? Or are they shaped by larger social, economic, and political forces at play in society, reflecting and amplifying these influences but exerting relatively little influence of their own?

History can help to answer such questions. There have been a number of points in the American past when reformers believed that education could change society, and much time and energy was devoted to improving society through schooling. But such efforts also raised nagging questions: Is relying on educational institutions to address larger social problems a strategy ultimately doomed to failure or disappointment? The answer to this question is a persistent puzzle in American history, for people in this country have placed uncommon faith in the power of education to improve society. As historian Henry Perkinson noted more than three decades ago, education has been an "imperfect panacea" for curing the nation's ills (Perkinson, 1968). But even Perkinson did not say what the schools *can* accomplish.

As already suggested, education includes a very broad set of activities, so as a way of focusing the discussion this book concentrates on schools and other institutions of formal education. It is not intended to be a comprehensive examination of these issues. Instead, as the title suggests, it is thematic, looking at particular incidents and periods in the American

1

experience with education that help to illuminate general tendencies and patterns in the past. The book has been designed to feature moments in history that were especially telling and influential in establishing the system of education that exists today. By examining key steps in the evolution of the current school system, after all, it is possible to comprehend ways in which education is related to larger patterns of social change.

Obviously, this book is somewhat different from other texts about the history of American education. For one thing, it does not pretend to include everything. Names and dates are hardly its major concern. Rather, the book's goal is to help one *think* about history, and the ways in which social institutions such as schools change, along with the rest of society. Of course, historical details are important. Good thinking requires attention to particulars, and evidence is critical to the assessment of any argument, historical or otherwise. So there is some exposition of developments, personalities, and even dates of key events in the past, matters every reader should pay attention to. Beyond the details of history, however, there is the significance of ideas, key concepts that are used to interpret history and think about historical change, past and present. Many of these ideas are drawn from the social sciences and have been developed to explain important patterns of social change in the past. Such concepts are critical tools to be used in thinking about processes as large and complex as meaningful social change. Without them it may be impossible to comprehend how shifts in the social structure have been linked to education and schooling. It is critical, in that case, to devote some attention to a few of the ideas and concepts that will be encountered in the narrative that follows. The issue of history and social theory is considered in greater detail later.

WHY STUDY HISTORY?

What is the value of history? This is hardly a rhetorical question; indeed, it undoubtedly is asked quite often, surely even about the history of education. To understand educational problems and their relationship to social change, the idea of studying history can seem patently ridiculous. Would one not be better served by examining contemporary issues, and devising solutions to present-day problems? What can the experiences of people who lived a hundred years ago or more possibly tell anyone about today? What has history got to do with education?

Things change. It is commonplace today for people to observe that society is different from not so very long ago. In fact, standing at the start of a new millennium, it is not unusual to hear someone say that things are changing faster today than ever before. The daily news contributes to this impression, of course, with its constant drumbeat of reports about shifting social views and attitudes, and political changes from one election to the next. There is a steady stream of information about "progress" in one sphere of life or another, and the ever-advancing march of technology. Given this, who can doubt that the present is an era of significant social development? Why should anyone look to the past to understand it?

History poses challenges to such questions. Are people justified in making such assumptions about the present? Because of the idea of progress, there is a tendency to believe that society today is somehow different—even better—than the social order of the past. After all, people then were "old-fashioned," and the public knows so much more today. Or does it? How does one know that the pace of change is faster today than in the past? It is possible, after all, that society in earlier periods of history experienced even greater shifts than can be discerned in the present. To many today this would come as a surprise. There is a natural inclination to see one's own time as the most interesting and dynamic, if only because the present is known so much better than the past—although many people today see the future as being even better. There are pessimists too, of course, and major problems loom on the horizon, but most seem to believe that progress has been good and expect it to continue. This is the lure of presentism, and what might also be called an intrinsic belief in progress (Nevins, 1938).

But in fact the present is not the only period of notable change. Things changed quite rapidly in earlier periods, in some respects at a faster rate than change is evident at this time. Indeed, in many ways the world today is in an era of considerable social stability, although this also is an era of significant shifts in many areas of life. Truly revolutionary change on a very large scale occurred in the more distant past (Aghion & Williamson, 1998). It was those earlier processes of change and adaptation that set the stage for the shifts evident in the present. One of the great values in studying history, in that case, is to better appreciate the dynamic quality of one's own times, by examining the challenges faced by those who lived in earlier periods. And everyone has something to learn from seeing how people responded to a rapidly changing social milieu in the past (Tuchman, 1978).

Of course it is not easy to comprehend the scope or impact of changes in one's own time; social change is a tricky subject. For one thing, it is everywhere. It is the very nature of society to constantly change, after all, just as individuals and communities develop from one year to another. But all change is not the same. There are major developments and small ones, and it is often hard to distinguish between those that are long-lasting and others destined to have little enduring impact. This is another reason to study history, to help one see how society has developed over time, and to understand the ways social change is influenced by certain events and circumstances, and by people. In this way too, history can help individuals and groups to understand how they arrived at the present state of affairs, although it never provides a formula for figuring out any particular dilemma. At its best, history may offer a point of comparison, to better understand a people's own circumstances, and themselves.

What does this have to do with education and schools? Like social change, education also is a difficult subject, even without considering its history. On one hand education is a complex human experience of individual growth and development, a process we encounter in our own everyday lives (Dewey, 1938). In other respects it also is the social and institutional activity of transmitting knowledge and values from one generation to the next, a process involving large segments of society and in recent times billions of dollars. And because education is linked to power and social status, it is a subject for debate on all sides of the political spectrum. In its institutional form, education also has become a means of imparting and certifying skills and knowledge essential to the welfare of society, a fact that has made it a topic of great public interest in recent years. Understanding education in its many dimensions, in that case, can be a challenging proposition.

Because of these manifold purposes and functions, education often has been closely connected to the historical processes of social development. Indeed, in U.S. history, education has been a centerpiece of important periods of change in American society. It has contributed to economic growth and political change, and it has helped to forge a national identity from the country's rich variety of cultural and social groups. Of course, the process of education itself also has changed a great deal in the past, and it has been influenced by changes in the economy, the political system, and other facets of the social structure. Schools today are quite different in many respects from those in the past, and the purposes of these institutions have changed from one period of history to another.

So one might say that education has been on both sides of the process of social development: both as a causal agent of social change and as an aspect of life that has changed because of other social forces. The link between education and social change, in that case, is complex and constantly evolving. This makes it potentially interesting as a topic of study, and as a vehicle for reflection on the present.

HISTORY AND SOCIAL THEORY

In the past several decades the study of history has grown more difficult and complicated. Historians no longer have a monopoly on the past; they have been joined in their studies by social scientists, especially those in sociology, economics, and political science. This has been a natural development, as many members of these academic disciplines—like historians— have become concerned with studying large-scale social change and its effects on individual lives. Indeed, historical study has become increasingly an interdisciplinary enterprise, with historical sociologists and economic historians, among others, contributing a great deal to the way people think about past events (Abrams, 1982; Rabb & Rotberg, 1982). These newcomers to the study of history have contributed more than just new information, however. The social scientists brought with them a number of ideas and propositions, or theories, about society, to test and refine with the use of historical evidence. These ideas and theories have proven quite useful and influential in the quest to understand how society has developed over the past several centuries and longer, and especially how the process of social change has affected people's lives in earlier times (Skocpol, 1984; Smith, 1991).

Some of these ideas are quite familiar, and have become terms of everyday use in conversation. Social critic Theodore Roszak has described the concepts that help to organize one's thoughts, those that precede information, as Master Ideas (Roszak, 1994). This is because they help one to think about the problems encountered in life, by organizing facts, values, beliefs, and theories so that people can understand the world more easily. Some of these are ideas commonly encountered in school; many have become a part of the conventional wisdom about how society has developed over the years. Roszak suggested that "all men are created equal" is such an idea, a notion that most Americans share as a basic proposition of social interaction. Others are a bit more obscure, but include concepts that are used to interpret facts and make sense of the events in people's lives. Some of the terms that are discussed here can play such a role, especially with regard to understanding such complex social phenomena as education and historical change. Even if they fall short of Roszak's definition of Master Ideas, these abstractions are useful in thinking about the process of social transformation.

Whatever we call them, it is important to have a clear understanding of how historians and social scientists have thought of these concepts, particularly if one is to make use of them in understanding the history of education. Briefly discussing them is also a useful exercise for beginning to think about how society undergoes transition, and how this process has been related to education and schools. It provides some interesting tools to reflect on history, and to consider the course of change that has affected the educational system.

A good example of master abstraction, and perhaps one of the most familiar in everyday usage, is represented by the term *culture*. Broadly defined by anthropologists as the way of life in a human society, culture can be thought of as a set of characteristics or traits that are typical of a social group. These usually include rituals or ceremonies, customs (established patterns of behavior), attitudes, and ideas that are passed down from one generation to the next. It is commonplace to think of these features of social life as especially evident in people from distant or exotic places, but they exist in contemporary American society as well. In fact, a person's own cultural traits are often difficult to recognize simply because they are so familiar. A handy definition of culture is "when one acts like his or her mother but didn't intend to." The tricky part is identifying these traits even when they are considered normal, what anthropologists have come to call "making the familiar strange." Regardless of the social groups in question, in that case, if people exhibit the same patterns of behavior and attitudes or values as previous generations, social scientists often use the term *culture* to describe it. Because it is so encompassing a concept, *culture* is a slippery term to define precisely. But it is indispensable in explaining the process of social change, particularly as it has occurred on a sweeping historical scale—as considered in this book (Kluckhohn, 1949; Kuper, 2000).

Culture is especially useful in thinking about schooling, because education can itself be defined broadly as the process of cultural transmission. If society is to function smoothly, after all, familiar types of behavior need to be taught to each succeeding generation. This does not mean that new generations have to accept the old patterns of behavior or the ideas and attitudes that accompany them. Indeed, younger generations have often rejected key aspects of the culture of their parents. When there is a pattern of new attitudes and behaviors that develops with the young, one can speak of cultural change. And because schools are directly involved in the process of teaching ideas and shaping attitudes, they stand at the very middle of the process of change in culture. A major question in the history of education and schooling, in that case, concerns the process of cultural transformation. How have identifiable patterns of behavior, customs, attitudes, and ideas changed in American history, and how have schools and other forms of education participated in these shifts (Spindler, 1963)? As suggested in the chapters ahead, the answer to this question is complicated and differs from one period of history to the next.

The question of culture gets even more complicated, however. Some social scientists interested in education have employed the concept of culture to pose yet another abstraction: *cultural capital*. This concept is premised on the recognition that all cultures are not equal; certain patterns of behavior, values, and attitudes are more widely admired and rewarded in society than others. Comprehension of classical music, for example, is often taken as a sign of sophistication, as is a taste for fine wines. Knowledge of this sort is taken to represent cultural capital, a command of certain types of information and skills that are venerated by others. Cultural capital can also be a well-developed understanding of history, or the ability to speak a foreign language—especially a high-status language, such as French. People possessing these skills generally are admired in the larger society because such capabilities are rare and considered a sign of sophistication. Cultural capital has more practical dimensions too, such as knowledge of how institutions function or knowing how to behave in certain situations, like being a good conversationalist, or even understanding the importance of doing homework in a timely fashion. Individuals who possess these socially desirable traits hold advantages in social life and often have access to higher status as a consequence. It is in this respect that the term *capital* is relevant. Because these characteristics or conditions allow individuals to do things that they otherwise could not, providing them certain benefits in society, they can be considered to represent a form of wealth (Bourdieu & Coleman, 1991; DiMaggio, 1982; Lamont & Lareau, 1988).

Schools can help to mediate the process of realizing such benefits if they reward the holders of cultural capital with greater claims to credentials or other forms of social recognition. Children with highly educated parents, for instance, have access to books, music, magazines, and media technology that may give them advantages in school. Parents who understand how complex institutions function can pass this knowledge on to their offspring. These are forms of cultural capital that are highly relevant to education today, but every historical period has been marked by one form or another of cultural advantage that can be transferred from one generation to the next. Consequently, *cultural capital* is a useful term in studying the history of education, even if the meaning of the concept is likely to shift from one historical period (or cultural setting) to another (Kalmijn & Kraaykamp, 1996; Lareau & Horvat, 1999; Roscigno, Ainsworth, & Race, 1999).

Another social science term that has gained wide currency in recent years is *social capital*. This idea is similar to cultural capital, but conveys a slightly different point. *Social capital* refers to advantageous attitudes, values, and behavior that are reinforced by the social groups an individual is associated with. It also can refer to networks of association and influence that can benefit people. Knowing the right people to secure a certain advantage, such as lawyers or bankers, can be considered a form of social capital. Tightly knit communities, where people help one another with all types of problems, provide social capital to their residents. When members of these communities share values that encourage socially responsible behavior, such as maintaining a job or attending school regularly, this too is a variety of social capital (Coleman, 1988).

With regard to education, perhaps the most straightforward example of social capital is the effect of local communities on school attendance. It has long been observed, for instance, that some social groups seem to encourage school enrollment more than others. The children of Jewish immigrants in American cities had unusually high levels of school attendance in the early 20th century, even though their parents often were poor and lacked formal education. Similar patterns have been observed more recently among Asian

Americans. Some of this behavior appears to have been due to attitudes in the community that attached great importance to school as a place where young people should spend their time. But historically these groups were poor and did not have conventional forms of cultural capital, such as knowledge of American customs or command of proper English. Such examples demonstrate that it is possible for a group of children to possess high levels of social capital, but relatively low stocks of cultural capital (socially valued knowledge and abilities). In the case of immigrant groups with little cultural capital, social capital may have been a resource that helped them to overcome disadvantages they faced, and perhaps to eventually acquire elements of cultural capital. If a community is quite cohesive and can exert pressure on the young to meet or exceed societal expectations regarding school attendance, we can say that social capital is enhancing their education (Perlmann, 1988; Rotberg, 2001; Zhou & Bankston, 1994).

Of course, this also can work in the opposite direction. There have been groups in the United States that have shunned the schools, for example, and they have discouraged their children from attendance. Such a group may also be quite cohesive and successful at exerting pressure toward compliance, but it is possible to say that these groups have not provided social capital because their values do not provide children any advantage in this regard. Indeed, if their behavior has had a negative influence on school participation, the children may have been disadvantaged in the larger society. In any case, a cohesive and broadly enforced set of community values and expectations defines social capital only if it results in a tangible benefit for the individuals or groups in question. The impact on education depends on the character of the attitudes in question and how they are enforced by the immediate community (Coleman, 1988; Portes, 1998).

Social and cultural capital are examples of ideas that are commonly used to examine the behavior of individuals and social groups. In particular, these concepts are useful for explaining why some individuals and groups succeed in the larger society and others do not. In this respect, both are related to the economic term *human capital,* which refers to differences in skills and knowledge that help explain why some people—and groups—are more economically productive than others. Lawyers and doctors, for example, can perform tasks routinely that would take less knowledgeable people much longer to complete, if they could do them at all. The same principle applies to nearly all jobs that require advanced levels of training. Consequently, people who possess such skills and knowledge typically command higher wages or salaries than those without them. This, according to economists, is the reason why people with higher levels of education usually earn more money than others. As demonstrated later in this volume, human capital has become a critical component of the modern economy (Becker, 1964).

These various conceptions of capital possessed by groups and individuals are important to understanding the development of modern school systems and the way that they function in society. The concepts differ in that human capital—skills and abilities—is usually seen as an outcome of schooling, whereas cultural and social capital—attitudes and behavior—are typically considered factors that help explain success in school. In all three examples, however, capital is generally considered a good thing to possess, whether it is human, cultural, or social. It represents a tangible resource that can be drawn on for social advancement. The terms *cultural* and *social capital* identify resources that contribute to achievement in school and in the larger society. *Human capital* is knowledge and skills that contribute to economic advancement. Together, these are ideas that have special significance in research on education today, and they are relevant to comprehending educational history as well.

Culture and capital are concepts that help one to characterize people and groups, and they can be thought of as properties that allow greater understanding of differences in people. Yet other social science ideas describe vast processes of change in society that create effects on a grand historical scale. One such example is *industrialization*, perhaps the most familiar and significant single concept in recent history. Although it is not as sweeping or universal as culture, it too is indispensable to understanding the process of social change. Industrialization is a term used to represent a host of shifts in society and the organization of work that accompanied the rise of mass production manufacturing. At the most basic level industrialization, or the industrial revolution as it is sometimes called, was a rapid rise in per capita output, or a sharp increase in the productivity of individual workers. This could only be accomplished, of course, by instituting other changes, such as the introduction of new technologies or organizing production processes in new ways. Historically, this first occurred in Great Britain between 1750 and 1850. It happened a little later in the United States, in the mid to late 19th century. And it developed even later in Japan and other countries. Wherever it occurred, however, industrialization had a profound impact on the people who experienced it directly, and it has produced a lasting effect on the organization of society (Ashton, 1948; Brownlee, 1979).

This can be seen in history. Before the industrial revolution the vast majority of people lived in the countryside and worked on the land, in agrarian settings. Most consumer goods were made by artisans, often by hand, and people purchased goods produced locally. This changed dramatically with industrialization. After the industrial revolution large numbers of people were employed in factories and related occupations (such as transportation of industrial goods), and lived in cities where they consumed goods produced elsewhere. They found themselves working longer hours, often performing relatively simple, repetitive tasks, and they exercised little control over their work, as it was often dictated by machines. Altogether, people's lives changed drastically, sometimes in a relatively short time. Industrialization, in that case, meant more than just a shift in production; for many people it meant a whole new way of life, and this in turn certainly affected culture (Laslett, 1965).

The process of industrialization caused many aspects of society to change. This was partly because of the sheer volume of goods and services produced. It enabled cities to be built, and fortunes to be made by a select few. For many people—perhaps most—the increased quantity of commodities meant a rising standard of living. But for others it was a time of wrenching dislocation, especially for those who left the countryside to seek work in distant cities. In the United States many industrial workers came from Europe, traveling thousands of miles to seek employment. The large-scale movement of people from one part of the world to another often led to cultural conflict and political instability. It also meant important changes for education, as schools struggled to prepare students for a new world (Rabb and Rotberg, 1981).

As has been already suggested, industrialization is also associated with the concept of technology, or the use of machinery or other devices to conserve or enhance human labor. Factories called for new forms of work controlled by mechanized processes. This, in turn, had important implications for the development of education, as new forms of knowledge and skill were called into play. It also required new work habits, and close attention to organization and efficiency. Eventually, as a complex industrial society began to emerge, new roles for management focused on planning and the disposition of time. This too would have important implications for education, to meet the requirements of these rapidly changing social roles (Cowan, 1997).

Yet another concept associated with social change—along with industrialization and technology—is *urbanization*. This term refers to the changing spatial arrangement of society, and particularly to the growth of cities, and all of the social problems that became associated with them. Historically, cities grew as markets for the exchange and distribution of goods, and the location of specialized services. With industrialization, however, cities became centers of manufacturing, which required large numbers of workers and complex transportation networks. Expanding cities meant ever more people crowded together, sharing space and struggling over the goals and values that would prevail in the future. This, in turn, entailed the development of social institutions such as schools, but also churches, law enforcement agencies, charities, and a host of governmental entities to oversee social amity. As cities grew they became more complicated, and finding new ways of managing the diverse social groups that made up the population became a major challenge (Monkkonen, 1988; Rabb & Rotberg, 1981).

These changes augmented the importance of formal education. With the growth of large cities, people's relationships with one another seemed to change. Here one encounters the concept of culture once again, this time as a pattern of social behavior peculiar to cities. It was no longer possible to know everyone in the immediate community or on the job. In rapidly growing industrial cities people were constantly coming and going, and close personal relationships, built over a long period of time, became more difficult to sustain. In this context, people began to relate to one another in largely functional terms, based on their occupations and other social characteristics. This also led to changes in social capital, as the social cohesion of communities began to weaken. Historically, it often appeared that social capital was dissipated with these events; shared norms and expectations eroded, and familiar social controls lost their significance. More formal systems of socialization and control, such as the schools and police, gained additional importance as a result. A new institutional culture began to take shape in the largest cities because of these developments (Schnore, 1965, 1974).

All of this made education especially important as a way of certifying a person's knowledge, abilities, and even moral character. If it was impossible to know a man's history, for instance, or even to investigate it by asking others about him, credentials such as diplomas and degrees could at least certify a modicum of understanding and reliability. As the social scientists have put it, *secondary relationships* were substituted for firsthand knowledge of a person's past, and as a result mediating institutions such as schools became especially important in the evolution of society. Established patterns of behavior changed dramatically, and social scientists described the development of a historically new and distinctive urban culture in the largest cities (Palen, 1997).

Social scientists and historians have long noted that both industrialization and urbanization have been linked to a more highly defined social division of labor. Indeed, increased specialization in productive activities is virtually axiomatic during the process of industrial development; it is one of the chief ways productivity gains (the production of goods and services at lower cost) have been realized historically. At the same time, as urbanization advanced, there was a sharpening division of labor in the occupational structure of cities. Larger cities developed more specialized occupations and services. The effects of this are easy to see today. One usually finds the most skilled surgeons in hospitals located in the bigger metropolitan areas, for instance, along with the most exotic health food stores, specialized music distributors, and costume shops. It is only in the biggest cities, after all, that there is a large enough population base to support such specialized activities and interests. The historical development of the division of labor has thus been linked to both industrialization and urbanization. And because the division of labor is closely tied to the need for new and different types of knowledge and skills, it has had profound implications for the development of education in American history (Hawley, 1950).

The division of labor in society is tied to yet another classic concept in social theory: *class conflict*. This idea usually is associated with social inequality and the development of the capitalist economic system. Karl Marx, the famous German revolutionary and philosopher, was probably the best known proponent of the view that capitalism inevitably produces such inequities, but it has had many other adherents too. Today social scientists continue to debate such questions, but few dispute the importance of systematic inequality based on the type of work a person does or how much property he or she owns. And when such inequalities grow extreme, conflict can erupt. Put another way, as the division between owners of capital and workers widened, Marx and other social theorists predicted that people who had nothing but their labor to earn a living with—the working class—would come into conflict with those who owned or otherwise controlled the means of production. There is much evidence of this in history, even though the apocalyptic vision of the Marxists has yet to be fully realized. With industrialization, and particularly the development of the factory system, differences between social classes were aggravated. This led to socialist movements, relatively small in the United States but larger elsewhere, and the development of modern labor unions. Historically, there was considerable strife over the rights and living standard of workers. As discussed later, these incidents included battles over education and schooling, even though class conflict of this sort does not seem to have been a major factor in the evolution of American education (Bowles & Gintis, 1976).

People who occupy conflicting positions in society, of course, often view the world in altogether different ways. And the manner in which they perceive problems often gives shape to their responses to them. Social scientists use the term *ideology* to represent the system of ideas and beliefs that people use to interpret their circumstances and to guide their actions. This is yet another critical concept in comprehending the relationship between education and social change, and it is clearly connected to the definition of culture discussed earlier. One useful way of distinguishing between these terms is to think of culture as principally representing patterns of behavior, and ideology as limited to beliefs and ideas, even though each influences the other. As historian Carl Kaestle has noted, in the United States ideology has been strongly linked to Protestant religion—or, in historical terms, to the Protestant Reformation—and a battery of ideas revolving around the capitalist economic system: private property, hard work, and self-denial for purposes of enrichment. These somewhat disparate elements have worked together through American history to form a coherent worldview that has shaped attitudes and the development of institutions. There are other aspects of ideology that are touched on later, but as noted earlier, the development of values and attitudes clearly is a crucial component of schooling as a social institution. Ideology—and changes in it—consequently have been critical factors in the development of education in the United States (Kaestle, 1983).

Like culture, ideology is a tricky concept. Because ideology also affects the way people see the world, sometimes it is difficult to recognize its impact in everyday life. History provides a useful vehicle for examining the effects of ideology on familiar institutions and events. And some elements of ideology are more important that others. In history there are particular aspects of popular ideology that have been especially important, at least in the United States. *Racism* and *sexism* are batteries of ideas that hold certain groups of people to be inferior in important respects to others, and these ideas have had a profound effect on American society. Racism is an ideology that suggests African Americans and other groups should be seen to be biologically different and less deserving of social status than other groups, particularly Whites. Sexist ideology maintains that women are inferior in terms of intellect and physical stamina to men. Both of these elements of ideology have been powerful influences on popular thought and behavior in American history. Obviously they have had important implications for education, and for comprehending the development of schooling in the United States (Omi & Winant, 1994).

There is more to the question of ideology and its impact on education, however, than the troubling legacy of racism and sexism. Yet another aspect of popular ideology in this country has been equity—or the principle of equality of opportunity. This idea is associated with such other familiar features of American ideology as freedom and fair play. This is contradictory, of course, to the influence of concepts such as racism and sexism, and other features of ideology that would withhold opportunities from one social group or another. It often has been noted that popular ideology in the United States is riddled with such conflicting elements. But these sorts of inconsistencies are part of what has made the United States such a dynamic society, and help to account for the rapid pace of social and institutional change in this country. The concept of equity became a rallying point for reform of schooling throughout American history, but especially in the latter half of the 20th century. It was in this most recent period that the largest wave of reforms to make the schools change society were instituted. And it is the legacy of those efforts that the nation's school system continues to struggle with today (Ravitch, 1983).

Concepts such as culture, industrialization, urbanization, social and human capital, ideology, and equity are useful only to the extent that they allow one to think clearly and creatively about how society changes and ways in which such changes have affected people's lives. In the case of education, these ideas are helpful in interpreting just why schools and related social institutions, such as families and other agencies of socialization, changed over the course of history. Schools have evolved a great deal in the past several centuries, even if certain aspects of education seem to have remained largely the same. But schools have developed in step with other social institutions, and they have responded to forces at play in the larger society.

On the other side of the coin, of course, there is the question of how the process of education, imparting knowledge and skills, and new ideas, has contributed to the course of social change. Popular movements have demanded changes in the social order, and in some instances education has been viewed as a way of ameliorating deeply seated social problems. As noted earlier, studying history enables one to see just how schools and society have interacted. Concepts like those just described make the process of historical assessment manageable, and provide insight into challenges the schools face at present.

THE EVOLUTION OF AMERICAN EDUCATION

Schools are among the most familiar social institutions people encounter in today's complex modern society. They have become an integral element of American culture. Nearly everyone has attended some sort of school for a lengthy period of time, typically during life's most impressionable stages. And for the most part, people's experiences in school have been quite similar, at least as regards the institution itself. Hallways and classrooms are nearly ubiquitous in contemporary schools, as are teachers and principals. Almost all schools divide the day into discrete periods of activity, and follow annual schedules set by state authorities. In the main, schools pursue goals dictated by sponsoring institutions and agencies, such as state governments or churches. And all of them share a commitment to individual growth or human development and responsibility to the future of society.

For most people, these and other aspects of schooling are so ingrained that they are virtually taken for granted, one of the most telling definitions of culture. Historians David Tyack and Larry Cuban have referred to some of these features as the "grammar of schooling," or rules and expectations that define the institution's structure and everyday operations. Because schools contain large numbers of children, for instance, they demand special attention to discipline and order, and they require adult authority in matters of supervision and dispute resolution. Schools also place great emphasis on the routine transmission of formalized knowledge, and the evaluation of learning with more or less standardized instruments of assessment. Of course, schools are also places where people make friends, play games, and do a variety of other things, but these features of our experience do not identify the institution as a school. Rather, it is the rules and formal relationships of power and authority that form the familiar institutional parameters that most people today associate with schools. Memories of these aspects of school life stay with individuals, and seem to be essential to the very concept of "school." If it did not have these characteristics it would hardly qualify as that type of institution (Tyack & Cuban, 1995).

But schools have not always been this way. Indeed, many of these taken-for-granted qualities of schools did not exist in earlier times. These are aspects of schooling that have evolved historically, in response to forces of social change, and to address social problems in the past. People like to think of schools as fixed social entities that do not change (indeed, some say that social stability is a goal of modern schooling), but in fact they have been quite pliable and subject to change throughout history. One of the purposes of studying the history of education, in that case, is to determine just how the familiar structures of today's schools evolved. This, of course, is a requisite step if one would like to change these structures in the future, to make a better school.

How did schools develop in the past, and what caused them to change? These are questions that are central to the history of education, and critical to anyone interested in educational reform. As a prelude to the more detailed discussions in the chapters to follow in this book, it is fitting to take a look at some of the big changes that have affected schools in the past, and consider how they may have been related to some of the concepts we have discussed thus far. Terms such as *industrialization, urbanization, ideology,* and *class struggle,* after all, help one to make sense of the confusing mass of information about the past, and to arrive at generalizations that make it possible to think about present-day problems.

Two hundred years ago, for instance, schools were held in makeshift huts or cabins, or in rented rooms in urban areas. Most of the population lived in the countryside, so small schoolhouses predominated, where any schools existed at all. Children of all ages attended, and teachers conducted many different lessons simultaneously. School sometimes only lasted a few months each session, and attendance often was intermittent. Teachers did not have regular employment, working from one term to the next, and many were hardly better educated than their students. Features of school that people often take for granted, such as a measure of age-grading and a common curriculum, all had to be invented and established as widely accepted routines, as they were in the 19th century during the common school revival and later reforms. But the process of change was generally slow, and it occasionally met with fierce resistance. Building the modern American school system was something of a struggle. This often is forgotten when observers complain about certain aspects of the schools today (Axtell, 1974; Cremin, 1951).

Other features of the now familiar education system developed later. Most teachers in the United States were not professionally trained until the 20th century, at least not in the current sense of the term, and bureaucratic systems of management for education were perfected then as well. New schools for children of different ages, grammar schools and high schools, proliferated at this time also. These changes were driven, however, by population growth and the ever-expanding numbers of children attending schools. This was especially true in the nation's major cities, which grew very rapidly at the turn of the century. Urbanization, in that case, was a central element of educational change. Without the growth of enrollments, modern, bureaucratic school systems would not be possible. Larger numbers of children made age-grading feasible, along with the long-term employment of teachers. These are yet other aspects of schooling generally taken for granted today (Tyack, 1974).

At the same time, the process of industrialization and the growing division of labor became associated with curricular differentiation in schooling, and the development of specific courses of study to prepare students for various careers. By the early 20th century, high school students could choose between industrial education courses, college preparatory programs, and such specialized subjects as home economics and stenography. The idea of linking schools closely to the world of work became known as *vocationalism*. As schooling became associated with a host of different types of jobs, school completion, sometimes called attainment, became an important factor in the allocation of people to various types of employment. Schools were becoming adapted to the development of modern, urban America as it grew more diverse and variegated (Rury, 1991).

Some would say that the education system at that time was becoming an important instrument for assigning people to different positions in the social order, a large-scale sorting machine (Spring, 1976). Others would argue that the schools were engines of opportunity, allowing individuals to aspire to whatever position their talents were suited for (Ravitch, 1978). In either case, the central question was the link between schooling and the growing complexity of the social structure, an outcome of industrialization. As the social division of labor became more complicated, the issues of schooling and training people for productive careers in the new society grew in importance. Linked to this was the question of providing individuals and groups with the skills and knowledge required by the development of the economy, particularly in the 20th century. As technology advanced, and the tasks people were asked to perform became more complex and difficult, the demand for human capital, people with appropriate skills and knowledge, grew significantly. By the latter 20th century there was a revolution in the importance of human capital, and public interest in schooling reached new heights (Goldin, 2001).

These developments, of course, made education a potent political issue, especially in cities but in other settings as well. As schooling came to be seen as an economic and cultural advantage, it also became a point of contention. The history of American education is rife with instances of groups organizing to demand changes in the schools. Such incidents were commonplace in the 19th century, but seem to have increased in frequency with the growing importance of education in people's lives. In the latter half of the 20th century education became an increasingly volatile issue, especially as it was perceived to be related to social and economic status (Ravitch, 1982; Vinovskis, 1999). Historically, much of this agitation has focused on the question of equity, and whether one group or another was being denied equal access to education. In the early 19th century there were debates about working-class children in schools, along with women in secondary and higher education. In the 20th century political conflicts often concerned new ethnic groups, along with questions of school funding. As a consequence, many of the greatest inequalities in American education have been reduced or eliminated, although important disparities still exist. Today the issue of equity in education continues to be a point of frequent partisan contention, and schooling has become a major issue in national politics. Looking at the history of this issue can help one to understand its most recent manifestations (Katznelson & Weir, 1985; Peterson, 1985).

This basic outline demonstrates some of the general ways education has evolved in the United States over the past 200 years, as society has developed in response to industrialization, urban development, and the growing complexity of modern life. The educational system that exists today is the result of a long process of adaptation to changing social conditions. Most of the features of modern schools that are known so well at present were formed in response to specific historical circumstances. And schools will continue to change as they adapt to shifting social forces in the future.

SCHOOLS CHANGE SOCIETY

We have seen that society shapes the evolution of schooling, but what about the converse? How has the development of education changed society? There is, of course, the process of individual development that education typically entails. But what has been the cumulative effect, if any, of this sort of individual change on society writ large? This is a problem that historians have not devoted much attention to. But there are some examples one can highlight.

One is the case of women's education. Early in American history women were largely uneducated. But after the Revolutionary War there was new attention given to education for women. As public school systems were established by the states in the 19th century, most were coeducational, providing boys and girls the same educational opportunities. Female enrollment grew, and by midcentury literacy rates for women in Northern states were just about equal to those for men. Women began to attend academies, high schools, and colleges in greater numbers at this time also. All of these changes preceded the movement of women into jobs requiring higher levels of skill, and the development of the first women's rights movement. Did education "cause" these latter developments? Not entirely, but it certainly contributed to them. It is probably safe to speculate that neither of these large-scale changes in society would have occurred as soon without changes in women's education (Rury, 1991; Tyack & Hansot, 1990).

There is a parallel case of education affecting social change in the case of African Americans. The ancestors of most African Americans came to this country as slaves, and as such were excluded from most forms of conventional schooling, even if they cultivated their own rich forms of informal education. Following the Civil War, after gaining freedom, African Americans enrolled in schools on a mass scale for the first time in history. Although their schools were inferior to those for Whites, these opportunities did result in the development of an educated elite that was able to articulate effective challenges to racism and discrimination in the 20th century. Eventually, African Americans made schooling a defining issue in their struggle for civil rights, with the historic *Brown* case in 1954 standing as a turning point in the movement for equality. Without the development of education as a resource for the Black community, and as an object of struggle, it is doubtful that these changes would have occurred quite as rapidly as they did (Anderson, 1988; Sitkoff, 1993).

These are just two of the most dramatic and profound changes in American society that have been affected, at least in part, by the development of schooling as a formal institution (and they are discussed in greater detail in chap. 4). There are many others, as seen elsewhere in this book. And of course there were other changes, concerning ideology or the larger question of American culture, wherein schools have played a less dramatic but nevertheless important role in the evolution of popular ideas such as equality, democracy, and fair play. Ideology often changes at a slower pace than other aspects of society, so shifts such as these are more difficult to identify and attribute to the schools. But this does not mean that they did not occur. A part of the problem of education and social change, in that case, is to identify less obvious developments such as these, and to make judgments about just how they fit into the relationship of education and society.

In any case, there is evidence that schools have had a considerable impact on society at particular moments in time, even as they have been shaped by industrialization, political developments, and other social changes. All of these events have established the features of modern education that people often take for granted today. It's the analysis of the process that makes history interesting and worthwhile as a mode of analysis, for understanding how the present has arrived, and perhaps what the future holds.

A FINAL WORD ABOUT HISTORY

Henry Ford once said, "History is bunk." Generations of students also have declared it boring. At its worst history is a lifeless list of names and dates, or a set of formulas for describing otherwise intricate and complicated processes of social development. But at its best history is a story complete with human drama, memorable characters, struggle between forces of progress and retrogression, elements of mystery and suspense, and lessons for life writ large. For historians it also is a science, one that requires scrupulous attention to getting the facts straight and testing explanations against the best available information about the past. This means that good history is reliable, at least in the sense that it cannot be disputed on basic matters of evidence. It also means that history is more than just a story, in the sense that it has to strive to achieve a higher level of reliability than mere plausibility or internal consistency. History is also a matter of setting the record straight, attempting to identify what in fact occurred in the past.

Throughout the narrative that follows, the reader will find references to other works, usually contained in parentheses with the date of publication so that the full citation can be located in the bibliography at the back of the book. The text also refers to important authors who have studied a particular topic and who have been especially influential in shaping the work of historians. These references have been included as a way of verifying the facts in this historical account, but also as resources for readers to utilize in investigating particular topics themselves. One should follow up on any questions that may arise in reading this book by looking at some of the relevant citations provided. The book's bibliography, moreover, is hardly exhaustive; there are many other studies in the history of education and related topics that readers may also want investigate. Let this volume mark the beginning of one's thinking about these issues, not the end.

Of course, history is more than just identifying "what happened." The historical record is always incomplete, and the historian has to make judgments about just what is truly significant in the great mass of surviving materials. But the expectations of history as a scholarly field exert a powerful discipline: The story the historian constructs must conform to the historical evidence. The same is true, by the way, of the major ideas just outlined briefly. The use of ideas such as *industrialization* or *ideology* must fit the evidence at hand as well. And historians argue constantly about whether these terms are appropriate to describe a particular period or series of events. Constructing historical explanations, it turns out, is a complicated business, at least if one wants to be faithful to the factual record. And of course, new evidence is constantly being turned up, overturning established explanations and theories and posing challenges to the way people think about the past. The narrative of American education and social change that is presented in this book is informed by the most recent research, but eventually there doubtless will be new perspectives to consider and evidence that challenges some of the interpretations offered herein.

This means that readers have to pay attention to the details of educational history at the same time that they work to construct useful and interesting explanations of social and educational change. Names, dates, and statistical data, consequently, matter to some extent, although not as ends in themselves. They are meaningful insofar as they help to establish and to ratify the ideas and theories that are used to explain and understand the past. In addition to this, there is the task of straightforward historical description. A major part of the historian's task is to paint pictures of the past, to reconstruct the world of the people whose lives and behavior one is trying to understand. In doing this, the goal is to comprehend these people and their social setting in terms of their own understanding of it. It is possible to explain and comprehend; judgment is another matter. The historian aims to reconstruct history as it occurred, while offering explanations that help one understand the past in terms familiar today.

The task of the historian is complicated, in that case, and the challenge of reading history is to construct and test one's own understanding of patterns in the past. In the accounts of historical events presented in this book there are many names and dates. These comprise important place markers in the historical development of American education. They are not furnished for memorization, but rather to provide points of reference in developing one's own comprehension of the development of American society and the educational system that grew out of it and helped to shape it. Names and dates, in this case, are important pieces of the historical puzzle, and it is up to each reader to judge the way they are used in the narrative that follows.

The book also features somewhat detailed accounts of certain events, or chains of events, that have marked the development of American education. At points in the text, these instances, descriptions of particular moments, are used to illustrate certain themes in the history of education. In the narrative that follows, each one is labeled *case*. These episodes are intended to help bring an issue to life, to illuminate the broad trends that a book of this length must dwell on. Education, after all, was a topic that people often were passionate about in the past, and the struggles they engaged in helped to create the school system—and the larger culture—that exists today. One such instance in the history of American education has been chosen to start most of the chapters, and there are yet others sprinkled throughout the narrative. It is hoped that these glances into the lives of people struggling to make education better—even when they encountered determined opposition—prove to be interesting and revealing. They are intended to help illuminate the connection between education and social change as it unfolded in the past. These short case studies touch on a variety of themes, but several of them are concerned with the changing conditions of childhood at different points in time. Others provide a glimpse of conflicts that marked a particular era, or other events that help illuminate a period or historical movement. In each, the intention to offer something of a taste of how people experienced and thought about education, and how educational ideas and institutions changed in different eras. Although these are not highly detailed historical descriptions, hopefully they will lend a greater appreciation of the process of change today as well.

So now the story is ready to begin. The narrative that follows is a history of the institutions and experiences that people have come to call "education," and the way it fits into the larger process of change that has defined modern society. Hopefully, it will help illuminate the educational and social problems that exist today, and stimulate ways of thinking about them a little more clearly and expansively.

CHAPTER TWO

Colonial Origins: Education in a Preindustrial Society

The story begins by considering the development of education and society during the colonial period of American history. Extending from the beginning of the 17th century (1600s) to the time of the American Revolution (1776–1783), this period encompassed nearly two centuries, and witnessed the appearance of a nascent Euro-American society on the North American continent. It was a time of beginnings for many aspects of what has come to be known today as American culture, patterns of behavior and attitudes distinct from those found in Europe. And it was an era of sweeping social changes, even if it predated industrialization and large-scale urban development. Colonial society was agricultural, and it was cast on a small scale. But it was a society in transition, experiencing growth and a process of change that eventually led to the Revolutionary War and the dawn of a new era in American history.

A good way to begin an exploration of colonial society is by considering the experiences of one of its best known and most historically controversial figures. This will provide a glimpse of what it meant to live at this time, and to learn about what is perhaps the most essential aspect of education: the difficult process of growing up.

CASE: PARENTS AND CHILDREN IN A NEW WORLD

Cotton Mather, who lived between 1663 and 1728, was one of the most influential and widely acclaimed men of his time. He was perhaps the leading cleric (minister) and intellectual in New England during the 18th century. He had been named for his maternal grandfather, the well-known English cleric John Cotton. Mather was the pastor of Boston's famous Old North Church, having followed in the footsteps of his father and grandfather in that pulpit. In short, the Mathers were a renowned family; Cotton's father, Increase, even served for a time as president of Harvard College. Cotton was appointed an overseer (or trustee) at the college twice during his lifetime, and is widely credited with being responsible for the establishment of Yale, later turning down its presidency. He also was a controversial figure in the infamous Salem witch trials in 1692, having published a tract against witchcraft a few years earlier. Altogether, he authored hundreds of works, including the famous *Magnalia Christi Americana*—a history of Puritanism in America (Silverman, 1984).

In addition to all this, Mather was an inveterate keeper of diaries, and his daily reflections, unusual even for the most literate of ministers, provide a unique window on the society of his time. For purposes of this account, Mather's chronicles of his family life are most interesting, for they provide insight into the trials and tribulations of a well-known 18th-century parent (Hiner, 1979).

In 1717 Cotton Mather was profoundly troubled. The reason was his children, and his 18-year-old son, Increase, in particular. "Creasy," as his son was nicknamed, had been accused by a local "harlot" of fathering her child out of wedlock. Mather was mortified, writing in his diary, "Oh! Dreadful Case! Oh, Sorrow beyond any that I have met withal! What shall I do now for the foolish youth! What for my afflicted and abased family?" Mather managed to keep the case out of the local courts, and he also kept Creasy confined at home, plying him daily with sermons and remonstrations for piety and good behavior (Hiner, 1979). But Creasy was not altogether contrite. Just two weeks after being accused, Mather wrote that young Increase had "made a worse exhibition of himself unto me ... than I have ever yet met withal."

Seemingly desperate, Mather wrote in his diary, "Oh my God, what shall I do? What shall I do?" He had harbored great hopes for Increase, consciously naming him after his own father in expectation that the child would continue the Mather tradition of conspicuous piety and religious stewardship in colonial Massachusetts (Silverman, 1984). What he found instead was a continuing source of anguish and pain, disappointment tempered by love but nonetheless humbling and humiliating. It was a telling trial of 18th-century parenthood.

Altogether Cotton Mather was father to some 16 children. This was a high number even for colonial America, where the average rate of fertility was about eight children per married woman (four times today's birthrate). But Mather also lived to see all but five of his children die, most of them before the age of four. He buried two wives also, and had married a third just two years prior to learning about the accusations against Creasy (Hiner, 1979). It is possible that the large size of Mather's family, at least in part, represented an effort to compensate for these losses. Some historians and demographers have speculated that high birthrates were a rational response to the terrors of death and uncertainty in the New World; if children were likely to die a family needed more of them (Moran & Vinovskis, 1992). No doubt the revelations about young Creasy did little to assuage Mather's anxieties about his children. To a man of such renowned piety and faith, a wayward son was a test at least as great as the loss of an infant child.

Yet there is abundant evidence that Mather cherished his son deeply. Less than two years after the implications of an illicit union, Creasy was charged with "bearing a part in a night-riot, with some of the most detestable rakes in town." Once again Mather was distraught. "My miserable, miserable, miserable son Increase," he wrote in his diary, at the same time asking, "Oh what shall I do?" After pondering the situation, he decided to send Creasy to stay with his grandfather, who also was upset at his behavior, and to write him a "tremendous letter" threatening that he would "never own him or do for him or look upon him" until he earnestly repented.

Shortly after sending his son away, however, Mather found himself in tears as he asked God to help his son. "Ah poor Increase," he wrote in his diary, "Tho I spake against him, yet I earnestly remember him, and my bowels are troubled for him." A little later, in writing another pastor for help with Creasy, Mather predicted that "when you see him, you will certainly love him" (Silverman, 1984). Creasy continued to be a test to his father's faith until his untimely death at sea in 1724. But Mather's torment upon hearing the news suggests the depth of his affection for the wayward son. "Ah vain world," he wrote, "how little is to be expected in thee and from thee ... disappointed harvests, how frequent are you ... this world will afford us no substantial happiness." In this respect Mather's feelings toward Creasy were not unusual: Mather grieved openly and sorrowfully when each of his children died. The fact that it occurred so frequently, or in the case of Creasy so far away, did nothing to diminish the pain these events occasioned. Youthful indiscretion, sickness, and death were all a part of life for Cotton Mather and other parents in 18th-century British North America. Yet families were bound together with genuine love and affection, even if they were separated by vast distances and long stretches of time. And it was these sentiments that defined parenthood more than any other.

In many respects, Cotton Mather's behavior was quite contrary to what one might expect of an accomplished and didactic 18th-century cleric of his reputation. He did not assert the authority of patriarchy or parenthood, and he did not command his son or threaten him with terrible punishments (apart from an apparently hollow warning of banishment). Nor did he throw him out on his ear, or condemn him to damnation and suffering. Rather, he fretted for him like a dear friend, one who identified with his plight and cared deeply about his prospects for future happiness. Despite his conservative religious background, in this respect Cotton Mather was quite a modern parent for his time, but behavior such as his eventually would come to be characteristic of familial relations in British North America (Morgan, 1966).

Historians have suggested that the Europeans who settled in the New World acquired a distinctive view of life and social relations (Bushman, 1967; Butler, 2000). Part of this was a reaction against Old World traditions of upholding inherited authority, and hierarchical rules dictating status and delimiting opportunity. However much these European settlers may have missed their former society, the New World imposed a different set of expectations on them, and a distinctive way of life that was free of many of the constraints posed by the old order. Even though many young men observed what historian Harvey Graff has described as the "traditional pathways" of following in their father's vocation and station in life, others did not. American children did not even have the memory of European society to constrain them, and alternative pathways may have proved inviting (Graff, 1995).

Cotton Mather, for all of his regard of tradition and respect for authority, was a product of this new social environment. He did not dictate orders to his children as much as he educated them. In this respect it is possible to say that he attempted to transmit a high level of cultural capital to his offspring. But the transfer of cultural capital was never automatic; nor was it often easy, as Mather's experience with Creasy suggests. Mather worried about his children's prospects, but all he could give them was training and wise counsel. It was up to them to make their ways in the world as independent, free individuals. And of course there was Mather's undying affection, the source of his great pleasure in family life and his extraordinary anguish. Such is the puzzle of education in the modern era: How does one prepare the next generation for the challenges of the future, while wanting to protect them from the dangers? It was a dilemma posed especially poignantly in the New World.

LIFE IN A NEW WORLD

As difficult as it may be to imagine today, North America seemed truly a "new world" in the 17th and 18th centuries, the time and place usually referred to as colonial America. At least this was true for the Europeans who came to the Western Hemisphere to settle—or to profit and plunder—between 1492 and 1776. This was a vast stretch of time, of course, and much happened between the moment that the first European settlers arrived in British North America and the American Revolution. A largely English colonial society was established, and it evolved rather quickly from one generation of settlers to the next. Recognizing the complexity of this process of change, it is still possible to make certain general observations about the period as a whole. It was a time quite different from today.

Throughout this time most of North America was an expansive wilderness, inhabited only sporadically by a native population numbering just a few million across the entire continent. It was said that during the 1600s visitors to New England could smell the pine trees more than a hundred miles off the coast. This was doubtless true of other parts of North America also. The first European settlements were tiny, and did not penetrate very far into the interior of the continent. The people in these colonies lived in close proximity to nature, and natural events were a major preoccupation for them, especially the weather, seasonal changes, and encounters with predatory animals or pestilence. Life in these settings was a constant battle against the elements, and hard work was required to forge a living from the wilderness.

Of course, the North American continent was already inhabited when the first waves of English settlers arrived in the 17th century. The Native Americans, or "Indians," as they had been dubbed by Christopher Columbus, were a diverse and occasionally contentious population, embracing hundreds of different social and cultural groupings. The vast majority of them lived in agricultural and hunting societies, cast on a scale considerably smaller than most European nations of the time, even if there were exceptions in certain vast tribal federations. Although the Native American population was substantial, it was spread thinly across the North American landscape. Divided into relatively small and isolated tribes, and without the military technology of the Europeans, the Native Americans were often unable to resist the demands of these newcomers when disputes arose over land or other issues. As a consequence, they were continually defeated, exploited, and pushed out of the way to make room for the expanding European population in the "New World." In educational terms, this was perhaps one of the most basic and profound lessons taught by the experience of colonial settlement: Native Americans were seen as an inferior people by the Europeans, a group that, when not feared, was to be crushed and discarded when they stood in the way of "progress," or to be pitied and "civilized" once they were defeated (Nash, 1974, 2000).

The self-righteous attitudes of Europeans who felt superior to Native Americans took different forms, and were not always expressed in hostility or violence. Some newcomers found themselves beguiled by the handsome features of the natives, or by their seemingly simple, natural lifestyle. But even the "friends" of the Native Americans often sought to convert them to a particular religion, teach them European morality, or alter their culture in yet other ways. This early contact between two vastly different social and cultural traditions marked what was perhaps the first great process of social change in what is today described as American history. It was a transformation that proceeded largely in one direction, with Native American society being gradually and forcefully pushed to the margins of the emerging European-based civilization in North America, even though Europeans certainly learned a great deal from Native Americans in the process (Axtell, 1985). In light of this historical turn of events, the term *New World* is both telling and ironic.

THE DIFFERENT WORLDS OF COLONIAL NORTH AMERICA

The process of cultural interaction and displacement that led to European domination of the Western Hemisphere was in full bloom by the time Englishmen came to settle in the opening years of the 17th century.

In time, British North America came to be a large, diversified land, strung out along the Atlantic seaboard in a series of colonies, each established under different circumstances. Some of these settlements were started by religious expatriates; others were established for personal or collective gain. It was a domain marked by different climates and a varied topography, and settled by people from a wide variety of backgrounds. Accordingly, it is difficult to make generalizations about the colonial population, and about the various educational practices and institutions characteristic of the time. It would be wrong, in that case, to speak of one unitary colonial culture. Instead there were several different societies in British North America during the 17th and 18th centuries. And although they shared a number of similarities, each was quite distinctive—especially when it came to culture and attendant educational practices.

Most historians divide colonial America into three general sections, each representing a large portion of contiguous territory and its corresponding colonial population (Henretta, 1973; Main, 1965). The first, in order of settlement, was the South, which began with the settlement of Jamestown in 1607. Representing the colonies of Virginia, Maryland, the Carolinas, and Georgia, the South was characterized by peculiar forms of commercial agriculture, along with a social structure and cultural tradition well adapted to the region's dominant commercial interests. Just to the north were the middle colonies, the largest of which were Quaker Pennsylvania and Dutch New Amsterdam, later named New York by the English. These colonies, which also included New Jersey and Delaware, featured a heterogeneous mix of peoples who had come to the New World for a variety of purposes. And to the north of the middle colonies was New England, perhaps the best known and most studied of the colonial regions, and often noted in regard to the history of education.

Each of these regions was characterized by a distinctive pattern of economic development and a correspondingly singular set of cultural and political traditions. All of the colonies were preindustrial and local economies were dominated by agriculture, but climate and land made for considerable variation in the way people worked and lived. The South, with its relatively warm climate and long growing season, quickly became dominated by an export economy trading in tobacco and to a lesser degree rice and other crops. At the start of the colonial era land was plentiful in this part of the continent, but labor was not. So Southern landholders turned to involuntary labor, indentured servants at first and then eventually to progressively larger numbers of African slaves. To the North, large-scale agriculture of this sort was rare, although not unknown, and the economy was characterized by small freeholder farms, usually worked by a single family. Such farms generally produced little for the export market, although many participated in expanding local markets, particularly those located near towns and cities (Henretta, 1973; Hofstadter, 1971).

Culturally, different traditions came to characterize each of these large regions, and of course there were innumerable localized customs as well. In the South, for example, the rich planters (or plantation owners) represented the cultural and political leadership of the local society. Even if they were a minority of the population, they set the tone for the prevailing values and patterns of institutional development—including educational practices. Elsewhere, the local colonial leadership was dictated by the circumstances of each colony's founding. Religion inevitably was a major factor in the cultural identification of the different colonies. Of course, religion is a key aspect of culture today too, but it is important to appreciate just how significant it was in the 17th and 18th centuries. In many respects, religious beliefs and practices were a major element of personal identification at that time, much the way nationalism or ethnic identity is today. It was an age of religious ferment, moreover, and there was considerable conflict between warring religious traditions on a world scale. The settlement of British North America followed closely on the heels of the Protestant Reformation and the Catholic counterreformation, events that shaped the way most people thought about the world and themselves (Fischer, 1989; Morgan, 1975). This was especially true when it came to the question of education.

Religion was a critical factor in the settlement of the Northern colonies. In the South, the wealthy planters were generally Anglican, the official Church of England, which had split from Catholicism during the reign of Henry VIII. The New England and middle colonies, however, were largely settled by dissident religious groups, seeking freedom to practice their beliefs outside of the purview of an English society dominated by the established church. The Quakers in Pennsylvania were one such group, along with the Catholics in Maryland, and a little later the so-called Scotch-Irish in Pennsylvania, New York, and elsewhere. But the best known and probably the most important of the religious colonies were those established in New England. And it is there that discussions of the connection between religion and education in American history usually begin.

RELIGION, CULTURE, AND EDUCATION

Most Americans today are familiar with the story of the Pilgrims coming to the territory that eventually became Plymouth Colony in New England during the early 1600s. Like the Pilgrims, many of the first settlers in British North America came in pursuit of religious independence. Other groups seeking to practice their own religion arrived in the same region, with the most important being the Puritans. The Puritans established Massachu-

setts Bay Colony and the city of Boston, which eventually became the most
important settlement in the New England colonies. Their beliefs and ideas
reflected elements of what eventually would become dominant features of
American culture in the years that followed.

The Puritans—along with most other religious groups that arrived in
North America—were resolute Protestants. In particular, they were followers, to one extent or another, of the French theologian John Calvin
(1509–1564), who had rejected papal authority in favor of a church based
on biblical interpretation and faith. They had departed England because
they believed it to be a corrupt and decadent society, and they hoped to establish a more perfect social order based on moral authority and religious
virtue. Like many other Protestants at the time, they rejected what they believed to be empty rituals in Catholic and Anglican religious practices. They
were convinced that each person bore an individual relationship to God,
based on piety and goodness, although they were hardly prudes either.
This, however, did not necessarily mean that they were willing to tolerate
the religious beliefs of others who differed with them. Consequently, there
were occasional conflicts that marked the first century of settlement in
New England (Miller, 1956, 1959; Rutman, 1977). Such clashes notwithstanding, most of the people who eventually came to live in this part of
British North America were Protestants, and believed that the grace of God
was manifest in the behavior of his subjects and the lives they led.

The religious beliefs of the Puritans, the Pilgrims, and other groups
that settled in New England held great significance for the development
of educational practices there. It would not be wrong, in that case, to view
religion as a principal component of the ideology of the age. Perhaps the
most fundamental tenet of Protestantism was the belief that each person
needed to form an individual relationship with God. To do this, of course,
one had to be able to read and interpret the holy scripture, catechisms,
and other religious documents; in particular it meant that every man, or
person, should be able to read the Bible and interpret it himself. This required literacy, and the ability to reason from principles conveyed
through a variety of socially sanctioned texts. It was a set of skills that earlier generations of Europeans had not cultivated widely. In the stalwart
world of Calvinist Protestantism, however, becoming literate and being
knowledgeable were taken as highly esteemed virtues, as long as they
were employed in the service of religion. This meant that historically new
importance was attached to education.

Social theorists have long debated the historical significance of Protestantism, and Calvinism in particular, as a transforming influence in the development of Western civilization. Max Weber, the famous German social
scientist of the early 20th century, argued that the Protestant Reformation
was linked to the rise of capitalism as an economic system, along with its

distinctive pattern of social and ideological practices. In particular, Weber suggested that Protestant, and especially Calvinist, predilections for self-denial (an ethic of simplicity and thrift), hard work, and self-improvement (education and careful investment of wealth) contributed to the development of a class of merchants, financiers, and forward-looking aristocrats who spearheaded the emergence of modern capitalist society (Weber, 1930). It was an ideological outlook especially well suited to capitalism as a social and economic system. In the New World, one might add, it shaped the thinking of thousands of small freeholding farmers and the entrepreneurs who served them as tradesmen, innkeepers, and peddlers. While the relationship between religion and economic and social development was not necessarily direct and immediate, there is broad agreement among historians that the appearance of Protestantism as a social movement in the 16th century presaged an era of unprecedented social change (Landes, 1998).

The movement of Europeans to North America, in that case, can be considered a part of a massive social and ideological shift that occurred between the 16th and 19th centuries (1500–1800). At least this can be said of the first settlers in what became New England. The rise of Protestantism in its various forms signaled a renewed commitment to human perfectibility and moral improvement. Migration to North America also entailed a grand experiment in economic development, one predicated on creating permanent settlements and a new extension of English society. This was different from the colonies of other European powers, which often viewed the New World as a source of immediate wealth rather than long-term development (Landes, 1969). These factors taken together helped to give residents of British North America a rather modern and capitalistic sensibility by the end of the 17th century. Such predilections eventually would contribute to the outbreak of revolution, of course, but they also contributed to new developments in the organization of society.

EDUCATION FOR A NEW WORLD

Schools were fragile institutions in the colonial world, existing alongside older and more familiar agencies of education, the family and the church. Even though there was a high level of rhetorical commitment to formal education in some colonies, in practice it appears that schools typically were attended infrequently, and only a minority of colonial youth would have been considered "educated" by today's standards. Big changes in the economy and the intellectual life of the colonies affected education, but it is not clear that formal schooling played a significant role in these events either. To understand education in much of colonial America, in that case, it is important to consider the ideological, social, and economic forces that shaped social development.

The cultivation of skills and the transmission of culture were major concerns of English settlers in North America, evident almost immediately upon their arrival. This was perhaps most apparent in New England, where early laws called for establishing schools and for educating young men—and eventually young women too. Another early sign of the importance of education and learning was the Puritans' decision to establish Harvard College in 1636. Massachusetts Bay Colony has been described by historians as a "theocratic" society, one that placed special value on the necessity of moral and religious leadership (Miller, 1956). Given this, preparing a cadre of educated leaders was considered essential to the moral and intellectual life of the colony. Such was the principal rationale for creating early colleges. In the wake of religious debates and schisms, other institutions of higher learning were started in nearby Connecticut (Yale College, 1701) and New Jersey (today's Princeton University, 1746) to train yet more religious leaders. Eventually some nine colonial colleges were established, providing a modest but important supply of educated men for the ministry and other professional roles in the colonies (Cremin, 1970).

The colonial colleges were small institutions,.attended by only a handful of the young men in the colonies. They typically possessed just a few buildings and enrolled no more than a couple hundred students, many of whom probably never graduated. Even the sons of colonial intellectuals, like "Creasy" Mather, often did not show an interest in higher education. For most children the principal opportunity for formal instruction was offered by the local schools, which were conducted under a variety of circumstances. These schools also were quite small, and those who bothered to enroll usually did so for less than 7 or 8 years, often attending only 4 or 5 months each term. They studied the Bible, along with spellers, books of prayers, catechisms, and other religious texts. The famous New England Primer was the best known of a wide range of reading materials used to impart lessons in spelling and grammar, along with morality and virtue (Axtell, 1974). In these respects, the school was an extension of the home and the church, where religious instruction and reading were started and developed further. Families with a greater stock of formal education, and the skills and knowledge that accompanied it, could give their children an advantage, of course, in the transmission of cultural capital. But most people in colonial America did not view schooling as a route to higher social status or cultural advantages. Rather, the purpose of formal education was simply to augment the development of reading and reasoning abilities necessary for active participation in the life of a society governed by religious values.

Schools were probably most common in the colonies of New England, where the theocratic and Protestant purposes of formal education were most clearly invoked. In 1647 Massachusetts enacted a law requiring towns of 50 families or more to establish a school, to confound the "Old Deluder Satan" in his never-ending quest to lead Christians astray. Connecticut enacted a similar law just a few years later. Although it is unlikely that most towns large enough to be covered by such actions complied by immediately establishing a school, the appearance of these measures signaled the importance that colonial leaders attached to formal instruction (Cremin, 1970). If the idea of a perfect society, based on a firm set of religious principles, was to be transmitted from the first generation of settlers to their offspring, some form of systematic educational process had to be established.

It would be wrong, however, to assume that such measures marked the development of a modern school system. Schooling in colonial New England was intended to supplement—not supplant—the central role of the family in transmitting religious values and basic literary and computational skills. It was left to local authorities, and the taxpayers, to decide whether formal schooling was even necessary in particular towns and villages. Consequently, the "Old Deluder Satan" law was often honored in the breach, especially if there was not a large number of families interested in providing a school for the children. Here it is possible to see the influence of social capital, or a shared set of values and behavioral norms that affected education. If local communities did not attach importance to creating schools, formal education languished. But the logic of Protestant values regarding education proved hard to resist, especially in Calvinistic New England. As the population of the region grew in the 17th century, the likelihood of schools being opened to serve the children of a town was enhanced. Education remained largely a voluntary affair, and it was left to individual families to decide just how much schooling was needed for their children, even if community norms increasingly influenced such decisions (Axtell, 1974).

Schools in colonial New England—and elsewhere in this period—usually were tiny institutions, run by a single teacher, or *master*, the term used at the time. Outside of Boston, New York, or Philadelphia, schools rarely were larger than a single classroom, and typically were attended by perhaps several dozen students. Although there were a few legendary teachers, such as Ezekial Cheever of the Boston Latin School, many were college students or recent graduates waiting to be called to a pulpit or some other profession. Yet other teachers were men of modest education who were ill suited by temperament or training for other lines of work, and managed schools for lack of better employment (Brown, 1902). Consequently, running a school was a relatively low-status occupation from the very earliest times in American history, even when schools were relatively few and education was at least nominally assigned some importance in the culture and by governing authorities.

The question of schooling notwithstanding, the effort to preserve the religious purposes and the theocratic culture of Puritan New England in the 17th century was generally a failure. This was principally due to population growth and economic development; as the next generation grew older and new waves of immigrants arrived, it became impossible to maintain firm standards of religious conformity. In the 1660s religious leaders loosened requirements for church membership in order to attract the next generation of parishioners, who often lacked the religious zeal of their parents. This was the so-called "halfway covenant." Other religious changes were important too, especially the Great Awakening (discussed later). By the end of the 1600s the original Puritan theocracy had virtually disappeared. Religion continued to be the preeminent factor in the cultural lives of most New Englanders, but church leaders were not able to command the same authority their forefathers had wielded just two generations earlier (Rutman, 1970).

These developments demonstrated just how difficult it was to transfer the values of one generation to the next; it turned out that the transmission of culture could not be legislated. Despite measures such as the "Deluder Satan" law, schools simply could not sustain the traditional religious values of the original Puritan settlers. As noted earlier, moreover, they probably served only a fraction of the children in colonial society. The distinguished educational historian Lawrence Cremin counted just 11 schools in Massachusetts in 1650, serving some 2,339 households (or one for every 212); by 1689 the number of schools had grown to 23 and households to 8,088 (one for every 352) (Cremin, 1970). And as seen earlier, the vast majority of these schools were quite small, and colonial families were rather large. A conservative estimate, in that case, suggests that fewer than 1 in 10 children attended school at any one time. Even if the number of schools increased significantly in the 18th century, as some historians have suggested, many children probably attended them only briefly, if at all (Woody, 1923). Clearly, these institutions were limited in their purview, even in the region with the greatest juridical commitment to education. This suggests that underlying community interest in formal education, a central dimension of the concept of social capital, often was not very strong in early New England, at least by present standards. Many families probably relied on other resources to help impart basic reading skills and other forms of knowledge deemed important (Bailyn, 1960). Schooling simply did not play the critical role that it does today.

But change was in the air. Colonial society was in a state of flux, especially in New England. By the time Cotton Mather endured the torment of observing his children flounder on the road of life, things had changed significantly. The population of British North America expanded inexorably, from less than a hundred thousand in the mid-17th century to about a million by the time of Mather's death in 1728. It would grow to about 3 million by the time of the American Revolution. This was a big increase since the first wave of settlers, even if it still was a relatively small number in the vastness of North America. This growth meant new opportunities for commerce and trade, as well as new lands to be cultivated and regions of the continent's interior to explore (Butler, 2000).

In the two decades following 1720 the volume of colonial exports to England more than doubled (Henretta, 1973). The next generations of settlers moved out of the old settlements, and established new ones. As the tide of trade grew, much of it in farm and timber products, new job opportunities appeared, along with possibilities for enterprising merchants and financiers. Colonial society, although still largely agricultural and technologically primitive, began to exhibit some of the characteristics of modern capitalism. Wealthy merchants controlled larger portions of trade, and farmers produced more crops earmarked for the international markets. People at all levels of society exhibited a new level of interest in acquiring wealth. With this, old commitments to religious ideals and practices began to weaken further. As historian Richard Bushman suggested, in cultural terms this process represented a transition "from Puritan to Yankee" (Bushman, 1967).

Perhaps the most popular single series of cultural events in colonial times marked the Great Awakening, a period of religious revivalism that occurred primarily in the 1730s. British evangelist George Whitefield, a young man gifted with extraordinary oratorical skills, arrived in 1739, and proceeded to travel up and down the colonial seaboard, speaking (or shouting) to growing throngs of listeners. While not directly challenging traditional beliefs, Whitefield recommended a doctrine of salvation based on faith and good works, a gentle revision of the strictly conservative Calvinism of the Puritan forefathers. Where the Puritans had believed in an elect leadership of learned ministers, Whitefield held that intensity of conviction and commitment to God was more important than doctrinaire matters of scriptural interpretation (Heimert, 1966; Hofstadter, 1971; Rutman, 1977).

Ideas such as these dealt a final blow to the Puritan orthodoxy, already weakened by in-migration and intergenerational differences in religious views and practices. But Whitefield and his many followers, including influential Puritan divine Jonathan Edwards, also infused new energy into the Protestant values that underlay colonial society. New colleges were started to train "new light" (or enthusiastic) ministers, and new emphasis was placed on the importance of basic literacy skills for reading the Bible and other religious texts (Cremin, 1970). In a short time, religion became both more accessible and more democratic in orientation.

Yet another important source of influence on the intellectual and cultural life of colonial North America was the broad scientific and ideological movement known as the Enlightenment. Even more diffuse and variegated than the Reformation, the Enlightenment was a revolt among European intellectuals against superstition and religious dogma, and an affirmation of the power of reason and scientific discovery. Its leading English figures included Isaac Newton and John Locke, but there were many others elsewhere. In general, these men stood for ending artificial status distinctions based on principles of "divine right," typically espoused by the European aristocracy. These Enlightenment ideas often are taken for granted today, but they constituted a revolutionary ideology at the time, a point of view sometimes referred to as *modernism*. Representing principles of natural equality between men (people), their ideas spread with the circulation of books, pamphlets, and magazines, and often found an appreciative audience in the New World. After all, the Enlightenment thinkers represented a perspective well suited to the expansive capitalist ethic of British North America, where solving practical problems often came to take precedence over the preservation of orthodoxy. Enlightenment ideas about social equality also were well received in colonial America, as aristocratic pretensions and claims for status had little relevance in a society of landowning farmers, merchants, and planters. Although the direct influence of Enlightenment figures may have been limited to the most literate and cosmopolitan colonists, the ideas of these thinkers were well suited to the social conditions emerging in the New World (Butler, 2000).

Colonial society, in that case, underwent a critical process of social and ideological change in the 17th and 18th centuries. It was shaped both by the changing atmosphere of European intellectual and religious life, and by the evolving economy of the North Atlantic world. But it is clear that the earliest schools in American history were not very effective agencies of change. Rather, the impetus came from the market economy, the arrival of new groups of people with values and religious beliefs different from the original settlers, and a growing populism in religion and politics presaged by the Great Awakening and the arrival of Enlightenment ideas. The changing intellectual, or ideological, atmosphere reflected the growing circulation of books and other reading materials in colonial society, and not the influence of formal education. If anything, schools were intended to be conservative institutions, bulwarks against change that operated by reinforcing traditional beliefs and moral virtues. Insofar as they contributed to a rising level of literacy in colonial America, schools also may have helped to lay the foundations of the period's most far-reaching process of social change: the American Revolution. But more about that later.

SCHOOLS AND LITERACY

New England may have been the most self-consciously religious region in British North America, but it certainly was not the only group of colonies concerned with the transmission of culture. Other social and religious groups settled in the colonies to the south, and they had different traditions of education and cultural transfer. The Dutch brought their own religious practices with them to New Amsterdam, later called New York, and the Quakers (an English dissenting religious group) established the colony of Pennsylvania. Virginia, the Carolinas, and other southern colonies were divided, with the tidewater regions settled by planters interested in exporting tobacco, rice, and other agricultural products, and the Piedmont or backcountry populated by yeoman farmers. The planters generally remained solidly Anglican, whereas other settlers represented a variety of Protestant denominations, although there were small pockets of Catholics in Maryland and elsewhere. Like New England, these colonies also grew substantially in the latter 17th and early 18th centuries, and as new generations of settlers set out on their own, questions of religion and culture inevitably were raised (Greene, 1988). Even if newcomers did not challenge orthodoxy as dramatically as in New England, all were affected by the Great Awakening and the newfound enthusiasm for popular religion it signaled. The result was a gradual lessening of religious differences among the various colonies as time passed. A more populist and liberal (or tolerant) Protestantism, and the values it represented, became a shared feature of all the British colonies in North America by the 18th century (Hofstadter, 1971).

Even so, in the colonies outside New England the number of schools was smaller than in Massachusetts and its neighbors. By Cremin's estimate, in 1689 Virginia counted only 8 schools for more than 7,000 households (or about 1 for every 900); and New York had 11 for about 2,200 families (1 for every 200) (Cremin, 1970). For most colonial children, schooling was not a major element of life, although it appears to have been more important in Northern colonies than in the South. This, of course, points to the connection between religion and education. Children went to school to learn to read for largely religious purposes, and not to prepare for work or for other aspects of life. In New England, the local theocratic authorities had tried to mandate the provision of schooling for religious purposes, and families there clearly valued schools more than in other colonies. Governments rarely advocated schooling elsewhere, especially in the Southern colonies. In a famous statement, Lord Berkeley of Virginia stated in 1671, "I thank God that there are no free schools nor printing, and I hope that we shall not have these [for a] hundred years." Berkeley, who was governor at the time, echoed the view of many aristocrats and wealthy planters, saying that "learning has brought disobedience, and heresy and sects into the world" (Fischer, 1989). As a consequence of attitudes such as this, there was less schooling provided or utilized by the people in the Southern and middle colonies.

Statistics on literacy, the ability to read and write, seem to bear this out, although it is not clear that literacy was always linked to schooling. The region with the highest rates of literacy, measured by counting signatures on wills, was New England. Historian Kenneth Lockridge estimated that about three-quarters of the male population there was literate in the mid-18th century, and nearly 90% by the time of the Revolution. Literacy rates appear to have been somewhat lower in the middle colonies, New York and Pennsylvania, but they were the lowest in the South. Lockridge placed the male literacy rate in Virginia at about 70% by the end of the 18th century. Interestingly, literacy levels in England were comparable to those observed in Virginia. Indeed, historians have noted that schooling and literacy practices in the areas of England that colonists migrated from appear to have been similar to patterns noted in the various colonial settlements. There does seem to have been a general correspondence, in that case, between the amount of schooling provided in the colonies and the levels of literacy observed by historians, an association no doubt linked to cultural practices carried over from the Old World (Fischer, 1989; Lockridge, 1974).

It is uncertain, however, whether literacy was strongly related to formal instruction, particularly in schools of the sort counted above. Lockridge attributed much of the growth of literacy to changing "functional demands of society." By the latter part of the 18th century, he wrote, "land was obtained by purchase, often from an entrepreneur, and deeds were registered in the county court" (Lockridge, 1974). In other words, reading and writing skills became increasingly important for the performance of essential commercial tasks, such as transferring property and keeping accounts. Here again, economic growth appears to have been a cause of social change, along with the development of the legal system and the advent of public record-keeping. In this case, the expansion of commerce and government made basic literacy skills indispensable. And once there was a clearly recognized need for these abilities, people began to find ways of attaining them.

As it turns out, it appears that there were multiple avenues to the attainment of literacy in colonial America. The wealthy often hired private tutors to teach their children to read, especially in the South, and others were taught at home or in other settings, as apprentices, for instance. No doubt there was considerable "on-the-job" learning of requisite skills, and bright, enterprising boys (like young Benjamin Franklin) picked up knowledge from their employers and fellow workers. There was more specialized training for certain jobs also. In the larger cities it was possible to gain essential skills in "writing schools" and commercial classes run by entrepreneurial masters, providing lessons in a variety of subjects deemed important in the growing world of mercantile commerce (Cremin, 1970; Kaestle, 1973a). As literacy became more important, new routes to its achievement became available. And in the most commercially expansive regions of the country, literacy rates among men rose sharply in the 18th century.

The literacy statistics are interesting, in that case, but difficult to interpret. Not surprisingly, in all colonies literacy was highest for those with property and wealth, and it was considerably higher for men than it was for women. But literacy rates among the poor were highest in Puritan New England, a fact that seems to support arguments for the importance of religion and schooling. It was probably the case, moreover, that individuals with greater amounts of schooling possessed higher levels of literacy. Simply put, they could read better. There is little historical evidence about proficiency in reading, however, apart from the general circulation of books, newspapers and other forms of reading material. And on this score there seems to have been only a small variation among the colonies, some of it a function of population size. By and large, British North America was a literate society, even if schools were better developed in one region than another.

Literacy of one sort or another was essential, of course, to the development of colonial society. It aided the transmission of information and knowledge, a process that became increasingly important with the growth of commercial enterprise and political affairs. In general, the circulation of printed materials was quite wide and the number of published items rather large throughout colonial America, especially in towns and cities (Cremin, 1970). Newspaper and magazine circulation figures and book sales (press runs), on the other hand, were generally modest. This suggests that reading materials were not kept or discarded by individuals, but rather were passed from one group of readers to another. In this way, a relatively small volume of printed material probably reached a wide audience. In other words, literacy appears to have had a strongly communal flavor in 18th-century America. As a result, uniformly high levels of literacy proficiency may not have been very important, as long as at least some members of colonial society were relatively good readers. After all, if a man was unable to read something, he may have been able to have it read aloud or the contents described (Brown, 1989). This was done with all types of reading material, from the Bible and religious sermons and commentaries to the hundreds of political tracts and pamphlets that circulated in years preceding the Revolution (Bailyn, 1967; Hofstadter, 1971). Thus the benefits of literacy probably were spread quite widely, and much informal literacy instruction undoubtedly was conducted simply in the everyday exchange of information on a wide variety of topics.

It is likely, in that case, that the levels of literacy that historians have identified in the various colonies were caused by a number of factors, including the availability of schooling, religious values, the volume of reading materials and overall levels of trade, and information exchange. As a consequence of these influences, literacy was considerably more widespread in the New World than in the Old at this time, and the highest levels were to be found in New England, which also had more schools than any other region (Bailyn, 1960; Fischer, 1989; Lockridge, 1974). The precise relationship of literacy and schooling remains something of a historical puzzle, but schools alone did not produce the high levels of reading observed in some of the American colonies.

Literacy is an intriguing problem in itself, but it also raises a number of questions about colonial education. If so few children attended school at this time, and schools played such a small and uncertain role in the educational process, just how was culture transmitted from one generation to the next? How were skills developed, and information imparted about the facts of life in the New World? To answer these questions and others, it is necessary to consider the realm of informal education, or the ways people learned and lived on a daily basis in colonial society. And it is this set of processes that may have constituted the most important educational activities of the age.

EDUCATION BY OTHER MEANS

Society in the New World was cast on a very small scale. As indicated earlier, this was a preindustrial time, when most things were made by hand and people rarely traveled long distances, although commodities increasingly did. Cities were small in comparison to today, and the vast majority of the population rarely set foot in them. Most settlements numbered no more than several dozen families, and visitors were few and relatively far between. Even in such relatively densely populated regions as New England there was a pervasive sense of isolation in many small communities. But most people at the time did not even live in towns or villages. Instead they were on farms scattered across the countryside. European North America was an agricultural society. Even though there was a growing commerce in agricultural produce, lumber, and other goods, most people lived in worlds circumscribed by their immediate families and neighbors (Butler, 2000; Main, 1965).

For most colonial settlers comforts were few, at least by modern standards. Their dwellings were small and cramped, lighting was sparse, and other amenities were rare. Virtually every household chore, even one as simple as drawing water, was performed by some variety of human labor. There was little of what one could call manufacturing on a large scale in colonial America; there was limited economic development. Most things people owned, consequently, were produced by hand, often not at a far distance from where they were used. Skilled labor, necessary to produce many commodities of utility and value, was at a premium. Although the

New World certainly offered abundant resources, long hours of hard work were required to produce the goods that people needed to survive and prosper (Demos, 1970).

Even if life was difficult in colonial North America, however, it was better in many respects than what people endured in Europe. Although there was a great deal of variation on this score, life expectancy was greater in New England than in most parts of the Old World, and there was considerable social stability as well. Compared to Europe, land was abundant, and a man only needed to toil hard to make a living and, with a little luck, to succeed. These favorable conditions also contributed to the lessons of life in the New World (Fischer, 1989; Vinovskis, 1979). People came to believe that hard work was eventually repaid with tangible rewards. In the face of abundant resources, on the other hand, poverty came to be seen as the consequence of an inability or unwillingness to work. Beliefs such as these, reinforced by the resource-rich environment of a sparsely settled colonial society, eventually would become a cornerstone of traditional American ideology.

Given the wealth of natural resources and the small but growing population, labor quickly became the most critical element of the colonial economy. This had profound implications for the social structure of different colonies, depending on the types of labor needed and commodities produced. Shortages of labor in the Southern colonies, where unskilled workers were needed for clearing land and harvesting tobacco (the chief export of the region until after the Revolution), led to the widespread use of White indentured servants and Black slaves. In the North, where agriculture was dominated by subsistence products and local markets rather than export crops, these forms of labor were less prevalent. From the very beginning, in that case, the differing economic conditions of the various colonies, dictated in large part by climate and agricultural production, created distinctions between the principal regions of European North America (Main, 1965). As will be discussed later, this had important implications for education.

In sparsely settled colonial settings there were few institutions. By and large, life revolved around the family, the central unit of productive activities performed today by a host of other institutions. As a rule, families were large in British North America, averaging about eight children per household through most of the 18th century. This was a higher level of fertility than was found in England at the time, and reflected the premium attached to labor in a society where land was acquired relatively easily. Economics historians have suggested that family size was greater in societies with an abundance of land and scarcities of labor: Children were potential helping hands. Historians also have noted that high birth rates were sustained even when certain colonies became densely populated, however. Like Cotton Mather, settlers in British North America valued their children, and sought large families even when circumstances might not have recommended it

(Demos, 1986; Henretta, 1973). In terms of population, early American society was expansive, and the New World conveyed a sense of optimism about the future that often was less evident in European settings.

About 9 out of 10 European settlers in the colonies were farmers of one type or another. Although there was considerable variation in the types of crops they cultivated and the ways they made a living from them, the majority consumed much of what they grew or traded it locally for a limited range of goods and services. This meant that most of their time was taken up with daily tasks of caring for crops, with the busiest times at planting and harvest, and minding animals, preparing food from raw produce and meat, and maintaining the tools, farm implements, and other meager elements of technology at their disposal. They also built and maintained their houses, barns, and other structures necessary for life in relative isolation. Added to this were innumerable other household tasks, such as cleaning, child care, and making and repairing clothing.

For the men of these households, this way of life usually meant caring for 10 or 12 acres of crops, the most that could be planted and harvested with a family's manual labor, along with tending draft animals (horses, oxen, or donkeys), working on buildings, and performing other tasks counted as heavy labor. For the women it meant food preparation, cleaning, clothing repair, and child care. The latter was especially important, given the high fertility rate. With eight children, a colonial woman could be pregnant or nursing a baby almost continually for as many as 24 years. Given the fact that the women typically married in their early twenties, this meant that their years of greatest strength and vitality were preoccupied with childbirth and caring for young children (Henretta, 1973; Mintz & Kellogg, 1988; Norton, 1980). And this was accomplished in a setting with few modern comforts and conveniences. For most families, prospering in conditions such as these required hard work and perseverance. It also called for a special type of education.

With so much to be done, and so much dependent on accomplishing these largely manual tasks, children contributed a great deal to the success of most colonial households. This, of course, provided a strong incentive for having large families. But it also dictated a peculiar form of socialization. Children were raised with the expectation that they would contribute their share of responsibility for the family as a whole. Hard work was not to be shirked; indeed, it was considered a virtue. Relevant skills and bodies of knowledge, ranging from farming, carpentry, husbandry, and hunting to food preservation, soap making, cooking, and sewing, had to be imparted along the way, so that children could perform these tasks and be ready to maintain their own households upon reaching majority. By and large, these were not subjects associated with schooling. At the same time that families worked to survive, consequently, a continuing process of education and training unfolded in most colonial homes. It was a system of social learning well suited to the conditions of the New World; indeed, it was essential for survival (Demos, 1970, 1986; Morgan, 1966). And it set the stage for subsequent developments in the history of American education.

Contrary to some stereotypes of harsh colonial ideas about children, parents in British North America had great affection for their children. The anguish Cotton Mather suffered over the fates of his own children was doubtless felt by many other parents whose offspring were beset by similar catastrophes. Jay Fliegelman has observed that the most popular books in colonial America often dealt with childhood and the transition to adulthood. Colonial Americans appear to have been notably drawn to stories that emphasized the independence of children and the effects of learning lessons from life away from parents and family. This literature was influenced by the ideas of John Locke and other early-18th-century Enlightenment thinkers who suggested that individuality and reason were characteristics parents should foster in children, and not obedience and obsequious loyalty. Colonial fathers were advised, consequently, to forge relationships of friendship and mutual respect with their children, and not to assert their authority or to exert undue control over their families. The result, Fliegelman suggested, was an "American revolution against patriarchal authority" in the 18th century, which defined distinctive patterns of childrearing in British North America (Fliegelman, 1982). Parents loved their children in British North America, but they also wanted them to grow up to be free and independent members of the larger society.

Historians of the colonial family have noted a peculiar custom among many households, particularly in New England and other Northern colonies: sending older children away to board with other families, especially neighbors or relatives. Historians have surmised that this was done to provide training, a sort of apprenticeship in a variety of tasks useful around a colonial household. But why send them away when there was so much work to do at home? Children were sent out, it is speculated, so they could be disciplined more effectively. It undoubtedly also served as a way of imparting independence, helping children to pull away from their immediate family and to form relationships in the larger world (Norton, 1980; Rury, 1988a; Smith, 1980).

Colonial parents worried about pampering their own children, or giving in to their resistance to the regime of hard work in colonial society. They also were concerned about children becoming dependent on their parents or each other. So they sent their children to other households, at the same time that they took in teenage children from other families. This practice principally affected young women, but boys were occasionally boarded out as well. In this way the family served as an institution for somewhat more formal expectations about education. The critical task of imparting knowledge and skills relevant to the challenge of maintaining a household in the New World made this a necessity.

Of course, there were traditional forms of apprenticeship for young men interested in learning a trade. This was a practice with deep roots in European society, and it was observed widely in the colonies. In many respects, boarding children out to other families comprised a special form of apprenticeship. In both cases formal contracts were drawn up, periods of service were outlined, and lessons to be learned were agreed on. It was typical for the host household, or the master in the case of an apprentice, to provide food, lodging, and other necessities of support in exchange for work, and to train and educate the child in the period specified by agreement. As colonial society grew, there was concern about the quality of education and training received by apprentices. Benjamin Franklin, for instance, railed against cruel masters who summarily ordered their charges about and who did not take their education seriously. Franklin himself had suffered such an apprenticeship for a time (Cremin, 1970). Such controversy was testimony to the importance this form of education came to assume in colonial society.

Thus, even if relatively few of North America's European settlers attended school, all of them received an education. They learned from their parents and from the churches they attended, along with the apprentice and "boarding out" arrangements that were so ubiquitous in this period of American history. Given this, it is hardly a wonder that so few institutions of formal learning existed during much of the colonial period. Education was largely an informal affair, embedded in a host of other social relationships and guided by the necessities of life and work in a New World. This would change—somewhat remarkably—in the years to come.

CASE: EDUCATION AND SOCIAL BETTERMENT

The most dramatic change in 18th-century British North America, of course, was the revolution waged by the colonies for independence. Like most political revolutions, this war was accompanied by a larger process of social change, and education was affected profoundly. The American Revolution brought new ideas about schooling and its role in the social order, and these notions eventually led to the appearance of new educational institutions and practices. One example of this new way of thinking about education appeared in New York City in the years immediately following the Revolution.

In the year 1785 the American Revolution against King George of England was drawing to a close. Members of the newly formed New York Manumission Society came together in a large room for their second meeting. Comprised of many of New York's most prominent citizens, including such famous figures as Alexander Hamilton and John Jay, the group was formed to protect recently freed slaves from being kidnapped and shipped to the South, where they could be sold back into slavery. The war had changed New York's population visibly. The city had grown, and it became the temporary capital of the new nation, but there were social changes too. Among other things, the war had increased the number of ex-slaves in New York, as many had run away when their Tory masters fled the country, and ruthless slave traders were rumored to be preying on them. There was the danger of anarchy, as violent abductions of innocent freedmen (ex-slaves) were reported. It was a situation that called for an organized response on the part of New York's leading lights (Rury, 1985).

The men of the Manumission Society were 18th-century liberals, influenced by the ideas of Locke and other Enlightenment thinkers. Given this, they were opposed to slavery and considered it a violation of basic human rights. Yet, being men of means themselves, they also were concerned about the enormous investment that existing slaves represented. Here the ideals of the Enlightenment encountered the hard realities of property relations that underlay the emerging capitalist economy of the New World. Consequently, these men supported a "gradual abolition" of slavery, whereby the children of slaves would be granted freedom upon reaching the age of majority, 21 years old. This, of course, would eventually lead to the end of slavery, when adult slaves all passed away. It was not personally beneficial for slave parents, but it did promise to eliminate slavery in the future, as was eventually done in New York and other Northern states. The wealthy and influential members of the Manumission Society, after all, were interested in social reform, but they did not advocate radical measures that would threaten property. They did not want to upset the existing social order, especially after the chaos of the war, but they were interested in improving society in accordance with principles of freedom and republican democracy articulated in the Revolution (Zilversmit, 1967).

At their second meeting, however, members of the Manumission Society were presented with some troubling news. It was reported that freed slaves had been involved in a series of disturbances in the city. In particular, there were reports that they had become associated with sailors and other individuals of questionable repute, and that they had been observed "playing music" and dancing "in their homes" into the late hours of the night. This information was not happily received, and the conversation quickly turned from the issue of saving ex-slaves to questions of proper behavior and propriety among the freedmen. It was resolved that the society would make its concerns known, and that it would "withhold the benefits" of its association from those parties engaging in such activities. Clearly, the good men of the Manumission Society did not approve of the behavior attributed to certain members of New York's free Black population. At subsequent meetings they considered measures intended to forestall reports of this sort of behavior in the future. They voted to establish two new institutions for New York's free Black residents: a church and a school (Rury, 1985).

The New York African Free School, the Manumission Society's "charity school" for free Black children, opened its doors in 1787, the same year the Constitutional Convention met to discuss a legal framework for governing the new nation. From the beginning the school was intended to provide an education in traditional morality for the children of ex-slaves. Its purpose was to see that they did not "inherit the vices of their parents acquired in slavery or to learn similar ones through want of a proper education." As historian Carl Kaestle has noted, in this regard the school was intended to intervene between these children and their parents, whom the Manumission Society did not believe were fully capable of teaching properly traditional values. Here the purpose was different from the town and district schools of New England and other colonies, which were intended to supplement the education children received at home. Charity schooling, largely confined to the cities of the New World, was supposed to reform the poor, not necessarily to reinforce and extend the values of their parents. And the key to this was teaching them how to behave properly (Kaestle, 1983).

The curriculum of the African Free School, like similar institutions established elsewhere, was dominated by Protestant religion and morality. The school was not large, enrolling just a hundred students at its start. It doubtless was greeted with an understandable suspicion by many members of New York's free Black community. But before long it had succeeded in one of its principal aims: identifying a core of respectable families within the free Black population who could be called on as leaders. It was the members of this group, the Manumission Society's members hoped, who would serve as examples to others, and who could exert pressure on less reputable members of their community to behave properly (Rury, 1985). The men of the Manumission Society were liberals, after all, and believed that even the most recalcitrant and untrustworthy individuals were subject to improvement. It was their considered opinion, however, that the best course of change was in one direction—toward greater conformity with the norms of Protestant rectitude and the values of mercantile capitalism. For them, schooling was an instrument of reform, a way of changing individuals and groups—and ultimately society—for the better.

This was a form of 18th-century education that went well beyond the confines of the immediate community and the family for certain groups of children. The Revolution signaled a distinctive set of attitudes about society and the role of education in changing it. But the ideas and approaches adopted by reformers were not altogether new either. The New York African Free School was a prominent example of a certain type of schooling that had deep roots in the evolution of British North America. As historian Gary Nash noted, European settlement had created a diverse society by the mid-18th century (Nash, 1974/2000). The institutions and methods developed by the Europeans to train and educate other groups, especially Native Americans and Africans, were distinctive, and quite different from those established for their own children. This too was a vital part of the development of education and the transmission of culture in the New World. And it was one that would have important implications for schools as they took shape in the decades following the colonial period as well.

EDUCATION FOR CIVILIZATION

The issues that faced the New York Manumission Society were not entirely new ones in the 18th century. One of the central questions that emerged with the growth of colonial society, one that did not exist in the "old world" of European society, was just how people from vastly different racial and ethnic groups were going to coexist. The answer, by and large, was on terms dictated by the European, White Protestants who comprised the leadership of the various British colonies. This held important implications for the education of non-Europeans, who represented the majority of North America's inhabitants in the 18th century.

By the mid 1700s British North America was home to people who historically had come from three different continents. As noted earlier, they included European settlers and Native Americans. The third group, of course, was Africans, who were brought to resolve the labor crisis, especially in the South but in other colonies as well. Each of these groups comprised a substantial portion of the population in each colony, even though Native Americans generally were pushed to frontier areas, on the fringes of European society. Africans grew significantly in number as the slave trade picked up after the 17th century, and a host of new laws solidified their status as slaves, a category of bondage that had not existed in the English legal tradition prior to that time. By the second half of the 1700s, Africans constituted about a fifth of the colonial population (almost double the proportion of African Americans in the United States today). In some parts of the South, such as South Carolina, Africans outnumbered both Europeans and Native Americans; in the words of historian Peter Wood, they were a "Black majority" (Wood, 1974). And even in such Northern cities as Philadelphia and New York, Africans counted nearly a quarter of the residents—about the same proportion as Blacks in New York City today. All things considered, in that case, colonial America was a multiracial society. Statistically it was not unlike parts of the present United States, even if various groups interacted less frequently. And this raised questions about acculturation and socialization that were impossible to ignore.

The Europeans who settled in North America were acutely aware of the social and cultural diversity posed by the New World. In the South, elaborate legal barriers were erected to separate Whites and Blacks during the 17th century, among them widely different provisions for education. It took time for the institution of slavery to develop completely, but by the early 1700s there could be little doubt that Africans occupied a distinctly inferior social position, even compared to the most destitute European indentured servants (Morgan, 1975). Explanations were constructed to account for these racial differences in social and legal status, with the early development of a racist ideology that would hold non-Whites inherently subservient to Europeans, and to Englishmen in particular. In some quarters there was greater sympathy for the Native American population. Schools were established to accommodate the education of Native Americans, of which the most famous was Dartmouth College, although this feature of the institution did not last long. Most such experiments, however, ended with very few non-Whites receiving an education. For the most part, the schools described thus far in this book were for Whites only (Cremin, 1970; Hofstadter, 1971).

But there were even more ambitious efforts to educate the other peoples of North America. The most important such campaign was launched by the Anglican Church. Concerned about the growth of the colonial population in the closing years of the 17th century, a group of influential Anglicans started the Society for the Propagation of the Gospel in Foreign Parts, or SPG, as it came to be known. The founders of the SPG worried that God-fearing Englishmen would drift away from the church in the relative isolation of the colonial wilderness, or that they would fall under the influence of various dissenting groups prevalent in the colonies, such as the Puritans, Pilgrims, and Quakers. There were yet other religions to worry about also, with the Presbyterians and the dreaded Catholics being perhaps the most prominent. And of course there was also the question of non-Christian residents of the colonies: Native Americans and Africans. Over the next eight decades, the SPG dispatched hundreds of ministers and teachers to the New World, with the aim of "saving" the English population, and converting the non-English people of the colonies to the glories of Anglican faith (Calam, 1971).

The SPG encountered a good deal of resistance to its plan, as one might expect, and in the end it probably accomplished relatively little in the way of conversion. Outside of the cities and large towns, its preachers and teachers found it difficult to find sufficient numbers of Anglicans to support churches and schools. And Native Americans and Africans presented troubling educational dilemmas that proved largely intractable in the end. Perhaps the biggest problem, however, was the failure of the SPG to consider its mission in terms of an educational exchange between cultures. Instead, the SPG believed its duty was one of proselytizing and conversion. In particular, its role was to make good Anglicans of the uneducated Native American and African (slave) populations (Cremin, 1970).

Not surprisingly, the SPG campaign of education for conversion engendered relatively little interest on the part of Native Americans, who generally found the religious content of the SPG schools to be irrelevant to their interests. Slaves, although interested in the skills to be gained in school, often were not allowed to continue by their masters. Indeed, a slave revolt in New York was blamed on a school. Both groups, moreover, had their own traditions of socialization, and doubtless preferred to teach the children their own values, customs, and beliefs (for more on this, see chap. 4). Thus, although the SPG did open many schools, most of them did not last very long, and their cumulative impact was slight. The SPG probably exerted greater influence in the area of publishing. The group printed many books and religious tracts, and thousands of Bibles, which circulated throughout colonial society, an effort that almost certainly reached many more people than the schools (Calam, 1971).

However ineffective the SPG may have been as an educational force in colonial America, it did represent a model of a different kind of educational institution that would become more prevalent in the latter part of the 18th century: urban charity schools like the African Free School described earlier. Often operating in a single classroom, sometimes in the evening or on Sundays, these schools would serve groups that could not afford other types of schooling. As American cities grew, especially in the years following the Revolution, this type of schooling became more commonplace. It is little wonder, in that case, that the Manumission Society decided to create a charity school for the children of freed slaves when given reports of troubling behavior in the city's Black population. They were drawing on a tradition in American education with deep roots in the colonial era. It was a practice that would be put to new uses, however, in the years to come.

BUILDING A NEW NATION

It is an old axiom that political and social upheaval is often accompanied by a revolution in education. The American Revolution, which started nearly a decade before the Constitution was finally drawn up, produced a wide array of social and political changes in British North America. The Revolution was influenced by the ideas of such Enlightenment thinkers as John Locke and Baron Charles Louis Montesquieu. As stated prominently in the Declaration of Independence, it was premised on an assumption that "all men are created equal." Notwithstanding the question of slavery and racial inequities, this view of the social order held profound implications for the political future of the new nation (Bailyn, 1967; Morgan, 1975). It also led to a number of potentially revolutionary changes in the educational arrangements of colonial society.

Among the most important challenges facing the newly formed United States of America was establishing a system of education that would prepare its people for citizenship in a republican political system. The ideals of the Revolution, informed by Enlightenment notions of equality and democratic governance, suggested a political system of citizen rule through popular elections. But this was a new and untried idea. Consequently, when the new government of the former colonies was being debated in the 1780s, many were pessimistic about the prospects for a truly republican form of government. The men who drafted the Constitution included some astute students of history, and experience suggested that republics were doomed to failure. Ancient Rome was often cited as a prominent example. The difficulty seemed to stem from the problem of popular rule by election. Could the common man, poorly informed and subject to agitation by fanatics, be relied on to uphold the principles of fairness and honesty that were vital to the country's future? Prevailing theories of government held that the aristocracy was naturally suited to rule, even if it needed the guidance of representative assemblies, such as England's Parliament. The very idea of a popularly elected government, without the stabilizing influence of a landed aristocracy, was dismissed by many contemporaries as potentially disastrous (Brown, 1996; Tyack, 1967).

Because of these sentiments, Jefferson, Madison, Franklin, and the other leaders of the emerging republic felt that if the new nation was to succeed, education was essential. Voters in a representative democracy, after all, had to be well informed, and prepared to critically assess the arguments and opinions of the day. If democracy was to take root as a political tradition, popular education had to become an American institution. This became a rallying cry of the movement to establish a government for the United States, and a point of departure for the elite men then forging a new political culture in the former British colonies (Cremin, 1970). The question remained, however, of whether such a system of education could succeed in a country as diverse and large as the United States.

A modest number of proposals and recommendations for establishing an educational system accompanied the Revolution. Education and schooling became topics of discussion and debate, the subject of speeches, addresses, articles, and pamphlets. Seven of the new state constitutions made reference to education, and this too prompted debate. Jefferson proposed his famous plan for establishing publicly supported schools throughout Virginia, in a "Bill for the More General Diffusion of Knowledge," even before the Revolution finally ended in 1779. Characteristically, he believed that widely distributed and free schooling would lead to the rise of a "natural aristocracy" of talent and accomplishment, which would provide leaders for the new nation. Jefferson's plan was never adopted, even after he reintroduced it later, but it reflected the significance attached to education in the minds of many Revolutionary leaders (Brown, 1989, 1996).

Among the most prominent of the advocates of a new education after the war was Benjamin Rush, a well-known Philadelphia doctor, professor, and signatory to the Declaration of Independence. Rush called for establishing schools across Pennsylvania, supported by taxes and land grants, citing "fewer pillories and whipping posts and smaller jails" among the chief benefits to society. In a famous statement, Rush advocated making American children into "republican machines" through improved systems of schooling. Noah Webster, author of the first American dictionary and speller, also advocated universal free education to foster national unity. Webster called for schools to establish "an inviolable attachment to their country" in the minds of children, and urged Americans to "begin with the infant in the cradle; let the first word he lisps be Washington" (Rudolph, 1965; Welter, 1962).

As quaint as these ideas may sound today, they represented a radical break with the prevailing educational views and practices of colonial North America. They stand in stark contrast, for instance, with Lord Berkeley's utterances against popular education a hundred years earlier. They also helped to make education a national concern. These new proposals and others like them called for an end to schooling as a purely localized set of practices, undertaken largely for religious purposes or more generally for the "transmission for culture." In the wake of a political revolution, schools suddenly assumed new importance as agencies of political socialization, even though this term—a product of 20th-century social science—was never used at the time. The United States has been described as the world's "first new nation," and in the context of forging a new national identity, especially during the years immediately following the revolution, education gained new significance (Lipset, 1979).

Of course, these were merely proposals offered by elite and well educated national leaders, and the question of whether American schools did in fact come to perform these functions is another matter. In fact, none of the radical calls for new statewide or national systems of education were adopted in this period. Schooling, after all, was largely a local concern, and most Americans at the end of the 18th century had far more pressing concerns to occupy their attention—such as making a living. The creation of systematically organized, state-controlled systems of public education dedicated to purposes of mass socialization would have to wait for another generation of visionary leaders. But a new way of thinking about schooling had been broached by the Revolution, and yet other changes were set in motion that had a more immediate impact on educational practices.

REPUBLICAN MOTHERHOOD

Among the most important and underappreciated effects of the American Revolution was its impact on the lives of colonial women. Like most early modern societies of the Western world, British North America was quite patriarchal. Women had few publicly accorded rights inside or outside of the family structure, rarely worked outside of the home (unless widowed), and usually had little formal education. As noted earlier, statistics on literacy in the 18th century, collected by studying signatures, indicate that the majority of women in colonial society were illiterate. This was even true in New England, where male literacy approached 90% in the late 18th century. Women, it was believed, did not need to read, because they were not recognized as formal members of most colonial churches, a status reserved for men, and were expected to rely on their husbands to read the Bible and conduct business affairs (Brown, 1989; Kerber, 1980).

But there was change afoot. This was partly due to the liberal atmosphere of family life in colonial America, seen earlier in the discussion of Cotton Mather. It was also affected by the fact that women had been relatively few in number through much of colonial American history, a demographic trait typical of many colonial or frontier societies, which are usually settled first by men. This helped to informally raise their status, because men came to value them especially due to their scarcity. Added to these factors was the impact of the Great Awakening, with its sweeping liberalization of traditional religious views and practices. Even if George Whitefield and other leaders of the Great Awakening were not proponents of women's rights, their criticisms of traditional churches may have created more openness to women's participation in religious life. Developments such as these were part of a more gradual shift against patriarchal views and practices in colonial society leading up to the Revolution in the last quarter of the 18th century (Norton, 1980).

There also was evidence of changes in women's education during the colonial period. Kenneth Lockridge noticed a significant shift in women's literacy, growing from the latter part of the 17th century through the time of the revolution. In New England, the proportion of women able to sign their wills increased from less than a third to nearly half in this period. Although a less dramatic change than that observed for men, this development suggests a growing openness to female learning, and perhaps increased involvement by women in formal education (Lockridge, 1974). In the larger cities, "dame schools" appeared during the 18th century, classes conducted by older women intended to teach young children— both boys and girls—basic literacy skills, along with lessons in morality and good behavior. Girls also may have been introduced to domestic arts, sewing, embroidery and the like, and manners in special schools, particularly in the larger cities. As the number of schools increased in more commercially developed parts of the countryside, new opportunities for women's education appeared there also. For example, girls were allowed to attend the short summer sessions in New England schools during the latter 18th century. This may account for some of the observed improvements in literacy, along with greater openness to women's involvement in religious affairs (Sklar, 1993).

Historians suggest, however, that even more sweeping shifts in the lives of colonial women occurred with the advent of the Revolution. This was due in part to the disruptions of daily life that usually accompany war. Many women, for instance, found themselves alone when their husbands left to fight or were killed in the course of the conflict. As a consequence, women ran businesses and conducted the affairs of their husbands in their absence, or longer in the case of those who became widows. They negotiated contracts, paid debts (often without prior knowledge of their existence), managed employees, and conducted correspondence (despite poor literary skills). In short, women were required to fill a variety of male roles, and in doing this they implicitly—and sometimes explicitly—highlighted the question of female abilities.

Beyond this upheaval in gender roles occasioned by the war, there was the ideological impact of the Revolution, with its broadly egalitarian rhetoric and Enlightenment intellectual roots. The words "all men are created equal" in the Declaration of Independence, after all, inevitably raised the question of women's status too. As Abigail Adams famously wrote to her husband, John, "do not forget the ladies" (Norton, 1980). Even though the weight of popular opinion probably did not change much regarding differences between men and women, the possibility that women deserved more rights and greater social recognition became a subject of wider debate. The latter 18th century also saw the development of a nascent movement for women's rights internationally. This was the era of Mary Wollstonecraft's call for women's equality, and other treatises on equality of the sexes. A new view of women's roles was emerging (Rendell, 1985).

There was a shift in thinking about women's education as well, even if it was largely unrelated to more radical propositions for women's rights. Revolutionary leaders, faced with the question of educating citizens for the new republic, came to view American women as a vital resource. Benjamin Rush probably was the best-known proponent of women's education in the years immediately following the revolution, but there were many others as well. The reasoning was straightforward: If children needed to be trained in the virtues of republican government, the task of early education would fall to their mothers. Hence it followed that American women had to be educated, at least enough to read, write, and teach their children moral precepts and principles of American democracy. This is a view of female roles that historians have labeled "republican motherhood," and it became the rationale behind a surge of interest in women's education during the later decades of the 18th century (Brown, 1989; Kerber, 1980).

Benjamin Rush's celebrated "Female Academy" in Philadelphia was only one of perhaps scores of similar institutions established in the United

States in the decades following the Revolution. Unlike Rush's school, however, many others apparently were coeducational. These schools were not large, and many of them probably only lasted a short time. But the very fact of their existence pointed to a new set of attitudes about women's education. These institutions generally did not feature instruction in the classical languages, the curriculum that distinguished the more prestigious male academies of this era. Instead, they typically offered a course in literature, history, languages, and the "domestic arts," subjects deemed appropriate for young ladies (Woody, 1929). These were also subjects well suited for preparing women for the task of educating their own children, particularly their sons, and rearing them for citizenship in the new republican social order. This new female role of "republican motherhood" was ultimately quite conservative, and was tied more closely to the theme of nation building than it was to ideas of women's liberation. At the same time, however, it marked a radical break with the status of previous generations of women, and set the stage for yet other developments in the history of American education (Nash, 2001).

The movement to establish schools for women in the closing years of the 18th century was important, but it would be wrong to suggest that it represented a change in the experiences of most American women. These small and largely ephemeral academies, despite their numbers, could educate just a tiny fraction of the female population. As noted earlier, even in New England women probably attended school only during the summer sessions, and elsewhere few women attended any kind of school at all. In a largely agricultural society, where wealth was accumulated slowly and through painstaking effort, it is hardly surprising that relatively little energy was devoted to women's schooling. Yet the idea that women should be educated, once broached, would prove impossible to repress. In the years to come it would have a transforming effect on the development of the nation's school system.

EDUCATION AND SOCIAL CHANGE IN COLONIAL AMERICA

There can be little doubt that colonial society evolved significantly during the 17th and 18th centuries. As noted earlier, this was partly due to simple population growth; new patterns of behavior appeared as the numbers of Europeans multiplied more than threefold in the century prior to the Revolution. But there were other forces at play too. The value of land increased and the volume of trade surged forward, fostered by an expansive capitalistic ethic that eventually eclipsed the religious and cultural conservatism of the original settlers. This was a gradual process of change, but it was punctuated by such dramatic events as the Great Awakening and the Revolutionary War. British North America remained preindustrial and rural in character, but change was under way. By the end of the 18th century many aspects of an emerging national culture, embracing values of individualism and self-determination, were beginning to be evident. Colonial society was giving way to what is known today as America.

This was not an easy process. It entailed displacement of the Native American population and the movement of millions of people across the Atlantic to the "New World." As many as a fifth of these people were Africans, the vast majority of whom became slaves. Many Europeans, moreover, worked as indentured servants, often with few realistic prospects for freedom. Despite its growth and relative prosperity, colonial society was marked by inequality. This too would become a characteristic of American life.

For most of this period, education played a minor role in the transformation of colonial society. Schools were small and usually reinforced traditional values, and they touched the lives of a fraction of the colonial population. The various avenues of informal education that existed at the time, ranging from apprenticeship to literary circles, may have done more to transmit essential skills than the schools.

The biggest changes in colonial society, however, came with the approach of the Revolution. The movement to sever ties with England, culminating in the Declaration of Independence and the war that followed it, gave birth to a new republican sensibility in British North America, a development with enormous implications for education. In the ferment to establish a new nation on principles of popular rule and representative government, great significance was attached to education as an instrument of political socialization. At the same time, the purview of popular education was widened to include women and certain members of racial minority groups, even if such changes were isolated and episodic. A new vision of civil society was emerging, albeit in fits and starts, but it was one that held great moment for the future of American schools.

The 19th Century: Beginnings
of a Modern School System

The dawn of a new century in 1800 was a momentous time in the United States. The new nation was brimming with optimism and hope for the future as its citizens contemplated the vast continent they had begun to settle. It was a land of great abundance and natural wealth, and great challenges too. The decades to follow marked a time of important transitions in the development of American society, and the history of American education. The United States expanded across continental North America, and national systems of transportation and communication began to take shape. This period also saw the creation of state-supervised systems of public education, beginning with common (or primary) schools and eventually extending to high schools and universities. The reach of schooling expanded significantly as a result, with greater numbers of children attending school for even longer periods of time.

Perhaps the most basic changes in 19th-century America were economic and social: It was a time of industrial development and urbanization. This era brought the Industrial Revolution to the United States, a process that had started decades earlier in England. As suggested in chapter 1, there were important links between industrialization and the development of American schools. Economic development contributed to the expansion and improvement of education; as income grew and the economy became more complex, people attached greater value to schooling. Industry also provided important models for the growing school system. Like most forward-thinking Americans of their day, school leaders were impressed by the power and efficiency of early factories, and they praised the virtues of a disciplined and orderly workforce.

Industrialization stimulated sweeping social change, and this too influenced the development of schooling. Educators worried about the waves of immigrants that industrial growth attracted to American cities, and they devised new educational schemes to prepare children for changing work roles and for citizenship. Guided by an emergent ideology of Protestantism and republicanism, these men and women sought to utilize schooling to inculcate traditional values. Poverty also became a problem of large proportions in rapidly expanding cities. Changes linked to urbanization and inequity caused considerable uncertainty, and the 19th century also was a time when many Americans started worrying about maintaining social order and stability in their lives. This made some cling even more anxiously to the beliefs and practices that had characterized an earlier era, and it sharpened debates over the future course of education in this new and changing society. It was in this context that a foundation for the nation's modern educational system was established.

The 19th century also was a time of ferment in American culture. It was marked by lively debates over questions of childrearing and how best to educate children both in and out of school. Gradually the attitudes and practices of the previous century, with its emphasis on tradition and authority, gave way to more liberal views of education and the rights of children. But the process of change was slow and halting. The newly created American republic was large, and was undergoing rapid—if uneven—social and economic development. Old ways died hard, and new ones struggled to gain acceptance.

CASE: PARENTS AND CHILDREN IN AN AGE OF TRANSITION

No matter what the period, ideas about schooling are inevitably influenced by social norms and expectations regarding the behavior of children. This is an important aspect of ideology as it has affected education. Schools, after all, comprise an important element in the experiences of children, whatever the period. It stands to reason that these institutions will exhibit many of the same concerns that affect parents and other adults concerned with the growth and conduct of children. Looking at debates about childrearing in the 19th century can thus reveal much about the ideological context of American education during its formative years.

Francis Wayland was an important figure in the history of American education. The fourth president of Brown University and an advocate of reform in higher education, he was probably most famous as an author of textbooks on ethics and political economy used widely in high schools and colleges. In 1831, however, he published an anonymous letter in a local Baptist newspaper about an incident in the rearing of his own son, Heman (McLoughlin, 1975/1985). It is a revealing account, because Wayland both described his course of action in this case and attempted to justify it on religious grounds. It provides a rare glimpse into the thinking of a middle-class American parent concerned with the proper upbringing of a child, in a case that also engendered a bit of controversy.

The incident in question occurred when Heman was just 15 months of age (terms in quotations here are Wayland's own). Wayland observed that his son was unusually "self-willed" and that he had a quick temper.

One morning when Wayland took the young boy from his nurse, Heman began to cry "violently." Determined not to let the child have his way, Wayland decided to hold him until he stopped, and took away a piece of bread the boy clutched in his hand. When Heman stopped crying, Wayland offered him the bread, but the child threw it down. At that point Wayland resolved that Heman would not eat until he accepted food from his father and voluntarily welcomed his affection. Moreover, he was to be restricted from contact with other members of the household. Thus began a test of wills that would last more than 30 hours.

Wayland kept the child in a room by himself during the entire ordeal, and only allowed him to eat when he accepted food from his father. When Heman took the bread but refused to embrace his father, the food was taken back. The boy was obstinate throughout the first day, despite Wayland's regular visits, "every hour or two," and his speaking "in the kindest tones." Wayland described the boy "hiding his face in the bedclothes" and crying "most sorrowfully," but he refused to approach or embrace his father. Finally, in the late afternoon of the second day, young Heman finally relented, after nearly two days without eating. In the end he "repeatedly kissed" his father and "obeyed his every command."

Wayland clearly believed that his approach in this case was appropriate, if not exemplary, and wrote about it as a lesson to others. In justifying his actions, Wayland reasoned that if he had not confronted the child's will, "I must have obliged my whole family to have conformed in all their arrangements to his wishes." He noted that Heman's disposition toward other members of the household also changed as a result of the incident. Describing Heman as now "mild and obedient," he commented approvingly that "my whole family has been restored to order." In drawing principles from the incident he declared, "there can be no greater cruelty than to suffer a child to grow up with an unsubdued temper" (McLoughlin, 1975/1985). Wayland believed he had performed a great service in this case, both to his son and to society at large, and he wrote to provide a lesson to other parents confronted with similar challenges.

This incident is useful to examine because it captures a set of attitudes about parental responsibility and child development that were quite common among American Protestants in the 19th century. Willfulness in children often was compared to a kind of sin, parallel if not equivalent to original sin, that had to be overcome by learning obedience and respect for authority if the child was to become a useful member of society, a point Wayland made in his letter. The childrearing stories and advice books of the age, such as the popular works by Jacob Abbott and Lydia Sigourney, constantly warned of the dangers of children disregarding their parents, or engaging in selfish or self-centered behavior. The purpose of discipline was to teach the child a particular kind of self-control and conformity to the expectations of adults, especially the child's parents. Bad children were those who ignored the wishes and commands of adults, and such children ran the danger of becoming poor citizens, adults who ignored the rules of society and religion. Making the young conform to the expectations of adults was seen as being in their best interests, and representing the best possible course for society as well (Kaestle, 1983; Mintz & Kellogg, 1988).

It is important to bear in mind that Francis Wayland probably was not a typical American parent, insofar as it is possible to identify one. He was a man of intense religious convictions, and as a college president he was accustomed to exerting authority over the young. Being an educator, moreover, he probably was more didactically motivated than most parents. He deliberately seized on the use of feeding as an opportunity for confronting Heman's temper, even if he did not anticipate the ordeal that resulted. Although Wayland's account of the episode was published, not everyone thought that it was an example of good parenting. A second local newspaper published two responses criticizing the course of action described in Wayland's letter, one characterizing it as starving an "infant boy ... into a state of passive obedience" (McLoughlin, 1975/1985). Even in the 19th century, not all agreed with adult domination of children and the need for curbing the "willfulness" of their spirits. Certain parental advice books of the era cautioned against breaking the spirit of young children, instead urging that their natural playfulness and curiosity be nurtured and allowed to flourish. But few questioned the need for children to respect their parents and ultimately to adhere to paternal authority (Wishy, 1967).

In many respects the case of young Heman Wayland probably did represent traditional American conventions about children and education, despite the severity of his father's methods of instruction. Most Americans at the time certainly would have agreed with the proposition that children must obey adults, and should learn self-control at an early age. Many would have imparted such lessons quickly and violently with one form or another of corporal punishment, a course of action Francis Wayland pointedly rejected. And the belief that children should be taught obedience and respect for authority clearly dominated much of American education at the time. It was telling in this connection that Wayland's critics compared his actions to those of schoolmasters accused of flogging their pupils, yet another point of controversy in the 19th century. Wayland doubtlessly disagreed with this analogy, for he was opposed to corporal measures. Critical commentaries about such abuses notwithstanding, however, most American schools were founded on the principle that adult authority was paramount, and that children were to learn compliance before all else (Finkelstein, 1989; Hogan, 1990).

Social theorists since Max Weber have suggested that the ability to exercise self-control, to repress one's emotions and desires, was a key component of the development of capitalism. An ideology of self-denial, one that held various forms of deprivation in high esteem, was essential for the process of capital accumulation and economic development. This is one of the reasons pietistic Protestantism of the sort practiced by Wayland became one of the foundation stones of the modern social order. Good capitalists, after all, did not dispense their riches by following base impulses; they saved and reinvested them to advance the greater glory of Protestant civilization. Francis Wayland, in addition to restoring order to his own household, was teaching young Heman to exercise restraint, to control his feelings, and to follow the lead of the virtuous adults in his life. These were the lessons of middle-class American childrearing in the 19th century, however they might be imparted, and they were the ideological wellsprings of much of the nation's formal system of schooling. The ethic of improvement through self-denial and deprivation, glorified in Wayland's confessional and yet didactic letter, contributed to a transformation of American education and life (Greven, 1977; Rodgers, 1978).

THE AGE OF INDUSTRIALIZATION

The 19th century was a time of accelerating change in the American economy and the nation's social structure. Industrialization came to the United States during the 1800s, along with the manifold social changes associated with that process. As the volume of goods and income produced by the economy increased rapidly, a hallmark of industrialization, the extremes of wealth and poverty across the country widened. In sheer numbers, the population grew geometrically, increasing from 5.3 million to about 75 million over the span of the century. At the same time, the English-speaking populace spread to the West, establishing new towns and cities, along with such larger governmental agencies as deemed prudent or customary, principally counties and states. Geographically, the continental United States came to assume its now familiar shape during this time, spreading from Atlantic to Pacific and forming one of the largest nations in the world. Even more significantly, this territory was rapidly filling with fresh waves of settlers and came to represent a vast network of markets, and thus a powerful inducement to the development of industry. By the end of the 1800s the United States was no longer a slender string of settlements extending along the Atlantic coastline; instead, it was the largest economy and perhaps the most powerful nation in the world (Brownlee, 1979).

Even with rapid settlement, industrialization did not happen overnight. Factories capable of manufacturing vast quantities of goods needed access to markets for the sale of their products. They also required manpower, eventually in large amounts. The United States was a big country and its population was widely dispersed, making labor a scarce commodity. At the start of the industrial age American cities were small and most of the country's population lived in the countryside. A necessary precondition to industrialization was the development of a national transportation network, a means of moving products and people. This would become the infrastructure for the development of a national market, both for goods and for labor (Cochran, 1981).

The building of this network was the principal task of the opening decades of the 19th century. It was an age of large-scale projects, building roadways, canals, and eventually railroads to link the various cities and regions of the country together. Historians have variously dubbed this period the "transportation revolution" or the "market revolution" (Sellers, 1991; Taylor, 1968). In either case, it was a time when the distances that separated people seemed to shrink. It became easier to travel from one place to another, and, more important, goods produced in one part of the country became more widely available in other areas.

The transportation revolution held important implications for the social and political life of the nation as well. News and information traveled with people and merchandise, and hence they were communicated more quickly as well. Political parties could wage national campaigns more effectively, and public figures could travel more widely to promulgate political or religious views. With the growing national transportation network of roads, canals and railroads, a national consciousness of shared concerns and values emerged, spurred by debates over national issues and conflicts such as the War of 1812 and debates over land acquisitions in the West and the divisive issue of slavery. People found themselves less preoccupied with local issues, even if the vicissitudes of daily life continued to occupy most of their attention. Now a shared set of concerns and controversies gave new meaning to the term *American* as a source of identity and pride. The transportation revolution helped to hasten the evolution of a national identity (Sellers, 1991).

The transportation or market revolution also picked up the pace of economic life and contributed to the process of industrial development. Access to markets made the building of factories, already a central element of the economy in England, a practicable step in the United States. As it became cheaper to transport merchandise, the economies of scale in producing larger quantities of goods in factories made industrialization even more viable. With the New England textile industry leading the way in the 1830s and 1840s, the United States underwent a lengthy process of industrial growth that extended well into the following century. Between 1820 and 1860 the volume of cotton cloth produced annually in New England mills increased from less than 14,000 yards to nearly a million. And the pace of change increased even faster after the Civil War. Between 1860 and the turn of the century, the value of manufactured goods produced in the United States increased nearly eightfold, from less than $900 million to more than $6 billion. Textiles continued to be important in this latter phase of industrial expansion, but new industries led the advance, particularly iron and steel, paper, petroleum and chemicals, machine tools, and the processing of agricultural products, especially meat (Brownlee, 1979).

Over the course of the 19th century, manufacturing grew from less than 5% of the gross national product to more than half. Altogether, this process led to an unprecedented expansion of the economy, with the volume of manufactured goods growing more than four times faster than the nation's population. Per capita income, a figure that included children, increased at a similar rate. The impact of these changes was uneven, making great fortunes for some and creating impoverished pockets of industrial workers in the shadows of bustling factories. At the same time, however, it contributed to the wealth of most other Americans by enabling them to acquire a widening array of commodities (Dalzell, 1987). The foundation of what often is described today as the American way of life was established during industrialization in the 19th century.

The growing wealth produced during this early age of industrialism was extracted at considerable cost. The development of the factory system resulted in a loss of autonomy and independence for many workers. It also contributed to a devaluing of skills, and a replacement of skilled labor with machines. Apprenticeship, long an integral element of the educational experience of American youth, especially boys, gradually disappeared during the 19th century. As the scale of industrial production increased in size, thousands of workers were crowded together in drab factory towns or in industrial cities, where they often lived in conditions most would consider miserable today, as contemporaries did then too. Beginning in the 1840s and escalating quickly during the decades following the Civil War, millions of European immigrants came to the United States, many of them to take jobs in the burgeoning industrial sector of the economy. Industrialization appeared to have produced a new class of unskilled, impoverished workers in the United States, and was associated with a higher degree of cultural and social diversity. Cities and towns grew larger and dingier, and even the countryside was changed, as mechanized farming and large-scale agriculture slowly became more commonplace. Industrialization changed the face of America, but not everyone felt it was a change for the better (Laurie, 1997).

INDUSTRY, CITIES, AND EDUCATION

What did this process of economic and social change have to do with education? A great deal, as it turned out. For one thing, education and schooling became increasingly significant social issues as time passed, and as the process of industrialization unfolded. The nation's total investment in education grew dramatically, as larger segments of the population attended school for greater lengths of time. Economic historian Albert Fishlow estimated that the average American received just 210 days of formal education in a lifetime in 1800. By 1850 that figure had more than doubled and by 1900 it had jumped to 1050 days, about half of what it would be in 2000. Because these figures represent averages, it is important to note that some children, especially the well-to-do, benefited from more schooling than this; others received less (Fishlow, 1966a). In the course of these changes, however, formal education began to assume the familiar dimensions of school experiences as they are known today.

Apart from the sheer quantity of education, the character of school began to change as well. For many children, especially those in cities, towns, and other populated areas, school became associated with preparation for life, and for work in particular. This is not to say that education became vocationalized, although there were efforts to increase the amount of job preparation performed by the schools. Rather, schooling mainly was directed at the cultivation of proper "habits" of industriousness and responsibility, along with essential skills of literacy, numerical calculation, and knowledge of history, geography, and other subjects. This was education for citizenship, of course, but it also was preparation for life in the emerging industrial order, a society increasingly characterized by formal economic relationships and by the rule of the clock and efficiency. If the 19th century was an age of factories, the school became the best possible preparation for industrial life (Nasaw, 1979).

It would be wrong to assume, however, that there was a direct and immediate relationship between the rise of factories and the development of schools. In many instances the advent of industrialization meant that fewer children attended school in a given community. Early factory owners were interested above all in reducing costs, and it was not unusual for them to employ child labor, especially in Northeastern and Southern towns and cities. In such instances the factory became a school by default, even if the lessons it taught were usually quite harsh. Although some states had laws requiring factory owners to allow time for teaching child employees reading and other subjects, such measures often were honored in the breach. In cases when factories did not employ young children, they usually hired large numbers of teenagers and young adults, both male and female. These youthful workers often had the strength and stamina of adults, with higher levels of energy and a willingness to work for relatively low wages. The availability of work in factories, with low skill requirements, created a disincentive to school attendance. The immediate and direct effect of industrial development, consequently, may have been to lower educational attainment for children in industrial communities, typically the offspring of poorly paid industrial workers (Faler, 1981; Thernstrom, 1964).

Still, it is possible to argue that there was a tangible connection between the growth of the factory as an institution and the evolution of schools. Many 19th-century leaders were fascinated by the factory, and viewed it quite differently than most people do today. Exemplars of enlightened industrial development existed outside of the cities, and many observers believed it was possible to build factories that were clean and even morally uplifting to the young men and women that worked in them. The famous textile mills of Lowell were perhaps the best known instance of this, and their workforce of seemingly demure young women seemed to suggest that industrial development could be made wholesome. As industry expanded, however, and the demand for labor increased, conditions deteriorated. When larger numbers of poor immigrants came to dominate the industrial labor force, the character of even the most enlightened experiments in industrialization changed dramatically (Dawley, 1976; Dublin, 1979).

Some reformers rejected the idea of industry altogether, and attempted to establish ideal agrarian societies in isolated communities dotting the countryside. The best known of these communal experiments was Robert Owen's socialist cooperative in Indiana, called New Harmony. Established on principles of shared work and property, and an education system predicated on performing useful tasks without the imposition of discipline, New Harmony was a challenge to the emerging industrial order. Its practice of schooling was equally radical. Drawing on the work of European educational theorists, Owen and his followers were sharply critical of existing schools in the United States. Unfortunately, Owen's idealism did not suffice to ensure the success of New Harmony, and the venture ended amid disputes and misunderstandings. Although other communal experiments persisted considerably longer, they exerted little influence on the larger process of social development or on the educational system (Kaestle, 1983; Tyler, 1962).

Despite questions raised by Owen and other critics, many educators believed that industrial development represented the future. Because these men did not work in factories themselves, it was relatively easy to focus on the virtues of industry. To them, like countless other middle- and upper-class observers, the factory was a marvel of rationality, efficiency, and speed, along with power and reliability. Workers were required to conform to the demands of the production process, to be punctual, to follow orders, and occasionally to solve problems they encountered on the factory floor. In other words, they needed self-discipline and attentiveness, along with a good degree of deference for authority. Expectations such as these appealed to the Protestant values of early school reformers. They sought similar goals for the children in their institutions, claiming outright in some instances that the duty of the school was to prepare students for the demands of the emerging industrial social order. Even as some factory owners pulled children away from schools, many educators emulated the factory as a model institution of the new age. It was a powerful metaphor for the future social order (Kasson, 1999; Pollard, 1965; Vinovskis, 1970).

Carl Sandburg once quipped that America grew up in the country and moved to the city. It was an observation that might have been made about much of American history, but it was especially true of the 19th century. In 1800 fewer than 1 in 50 Americans lived in towns or cities; by the end of the century the number approached 40%. Industrialization was a major part of this story as well. Cities had been established and prospered during colonial times as nodal points of trade and essential services, but their growth accelerated significantly with the onset of industrial development. Many cities became centers of manufacturing activity and processing points for agricultural products, whereas others became distribution hubs for the rapidly growing volume of fabricated goods. The new urban industrial economy attracted millions of workers from the countryside and across the Atlantic, prompting rapid growth in the major cities. The 19th century also was a time of mass immigration, as the first large groups of destitute immigrants arrived in North America since the slaves and indentured servants of the 17th and 18th centuries. And successive waves of immigration were tied directly to the demand for industrial labor (Pred, 1966; Sharpless, 1977).

It was in the cities that the social impact of industrialization was most readily evident. The population of leading cities surged in the 19th century. Starting with fewer than 50,000 in 1800, New York became the first city in the country to surpass a million by 1860. Others such as Boston, Philadelphia, Pittsburgh, and Cincinnati grew nearly as fast, along with port cities in the South and West. With immigration from the countryside and abroad, the cities also became increasingly diverse socially and culturally (Blumin, 1976; Chudacoff, 1975; Ward, 1975).

As cities grew in the face of these developments, a host of institutions were established to cope with new social problems. Poorhouses, asylums, police departments, and jails appeared at this time. Questions of poverty and destitution, crime and social conflict, along with increased cultural diversity, seemed to call for institutionalized responses. Schools also were discussed widely in this connection. Although not a new institution, of course, the school did take on new social functions. In petitioning the city council for public support of their schools in 1828, for instance, a group of New York philanthropists declared that successful schools were necessary to forestall the need for more prisons. Similar arguments were made in other cities. For these school leaders, education was a means of social control, preventing youth from embarking on lives of crime and deviance. In conjunction with such problems as poverty and criminal behavior, these urban settings gave rise to many important changes in American schools in the 19th century. It is fair to say that the cities, particularly larger ones, were incubators of innovation in education, but a peculiar form of it: schooling for social order and control (Mohl, 1971; Schultz, 1973).

The earliest publicly supported schools in 19th-cer
called "charity schools" and were designated for the chi
Similar in most respects to the African Free School estab
York Manumission Society in the 1780s, these schools we
part proper norms of behavior along with basic lessons in literacy, mathematics, geography, and other subjects. Started by civic-minded members of
the urban elite, much like the Manumission Society, these schools started
as small-scale institutions but eventually were taken over by boards of education or similar governmental bodies entrusted to govern the public
schools. By the mid 1800s most large cities possessed the rudiments of a
public school system, but many of them had started with privately sponsored charity schools. With its New England roots, Boston probably had
the most venerable public schools, but New York and Philadelphia also developed rather large-scale systems in the opening decades of the 19th century (Boyer, 1978; Kaestle, 1973a).

Given the problems they faced, it is little wonder that the cities became
sources of educational change. It was in the nation's larger cities that one
of the first comprehensive systems for school organization and operation
was adopted: Lancastrian education. Joseph Lancaster was an English
schoolmaster who perfected a system for organizing schools efficiently and
inexpensively. Lancaster posited that a single teacher could manage the education of hundreds of children by using older students as "monitors," or
teaching assistants, to oversee the lessons of their schoolmates. Because
the knowledge of these assistants was very limited, most of the "instruction" consisted of "dictation," wherein the monitors pronounced words,
phrases, or numerical problems that were written down en masse by the
students and then inspected for accuracy. Monitors probably also listened
while children recited reading selections or presented answers to exercises (Kaestle, 1973b).

In employing these methods, the Lancastrian system of school organization demanded strict discipline and order among the students. Monitors,
consequently, often were little more than disciplinarians who ensured that
there was quiet while recitations and reports were delivered. Students
were given medals or other minor prizes for achievement, and the resulting competition provided motivation and a further way of catching errors,
by students monitoring their peers. With students divided into "classes"
supervised by a small number of monitors, a single adult teacher was capable of conducting a school with hundreds of children spanning many age
groups. It was a system well suited to the demands of the rapidly growing
cities and the low budgets of charity school sponsors.

Lancastrian education was also well designed for the demands of the
new industrial age. With a preoccupation with order and efficiency,
highly structured routines and uniformity of expectations, Lancastrian

schools represented a factory-like approach to mass education. This, of course, heightened its appeal among many reformers, who believed that Lancastrian schools promised to teach poor children proper habits of behavior, and a respect for order and discipline that would serve them well in life. Making children familiar with the routine and drill of daily recitations and exercises also promised to ready them for life in factory settings, where work was often repetitive and demanded a high tolerance for monotony. These schools also taught punctuality and respect for authority, as did most others schools, attributes especially important in an age when fewer children were likely to become independent artisans or masters of their own trade. If the factory and its industrialist owner were the heralds of a new era, Lancastrian schools for the children of the poor were institutions well suited to the future (Hogan, 1989, 1992; Mohl, 1971).

Lancaster's system was adopted in many urban school systems, most notably in New York, Boston, Philadelphia, Cincinnati, and other large cities. Most of these schools were not publicly supported at first; instead, they were sponsored by philanthropists interested in improving the lot of the poor and addressing the growing problems of poverty, crime, and disorder in the large cities. The New York Free School Society was one such organization, chartered in 1805 and comprised of many of the same individuals who had formed the Manumission Society two decades earlier. The Free School Society employed the Lancastrian system in its schools almost from the start, and helped to promulgate its virtues to education groups elsewhere. About 5 years later, the Manumission Society hired an English schoolmaster, Charles Andrews, to introduce Lancastrian methods in its African Free Schools as well. Such ready adaptation of the system to a variety of different schools was symptomatic of its popularity among urban school leaders at the time (Kaestle, 1973b; Rury, 1983).

The prevalence of Lancastrian schools continued through the first several decades of the 19th century. When Joseph Lancaster came to the United States in 1818, he was greeted with acclamation everywhere, and even spoke before Congress. He was killed by a runaway New York horse cart on another visit in 1838, just as his method of school organization may have reached the peak of its popularity. Following his death it came under criticism from a number of sources, and by the middle of the century it had decidedly fallen out of favor. Even so, the urban school reformers' preoccupation with order and routine remained inviolate elements of big-city school systems, long after Lancaster's peculiar method of monitorial instruction was a distant memory. As new generations of poor and unruly children poured into city schoolhouses, the basic purposes of urban education changed little, even if methods of instruction had evolved considerably (Boyer, 1978; Kaestle, 1983).

Charity schools were primary (or elementary) schools, but it also was in the 19th century that American secondary or high schools became popular institutions. These too were largely an urban phenomenon, as a large population base was required to provide enough students for such schools. It is widely acknowledged that the Boston Latin School was the first secondary institution established in the New World, in 1629, about a decade before Harvard, even though the modern concept of "secondary education" did not exist at the time. Most other high schools appeared much later, however. Because private tutoring and tuition-based academies prepared many young men for college and few occupations required secondary education, there was relatively little demand for high schools until well after the American Revolution. When the first high schools appeared, however, they quickly became the dominant form of education beyond the primary schools. Beginning in 1821, with the establishment of the first public high school in Boston, as distinct from a classical grammar school or academy, American secondary schools prepared students for a host of commercial and educational destinations. Although the numbers of students attending these institutions were small at first, high schools would eventually become one of the most significant educational innovations of the 19th century (Reese, 1995). The high school is discussed in greater detail later.

The most important educational developments of the early 19th century, however, concerned the common school, the primary institution that became a symbol of American education at the time. Urbanization and economic development helped to spawn a movement to improve the common schools and expand their purview. But the rise of urban industrial society also entailed the appearance of other institutions to help mediate the process of economic growth and social differentiation. These included public agencies for building and maintaining the transportation system, government offices for managing natural resources and industrial waste, and agencies for prisons, asylums, and similar institutions. These all were supported by the modernizing segment of 19th-century society, middle-class social reformers (Boyer, 1978).

The spread of school reform beyond the cities also was abetted by the growth of political parties, particularly those dedicated to national development through enhancing the institutional infrastructure. The early decades of the 19th century were a time of growing electoral participation in the nation's political system. Although the vote was still limited to white males, it was liberally extended to members of virtually all social classes. In light of these changes, politics was becoming an increasingly important aspect of life in the United States. Reformers, consequently, often worked through the national political parties then taking shape, and their corresponding state and local organizations. In terms of their general affiliation, these individuals usually were linked to the Whig Party, or later with the Republican Party. These groups were the driving force behind the development of common school reform. They found support in workingmen's parties and early labor organizations in the cities, longtime advocates of free public schools. But most reformers were middle class in orientation, and animated by visions of a more perfect society. It is possible to think of them as modernizers, helping to build the institutions that have become so familiar today. But they faced a daunting task in the early 1800s, for there was considerable resistance to these efforts. The process of building a coherent and uniform system of schools was marked by considerable conflict (Kaestle, 1983; Kaestle & Vinovskis, 1980).

A SLOW REVOLUTION: EDUCATION IN THE COUNTRYSIDE

Not everyone agreed that schools should change, or that new institutions were necessary for social advancement. There was opposition to the logic of urban industrial development and to the institution-building activities of reformers throughout the 19th century. This may seem surprising from today's vantage point, when urban industrial social institutions seem quite natural, as though they have always existed. But 19th-century society was in a state of transition. Although industrial development was the principal engine of change, most of the nation's population throughout the entire age remained rural and agrarian, and was quite isolated from the cities and other centers of industrial development. Consequently, many people were uncomfortable with the many changes that industrial society brought with it. Historian Charles Sellers has characterized this majority segment of 19th-century America as a "subsistence" society, one that spent much of life outside of the rapidly growing market economy that was associated with industrial development (Sellers, 1991).

People living in this largely rural social setting were generally self-sufficient, although they were drawn inexorably into the market economy as time passed. By and large, they were suspicious of the urbanite champions of industrial development and the institution builders who sought to transform and "modernize" the United States. They wanted to keep taxes low and preserve the way of life they had carved out of the land, or the livelihood their forefathers had started generations earlier. These people were hardly champions of a new and improved system of schooling, and therein lay the source of a major early conflict over education. In very general terms the question at the heart of the clash was this: Would education be utilized as an instrument of social and economic development, or would it remain a prerogative of individual families and local authorities? For the locals, it served personal tastes for improvement and literacy, and provided an introduction to Christian values. Modernizers approved of this, but wanted the schools to do more (Cremin, 1951; Graham, 1974; Sellers, 1991).

The answer to this question was by no means certain for people living at the time. And its terms of debate were not very clear either. In comparison to today, formal schooling did not occupy much of people's lives, and their futures did not hinge decisively on possession of educational credentials. Most people made a living, and developed careers, in one line of work or another without reference to education or formal training. Money spent on education, although high in comparison to other nations, was well below the levels of today as a fraction of the nation's economy (Goldin, 2001; Solomon, 1970). So it would be wrong to suggest that it was an issue that predominated in everyday public discussions. Rather, it was a facet of life that became an object of debate when reformers suggested making it a larger, more important and expensive aspect of the social infrastructure. By and large, these modernizers were intent on expanding and improving popular education, and they met resistance from people who believed change was unnecessary or undesirable. The changes being debated were hardly monumental; examples might be a longer school year or a state exam for teachers. Wholesale reform in the educational system did not occur overnight. But disagreements were often bitter just the same. In this way, schools evolved by degrees, with each step in the process marked by argument and conflict, as well as a good deal of apathy from a public too preoccupied by the uncertainties of daily living to worry about relatively small changes proposed for the schools (Larkin, 1988; Lasch, 1991).

If one were to briefly characterize the general terms of 19th-century school reform, it would be as follows: Modernizers, most of them representing the urban or market sector of 19th-century society, were intent on building institutions that could certify reliable criteria for achievement and impart a common understanding of moral principles and standards of behavior. Some historians have suggested that it was the commercial farmers and local merchants, those most closely connected to the market economy, who led the process of change in the rural districts. They heeded the reformers who articulated a set of parallel goals concerning new methods of instruction and humane treatment of children. But even these ideas were ultimately predicated on the expectation that more liberal forms of pedagogy would improve the outcomes of instruction: producing better educated and morally superior citizens. Above all else, the modernizers were dedicated to a system of educational institutions that worked efficiently and effectively to create an educated populace. Although reformers often employed idealistic, even messianic language, ultimately their task was a profoundly practical one (Kaestle, 1983; Parkerson & Parkerson, 1998).

In certain respects, the vision of schooling that common school reformers promulgated was parallel to the factory, the central institution of industrialization. Their concerns were similar to those of the charity school founders in the large cities; there was a universal interest in greater efficiency, and factories produced things more rapidly, and were thus eventually linked to the term *mass production*. But from the standpoint of the time, there was another issue that made common school reform different: a concern with improving the quality of education. Here too, ideas were influenced by the example of industry. Another virtue of factory production, after all, was consistently high standards of quality. Not only were products manufactured with greater efficiency, but they also were often better in terms of their appearance, function, and reliability. This was a result of standardization in multiple phases of the manufacturing process and the superior technology of industrial enterprises. If the various components of a product were designed to work together smoothly, it made sense that the finished product would represent an improvement over the handmade or "home-grown" commodities of the preindustrial era. This was a logic that reform-minded educators came to apply to systems of education (Hogan, 1990).

The effects of industrial development were plain for everyone to see, and were hardly limited to the cities. Mass-produced farm tools and a wide range of other products gradually came to replace the clumsy, makeshift and odd-looking items that had characterized the subsistence economy for generations. This was true of clothing, eating and cooking utensils, and a vast array of other products people used on a daily basis, wherever they lived. Consequently, for many forward-thinking people at the time, particularly those most directly connected to the growing national economy, the factory represented a downright revolutionary institution. In particular, the living metaphor of an integrated system of production represented by industry exerted a powerful influence on leading educational figures. This and the nation's rapidly developing transportation network, and improved communications, were symbols of progress and the superiority of American civilization. Reformers wanted to depict schools in the same light: They would improve each succeeding generation, uniting the country in a common set of values and forging a national identity (Cowan, 1997; Kaestle, 1983).

There certainly appeared to be much room for improvement in American education in the early 1800s. The schools that existed throughout much of the rural United States had changed relatively little since colonial times. They were isolated, small in size, conducted for relatively short periods of time, and taught by itinerant masters with little formal training. They also had become quite ubiquitous. By and large, the typical rural district school served an area of 2 to 4 square miles, to be accessible by walking, and was populated by some 20 to 50 families. Thus by the 1830s they literally dotted the countryside, particularly in the Northeast, serving millions of children in small, intimate settings bound by an immediate community. Levels of enrollment, attendance at any type of school for any part of the year, were already quite high in the opening decades of the century, over 70% for children aged 9 to 13. Americans clearly valued some form of formal education, as overall attendance figures were higher than for other major countries; only Germany had higher rates in 1830, and by 1880 the United States led the world. Following the Revolution, growing numbers of girls attended school along with the boys, at least in the Northeastern states and upper Midwest, marking yet another unique feature of American education (Fishlow, 1966b; Larkin, 1988; Vinovskis, 1972).

Even with high enrollments, however, it was not clear just what most children learned in such schools. The conditions of formal education differed greatly from one part of the country to another, indeed even from town to town in the same region. The length of school terms varied a good deal, and there was often considerable inconsistency in day-to-day attendance. For the reformers of the time, the issue was not one of persuading more Americans to send their children to school, but rather improving the quality of the schooling available to them (Rury, 1988b).

The rural common schools probably were not very effective educational institutions, at least by modern standards. Indeed, they usually just reinforced and expanded on lessons children had already learned at home and in church, the other two institutions that dominated the lives of Americans in the 19th century. No doubt, such schools helped to impart and enhance basic literacy skills, but they built on a foundation established by Protestant family values. Reading and writing were skills highly prized in most devout Protestant households, simply because they were considered essential to piety and to basic communication. Consequently, most rural children probably were introduced to reading at home and in church before they were asked to read anything in school. This was an early expression of social capital at work in the history of American education. A modicum of reading skill was a behavioral norm upheld in most local communities, particularly in the North, one reinforced by the local church, a central community institution. In a similar fashion, schools also conveyed basic mathematical and computational principles, along with a smattering of history, geography, and "moral philosophy" (Fuller, 1982; Gilmore-Lehne, 1989; Soltow & Stevens, 1981).

The success of these efforts doubtlessly hinged decisively on the attitudes of parents regarding the education of their children. The chief instructional technique was recitation, requiring students to repeat portions of text that they had memorized while reading either at school or at home. There were contests and games, such as spelling bees or multiplication tournaments, that served to break up the monotony. Storytelling occasionally helped impart memorable history and geography lessons. But there was scarcely any advanced instruction in a particular subject, as most teachers knew little beyond the basic elements of the usual school subjects, the "three Rs." On top of that, there was little continuity of instruction, because teachers seldom remained at a single school longer than a year or two. The schools were generally ungraded, which meant that children of all ages sat in the same room, and they endured the discomforts of poor ventilation and threadbare accommodations. And there was a heavy emphasis on discipline, with rules often enforced by means of harsh physical punishments (Finkelstein, 1989; Gulliford, 1991; Kaestle, 1983).

In short, much of school in the countryside was boring, repetitious, uncomfortable, riddled with conflict, and held little prospect of sustained intellectual stimulation. Without a great deal of parental support for the goals and objectives of such schools, it is unlikely that children would have undertaken such an onerous and disagreeable road to learning. The parental interest in these institutions was generally reinforced by the attitudes and values of other adults in the immediate community, whom children saw regularly at church and at other public gatherings. Thus it is probably accurate to say that the success of 19th-century rural schools was significantly dependent on the degree or amount of social and cultural capital possessed by students and imparted by their families and immediate communities. The importance of learning basic reading and mathematical skills was widely agreed on, and the necessity of mastering their lessons was impressed on children by a dense web of relationships in all areas of their lives. The schools probably did serve important socialization functions, especially for the children of Midwestern immigrant families, who may have been less aware of community norms and expectations. But even this purpose had to be upheld by the parents and other adults who supported the school in its everyday operations. The rural schools of the 19th century could hardly have succeeded without a high level of community support (Brown, 1989; Cohen, 1982; Gilmore-Lehne, 1989).

Given the close association between home and school in the lives of most rural American families at this time, it is little wonder that there was resistance to the efforts of reformers to change the educational system. From the standpoint of the opponents of reform, the existing schools functioned quite adequately, and there was no need for costly changes. But the logic of reform was inexorable, driven as it was by larger shifts in the nation's economy, social structure, and political system. Education clearly was linked to a larger process of social change. Even if the outcome of debates over school reform appeared uncertain at times, in the end resistance to the general logic of reform was futile.

COMMON SCHOOL REFORM

The time roughly between 1830 and 1860 is considered the first great period of school reform in American history. It marked the beginning of efforts to create a uniform system of mass public education, governed largely by the states, spanning the nation. It would take more than a century for this to be achieved, but it was the dream of a generation of reformers who started their work in the decades preceding the Civil War. Animated by a Protestant commitment to social perfectibility and the republican spirit of national advancement, along with the model of the factory system, these men and women presented the school as a solution to a host of social problems, and as a tool of economic and political development. As reformers, they were hardly unique in this respect. But they did articulate a number of ideas that might be classified as among the founding myths of the modern American educational system.

It is probably best to start with the problems they saw. First and foremost, school reformers were troubled by the enormous variability that existed as a consequence of the highly localized arrangements in American education during the early 19th century. They fretted over the haphazard training of many schoolmasters, the short terms that characterized rural education, often squeezed between harvest and planting seasons, and the chance provision of such basic school supplies as books and firewood. They dreamed of a school system with consistent standards of teacher preparation, long and uniform school terms, and generous supplies of books and other essential educational materials. They worried that without such a system, American schools would prove inadequate to the task of educating the nation's children for the demands of the industrial and urban age then dawning. And they also fretted about the growing diversity of American society, and the possibility of widespread social conflict in the absence of common values and a shared identity. For these reasons, school reformers proclaimed the cause of public education across the land. Consequently, historians have referred to the years between 1830 and 1860 as the "age of the common school" (Binder, 1974; Cremin, 1951).

The most famous proponent of common school reform was Horace Mann, an indefatigable lawyer and former state legislator who accepted the newly created post of Secretary of the State Board of Education in Massachusetts in 1837. Working with a modest salary and virtually no budget for his new position, Mann crisscrossed the state speaking to anyone who would listen to his message about the virtues of common schools. Mann undertook a wide range of issues in education, some of them still points of controversy today, and lobbied incessantly for the passage of new laws establishing the first elements of a modern educational system in Massachusetts. His annual reports, published by the state and distributed widely, became influential statements of educational reform. And other reformers across the country drew inspiration from his example (Curti, 1959; Messerli, 1972).

Looking around him at the changes occurring in 19th-century society, Mann was especially concerned about the divisions beginning to become evident in the social fabric. Early in his career Mann had witnessed an ugly mob attack a Catholic orphanage in a fit of anti-Irish hysteria in Boston. He recognized that religious sectarianism and cultural conflict posed a big challenge to the future of American institutions, especially the principle of democratically elected government. This made the idea of a common school, attended by children of the different groups in society and without affiliation with any particular religious viewpoint, essential to the future development of the republic. Mann advocated a nonsectarian form of Christianity for the public schools, and was roundly attacked by Calvinist church leaders in Massachusetts, who felt that schools without connection to churches were godless and immoral. Catholics also objected to the principle of nonsectarianism, seeing the religious and moral content of non-Catholic schools as essentially Protestant. Bedeviled by seemingly endless debate over these issues, Mann eventually prevailed in separating the public schools from the churches. In doing so he helped to establish the idea that publicly supported education was intended to serve children representing the full range of religious beliefs and cultural practices in society. This became one of the principal meanings behind the term *common school* (Binder, 1974; Messerli, 1972; Welter, 1962).

The common school movement, led by Mann and dozens of like-minded men and a few women across the Northern tier of states, and by some intrepid pioneers in the South, did not dramatically affect enrollments. These had crept up in the opening decades of the century, and common school attendance was near universal among children aged 7 to 12 by the 1840s, at least in the North. Instead, Mann and his fellow reformers focused on other problems, related to issues like those just touched on. In addition to nonsectarian instruction, they urged longer school terms, advocating 8- or 9-month sessions instead of the 4- or 5-month terms common in many rural areas. They pressed for systematic examinations and minimum training requirements for teachers, to raise the level of instruction and to help establish a professional identity for teachers. In particular, Mann succeeded in persuading the Massachusetts legislature to establish the nation's first publicly supported teacher-training institution, called a normal school, derived from the French word *normale*, in Lexington in 1838. Other such schools appeared in the wake of common school reform, providing modest numbers of professionally trained teachers to staff the nation's schools (Curti, 1959; Herbst, 1989; Kaestle, 1983).

Changes such as these required money, and much of Mann's time was spent in convincing the state's varied political and social constituency groups that public education was a cause worth supporting. Because schools were wholly controlled and supported by the districts, often defined by towns and villages, and not by the state, Mann had little alternative to exhortation as a reform strategy. He and other reformers worked largely in the realm of ideas, and it was in this domain that the mythology of modern public schooling was born. Local school authorities had to be convinced of the need for longer school terms, professionally trained teachers, more and better supplies, and other facets of school reform. Mann could get the legislature to pass laws requiring lengthier terms and exams for teachers, and even these steps occasioned political infighting, but without financial support for such measures, and sanctions to enforce them, there was little immediate impact. Mann and other reformers waged protracted battles against opponents of taxation to support the schools. Property taxes proved particularly controversial, as reformers were accused of undermining the very sanctity of private property. Childless adults also objected to school taxes, because they claimed to have no direct interest in education. But Mann sensibly argued that schooling was a public responsibility, a stewardship incumbent on all members of society, regardless of one's personal circumstances. Reformers also successfully fought against "rate bills" and other forms of partial tuition occasionally charged by the schools. Public education was to be free to all, and open to everyone. These were lofty—and expensive—principles, and it took time to resolve the debates they engendered. Consequently, school reform was often a slow and difficult process (Cremin, 1951; McCluskey, 1958; Welter, 1962).

Horace Mann was a shrewd reformer, however. He recognized the most important opponents to reform, and concentrated his efforts on winning them to the banner of change. In particular, Mann was concerned about the wealthy, who often did not send their own children to the public schools and may have been prone to thinking public education equivalent to charity schooling. Consequently, Mann devoted a great deal of effort to convincing the state's most affluent citizens, along with those who did not have children in school, that support for public education was clearly in their best interest. Taking a page from the philanthropic proponents of urban charity schools, for instance, he argued that moral education was the most important element of popular schooling, emphasizing the importance of a nondenominational Christian foundation to public schooling. Such an education, he maintained, would impart norms of proper behavior, teach respect for property and hard work, and help to prevent irresponsible behavior (Hogan, 1990; Messerli, 1972).

Beyond the question of morality, however, Mann also argued that educated workers were more productive, and that schooling could add to the value of Massachusetts's growing industrial output. In his Fifth Annual Report, published in 1842, Mann quoted industrialists who preferred educated workers for their reliability and tractability. Elsewhere in his writings Mann suggested that schooling also could help bridge the widening gulf that separated the wealthy from the laboring classes, and promote social harmony in an era of increasing disparities in social status. Using an oft-cited industrial metaphor, he argued that education could thus serve as the "balance wheel" of society, preventing inequality from leading to destructive conflict and helping all the varied groups in society contribute to social and economic progress. This reasoning became a cornerstone of the common school tradition (Curti, 1959; Vinovskis, 1970).

Mann did not campaign for school reform simply to advance a political cause or an economic agenda, however. He fervently believed in the power of education to resolve a wide range of social problems and to enhance the perfectibility of civilization. He viewed public schools as essential institutions of the emerging American republic. His annual reports, published in each of the 12 years he occupied the Secretary of Education office in Massachusetts, were circulated and reprinted widely by his contemporaries. Consequently, Mann became the most prominent national leader of the common school reform movement, even though he rarely left Massachusetts while engaged in his campaigns. In the mid 1840s he visited Europe to inspect the national education systems there, and returned with admiring reports of the Prussian schools. In Prussia he observed a state-run system of education with uniform standards of instruction, well-trained teachers, and child-friendly instructional materials and practices. Mann's description of these institutions created great interest in foreign models of education, and the Prussian schools in particular. Eventually, this was a further impetus to educational reform in the United States: Educational competitiveness would become a source of national pride. Only the Germans had higher enrollment levels than the United States, and eventually even they would be surpassed. American schools had to be as good as anyone else's (Binder, 1974; Kaestle, 1983).

Mann also was a great believer in women's education, and a strong proponent of the theory of republican motherhood first articulated in the Revolutionary era. True to his era, he did not necessarily think that women's schooling should be the same as men's, or that women ought to aspire to male roles in adult society. Rather, he believed that women had a special role to play in the development of the modern educational system as teachers. Mann thought that women were naturally suited to serve as teachers, as he believed that a maternal disposition of patience and affection helped them to work effectively with students—especially small children. Women teachers also cost less than men, even when professionally trained, so their employment could help to restrain the expense of improved schooling. Thus, the use of women teachers held benefits in terms of both their quality as instructors and the cost of educational reform (Bernard & Vinvoskis, 1977; Brown, 1996; Rury & Harper, 1986).

Women had been teaching for several decades in Massachusetts when Mann became Secretary of the Board of Education, so his ideas did not represent a major innovation in New England educational practices. In this case, too, it was Mann's role as a popularizer and advocate for reform that was most important. Mann's vigorous testimonies in support of women teachers helped to make school leaders elsewhere amenable to hiring them, particularly in larger cities. During the latter half of the 19th century the nation's teaching force feminized rapidly, especially in the Northern tier of states and large urban centers, areas where common school reform took root most rapidly. This was a critical aspect of social change, for it also altered the character of a major category of occupations at the same time that it opened up a new line of work for women. Some historians even have suggested that the job of teaching came to be seen as a uniquely female form of work during the 19th century, and that these views accounted for the rapid feminization of teaching. In this respect, common school reform left a particular stamp on American education; by 1900 about 8 out of 10 teachers were women. This is a statistic that has changed little in the intervening century (Perlmann & Margo, 2001; Rury, 1989; Vinovskis & Bernard, 1978).

At the same time that Mann was campaigning for reform in Massachusetts, a generation of school leaders who shared his vision of a uniform and professionalized system of education began their work in other states and cities. Many of these men also were Protestant New Englanders, committed to social perfection and concerned about the growing divisions in American society. Like others in their generation, they had migrated to newly settled regions in search of opportunity, and in the years following Mann's Massachusetts reforms they conducted similar campaigns elsewhere. They corresponded with Mann and with each other, creating a network of earnest school leaders who helped to fashion a national pattern of school organization across the United States (Kaestle, 1983; Tyack & Hansot, 1982).

Henry Barnard was a famous contemporary of Mann who held similar appointments in Connecticut and Rhode Island but did not enjoy the success Mann experienced in building state school systems. Barnard eventually became the first U.S. Commissioner of Education in 1867, but he endured a peripatetic career simply because political support for reform measures was always subject to change. Other leading reform figures had similar experiences. They included men such as John Pierce in Michigan and Calvin Stowe in Ohio, who struggled to expand the purview and raise the quality of public schools in their states. These reformers did not have a definite career path to follow. Instead, they made exhortation and inspiration their stock-in-trade. They were institution builders, but they also were engaged in a grand crusade to advance a particular vision of American civilization through education (Curti, 1959; Lannie, 1974; Soltow & Stevens, 1981; Warren, 1974).

Common school reformers shared a similar set of values and assumptions about life and learning, and this also helped to give continuity and force to the movement. Historian Carl Kaestle has catalogued this mélange of viewpoints, and described it as the ideology of common school reform. Much of this worldview was derived from the Protestant upbringing of these men and their faith in the moral superiority of their own cultural orientation. For example, Francis Wayland, whose childrearing practices were guided by his Protestant convictions about human nature, also exhibited many of these ideas in his writings and public utterances. Politically, school leaders shared a common set of concerns about the future prospects of the American republican form of government, which was still a recent experiment on the stage of world history. They all believed in the central importance of individual character development as a key element of social progress. Without virtuous people, in their opinion, society was doomed, so proper moral development—through families, churches, schools, and other institutions—was seen as essential to national survival. Personal industry and self-discipline were deemed key to moral development, as was private property. This was an ideological perspective well suited to the capitalist social order, and the common schools everywhere trumpeted the virtues of American capitalism as a superior economic system. There was a widely shared belief that women should occupy a respected but largely delimited domestic role in the social division of labor, although one might add that non-White women often were expected to perform hard labor. And there was widespread commitment to using education to unify the American people, so that the nation could realize its manifest destiny of world leadership (Hogan, 1990; Kaestle, 1983).

Most of these ideas were not controversial in the United States during the 19th century, and were espoused by the majority of middle-class, White Protestants—the nation's cultural center of gravity. Those that disagreed with one or more of these propositions—Catholics, immigrants, Blacks and other racial minority groups, and feminist activists—were believed to be a part of the problem that common schools were intended to resolve, a fact that eventually led the Catholics to form their own school systems. Most of the schools that were established under the aegis of common school reform, moreover, were for Whites. This shared set of values and purposes provided the common school crusade with a clear direction and a distinctive goal: the unification of American culture through the mechanism of universal schooling (Brown, 1996; Lannie, 1968; Welter, 1962).

The success of common school reform did not rest wholly on the shoulders of crusading reformers, however, nor on their messianic ideology. There was widespread support for education as a general principle in American culture; even if there often were heated debates over specific features of school reform, like reformers' ideas, the debates often were quite similar too. Historians have noted the effusive language in support of publicly supported education in many state constitutions, and constitutional conventions, during the 19th century, particularly in the Northern tier of states extending west from New England and the mid-Atlantic. Most of these constitutions provided for some degree of state support for education, along with a measure of state supervision, making it one of the few areas of public life to receive such attention at the time. As a consequence, some historians labeled the schools a "fourth branch of government" in the 19th century (Tyack, James, & Benevot, 1987).

In certain respects this was a legacy of the enthusiasm over education evident immediately after the Revolution. Beginning in 1797, the federal government passed the famous Northwest Ordinance, which provided for the sale of public (federal) lands to support education, as a condition for admitting new states to the union. Consequently, education was widely recognized as a legitimate and important function of governmental authority almost from the very beginning of the republic. It was on this base of broad public and historic commitment to education as an activity of the government that the campaigns of common school reformers were built. And this was a critical foundation for their ultimate success. The republican ideology of the new nation, holding that citizenship entailed responsibility and knowledge, dictated that schooling be made universally available, at least for those groups deemed eligible to be citizens (Meyer, Tyack, Nagel, & Gordon, 1979).

By the time of the Civil War the logic of common school reform had nearly swept its opposition from the stage of public discourse over education, starting in the Northern states. There was a great deal of work to be done, to be sure, but the ideas that schools should be supported by property taxes, should have greater uniformity, should be nonsectarian, should last for more than 6 months, and should be taught by trained, professional teachers no longer were sources of widespread controversy. This does not mean, of course, that all of these goals had been achieved. Great variation on all of these counts existed in virtually every state of the union, but even more significantly in the South and the West than in the northeast. But instituting these reforms gradually became a matter of enforcing standards that had become accepted by the political establishment. The cause had been aided by the ascendancy of the Republican Party and presidential candidate Abraham Lincoln, by inheritors of the modernizing mantle of earlier reformers, and by union victory in the Civil War. These historic developments represented the supremacy of the reform-oriented, institution-building ethos of the urbanized northeast. Struggles to establish the first compulsory school laws in the latter part of the 19th century marked the closing stages of this campaign. By then, the common school wars had been largely won, even if some battles remained unsettled; now it was time to turn to new challenges facing the nascent public school system of the United States (Graham, 1974; Tyack, 1978).

CASE: REFORMING PEDAGOGY

Horace Mann was an idealistic and tireless advocate for pedagogical reform; he also was a complex historical figure. Among other things, he held a compassionate belief in the inherent goodness of children and in their natural proclivity to learn and grow in the proper environment. In this respect his views departed from more conservatively minded educators, even if he shared many other aspects of the period's dominant Protestant ideology. Historians speculate that his own unhappy childhood experiences with the strictures of traditional Calvinist beliefs in original sin led him later to reject educational theories that emphasized submission to authority as a fundamental principle. No doubt he would have been a critic of Francis Wayland's tactics in the case described earlier (Messerli, 1972).

As seen earlier, beliefs that children needed to learn respect for authority and obedience were widely held in 19th-century America, although there was a growing debate over how such lessons should be imparted. One of the primary issues was the matter of how children should be treated. The controversy aroused by Francis Wayland's public airing of his own approach to childrearing was indicative of public interest in these questions. A much larger dispute raged during the 1840s over the question of corporal punishment in the schools. At issue was a basic question about pedagogy: Did children require fear to learn properly, or did such emotions make learning even more difficult to achieve (Hogan, 1990; Wishy, 1967)?

On returning from his first tour of Europe, Mann extolled the virtues of schools in Prussia. Although militaristic Prussia evoked images of authoritarianism and iron discipline, Mann found the schools there to be quite humane. Teachers actually presented the subject matter rather than demanding that students memorize and recite their lessons, and they used a variety of teaching aids to help stimulate student interest and assist learning. Most significantly, Prussian teachers eschewed any form of physical punishment, arguing that fear and pain inhibited learning rather than encouraging it. They were trained in special institutes, featuring the ideas of such humanistic thinkers as Swiss educator Johan Heinrich Pestalozzi and the German philosopher Friedrich Froebel, originator of the kindergarten. Mann found himself drawn to this perspective, and suggested in his *Seventh Annual Report* that American educators had much to learn from their European counterparts. In contrast to schools in Massachusetts and elsewhere in the United States, the Prussian educational system also was quite centralized and well funded (Messerli, 1972).

Mann's report provoked a negative reaction from one of the most prestigious and powerful groups of educators in Massachusetts: Boston's grammar school masters. These 32 men were the head teachers, equivalent to principals today, in the city's public grammar schools, which drew pupils from the primary or common schools and sent the best students off to high schools or academies for additional academic preparation. Most of the masters had gained their positions by virtue of long experience in the public schools, and they were widely held to be among the most knowledgeable and influential educators in the state, if not the nation. Their reaction to Mann's report represented a serious challenge to his authority, but it also offered a rare occasion of public discussion about pedagogical principles and differing views of children and education (Binder, 1974; Schultz, 1973).

In a lengthy response to Mann's report, the masters challenged many aspects of Mann's work as secretary of the state's board of education, but devoted special attention to the Pestalozzian principles he had advocated and his condemnation of corporal punishment. They dismissed the idea that children could learn through natural curiosity, and maintained that physical punishments were necessary to "focus" and "discipline" the minds of students. "Duty should come first," they argued, "and pleasure should grow out of the discharge of it." As longtime veterans of the public schools, they asserted that it was foolishly sentimental to believe that order could be maintained without the threat—and actual use—of physical coercion. As a matter of principle, they were strong believers in "faculty psychology," which held that the mind is like a muscle in need of exercise and training. The study of dead languages like Latin and Greek, for instance, was widely considered a virtue among 19th-century educators, because it helped to train powers of concentration and disciplined the mind to overcome difficult or wholly foreign subject matter. In this spirit, the masters affirmed the central importance of memorization and recitation as pedagogical techniques essential to "forming the habit of independent and individual effort." To them, upholding the long tradition of teachers exercising fearful authority over students, forcing them to train the "faculties" of observation and memory through sheer willpower, was of paramount importance (Katz, 1968; Messerli, 1972).

The masters may have had the force of tradition on their side, along with discipline-minded parents, but Mann seized on the opportunity afforded by their response to advance his agenda of reform in pedagogy. The central thrust of his reply to the masters was to charge them with base self-interest, and with defending their own privileged positions at the expense of children. He demanded that the regime of discipline based on unquestioned authority and fear be replaced by an education motivated by mutual respect, affection, and the love of knowledge. Mann also advocated authority in the classroom, but believed it was best achieved by observing courtesy and compassion. In defense of his office he listed the steps he and others had taken to establish a more comprehensive and effective school system throughout the state, and the salutary effects of the state's fledgling normal schools, which the masters had attacked. In particular, he rejected the suggestion that physical force was necessary for the success of modern schools (Hogan, 1990; McCluskey, 1958).

There were additional volleys of responses and replies over the next several years, with each side repeating many of the essential points without affecting the course of debate. The masters resolutely refused to budge on the issue of corporal punishment, declaring "all authority is of God and must be obeyed." In the meantime, however, several of Mann's allies in Boston gained seats on the Boston School Committee, the body charged with conducting inspections of the schools. Although such inspections were usually just ceremonial, Mann's friends turned the annual grammar school examinations into real tests of what students had learned, and the results were devastating to the masters. It turned out that the students had actually gained very little through fear and recitation, and that the haughty masters were almost totally dependent on textbooks and well-worn exercises in their teaching. As a consequence, the students performed poorly on the exams, and those that did the worst were in schools controlled by the most domineering and abusive masters (Messerli, 1972).

A report issued by the inspectors revealed that some masters had engaged in various forms of corporal punishment as many as 50 times per week. This led to a public outcry. It was a decisive turning point in Mann's battle to change attitudes about pedagogy. Even though some Bostonians continued to defend the masters, the tide of public opinion clearly had started to swing against the traditional pedagogy of fear and authoritarianism (Katz, 1968; Schultz, 1973; Wishy, 1967).

As a result of the investigation of the Boston Grammar Schools, four masters were dismissed from their positions. Others were transferred to other duties in the school system, a dramatic loss of face. In the wake of the controversy, a large group of civic and cultural leaders in the Boston area raised thousands of dollars to establish yet another normal school, concrete testimony of public support for Mann's ideas about children and pedagogy (Messerli, 1972). Although the weight of tradition would continue to make corporal punishment, recitation, and authoritarianism basic elements of popular schooling for decades to come, there were signs of change. The pace of reform was slow, but it also began to pick up speed as the 19th century gradually drew to a close.

THE RISE OF SECONDARY EDUCATION

The high school is sometimes said to be an American invention. An institution designed to teach the graduates of the primary and grammar schools, at about age 14 or so, it was virtually unknown until the early 19th century. Historians agree that Boston's English Classical High School was the nation's first such institution. Founded in 1821 to provide a more practical and accessible alternative to the famous Boston Latin School, it came to serve youth interested in acquiring certain of the "higher branches" of learning without undertaking a classical (Latin and Greek) education. It was not long before other large cities along the Atlantic coast and the major transportation arteries to the North and West came to establish similar schools. These institutions taught the growing number of primary school graduates who sought a well-rounded but practical education to prepare them for the urban world of commerce and social advancement. Consequently, the popularity of high schools grew. By the end of the 19th century they existed in one form or another in every type of city or large town in the United States. Even though the high school was hardly frequented by the majority of Americans, it had become an important element of the nation's institutional culture (Brown, 1902; Herbst, 1996; Reese, 1995).

The high school started as an innovation in urban school systems with large numbers of students and expansive tax support for public education. Popular demand for instruction in such advanced subjects as history, mathematics (algebra and geometry), literature and writing, political economy, science (or "natural philosophy"), and geography led to its rapid spread. Most high schools also featured instruction in some classical subjects, especially Latin, long considered a sign of achievement and status. From the beginning, however, there was little expectation that most children would attend these institutions; rather, they were intended to teach the very best graduates of the primary and grammar schools. The early public high school represented something of a contradiction, in that case. They were a part of the popular education system, yet they were designated to serve an academic and social elite. This accounted for both their great attraction and the controversy they engendered (Krug, 1964; Reese, 1995).

Most of the early large public high schools admitted students by examination, and many prospective students were turned away because their scores were not high enough. As one might imagine, these tests were anticipated with dread by both students in the primary schools and their teachers. In many respects, they represented a 19th-century equivalent of standardized tests in today's educational system. In time, the high school admission exams became important indicators of how well a particular school was performing and provided a convenient standard of comparison for parents interested in choosing a school for their children. In this way, the high schools helped to establish and enforce uniform academic standards throughout the nation's large urban school systems, simply by virtue of their position at the pinnacle of many children's (and parents') ambitions. Consequently, the development of the high school did much to help create better integrated and more unitary public school systems in the cities (Beadie, 1999; Labaree, 1988).

The high school was a controversial institution too, however. It competed with private or semipublic secondary institutions, most of them called academies, that had developed in response to demand for higher levels of education in the first half of the century. High schools eventually eclipsed such institutions altogether, but the process of change was fraught with conflict. The academies were rather numerous, especially in the northeast, and had many influential supporters who were not happy to see them displaced. Furthermore, the early public high schools were quite costly, and often occupied palatial buildings erected at great expense and with considerable fanfare. Critics decried the cost, noting that relatively few students were educated and that tuition-charging academies provided more or less the same services at considerably less expense and with little public funding. The fact that high schools turned away many students because of low examination scores or poor grades did not help matters. They were attacked as little more than finishing schools for the elite, paid for with public monies (Herbst, 1996).

Such attacks came to a head in 1874 in Kalamazoo, Michigan, where opponents of the local public high school unsuccessfully sued the school board to have it abolished. Legalities notwithstanding, educational leaders succeeded in persuading the public that the quality of public high schools was generally much higher than most private academies, and that the high schools helped set proper academic standards for the rest of the educational system. They also argued that high schools conferred economic and social benefits on talented students, providing them with reliable credentials, and that these students contributed a great deal to local communities. The high school was depicted as a valuable asset for a community to maintain, a resource well worth the cost (Goldin & Katz, 1999a; Reese, 1995).

This latter argument pointed to the high school's principal source of success. Probably more than anything else, the future of the high school hinged on its popularity with the relatively small but growing urban middle class. Parents in this social stratum, perhaps less than a tenth of the national population at midcentury, increasingly were concerned with passing advantages along to their children in the form of social, cultural, and human capital (even if they did not use such terms). They were the beneficiaries of industrial growth and the market revolution, but there was great uncertainty about how their offspring would gain positions in the burgeoning commercial culture of the cities. The establishment of public high schools with rigorous and exclusionary entrance requirements provided a clear and legitimate way for such families to confer status on the next generation. The rhetoric of the high school, free and open to all, gave the appearance of a meritocratic system of performance-based evaluations, whereby the talented succeeded. This clearly carried great appeal to middle-class urbanites, who instinctively eschewed the open display of social advantage or favoritism based on anything but ability and accomplishment. Competitive high schools, sitting atop the growing public system of education, proved irresistible to this social group. And this attraction accounts for the initial success of the high school and its rapid spread in the latter part of the 19th century (Hogan, 1996; Labaree, 1988).

For most working-class children, on the other hand, high school attendance simply was not a viable option, because most were expected to start working at about age 14 or 15. Unlike their middle-class counterparts, working-class parents usually could not afford to send their children to school once they were old enough to contribute to the household income. Thus, although the rhetoric of public education made the high school appear meritocratic, it was disproportionately enrolled with middle- and upper-class students throughout the 19th century, even if enough working-class students attended to legitimize the appearance of meritocracy. In this regard the critics were correct: It was a largely elite institution conducted at considerable public expense. The high school's popularity among urban society's most influential social classes, however, usually made such criticisms a moot point (Katz, 1968; Reese, 1995).

There was a great deal of variation in the size and character of high schools in the 19th century. In the big cities, where there was a ready supply of students and a large middle-class constituency, high schools could be sizable and widely admired for their academic standards. Philadelphia's Central High School, for instance, enrolled hundreds of students and was among the most famous in the country; its graduates commanded considerable prestige. Such urban high schools had large teaching staffs and attracted the best qualified faculty, with high salaries and opportunities to specialize in particular subjects. Institutions such as these, however, constituted less than 20% of high schools in the country (Labaree, 1988).

On the other hand, in smaller towns the high school often was little more than a single class where older students were taught advanced subjects by one or two teachers. The quality of education was much lower in these settings, and the credentials graduates received were questionable. But these classes often were the start of much larger and more comprehensive secondary institutions, built in later years as the community grew. In time, high schools came to represent local ambitions, and many boosters dreamed of institutions closer in size and function to the highly regarded flagship high schools in the cities. If the high school was becoming instrumental in conferring middle-class status, after all, it stood to reason that every growing community would eventually want to have one (Goldin & Katz, 1999a; Reese, 1995).

Yet another important feature of 19th-century high schools was the widespread practice of coeducation. Almost from the very start, high schools in many parts of the country enrolled male and female students together. For ambitious educators, this was partly a strategy for finding enough students to support these expensive institutions: Admitting girls meant twice as many potential students, and it widened the base of support among middle-class families. Coeducation also conformed to the logic of meritocracy: If girls could pass the exams and receive good grades, how could they be refused admission? Finally, female high school graduates became an important source of teachers for the rapidly growing urban school systems of the latter part of the 19th century. Educators predicted dire shortages of qualified teachers if women were not encouraged to enroll in the high schools. As a consequence, the majority of American high schools in the 19th century were coeducational. Most of the exceptions occurred in the largest cities and in the South, where separate schools for boys and girls often existed. In fact, by the end of the century, female students outnumbered males in the nation's high schools, in practically all regions of the country. The growth of secondary education and the rise of the high school helped usher in a unique era of (relative) gender equity in American education (Rury, 1991; Tyack & Hansot, 1990). This issue is discussed further in the next chapter.

At the end of the 19th century more than a half million students were enrolled in secondary schools in the United States, with the vast majority of them in public high schools. This meant that the high school had become a pervasive form of popular education, even though it served less than 10% of the nation's teenage population. Despite the populist rhetoric of the high school's supporters, it still served a fairly elite clientele. And even if most high school students were women, almost none were Black or Native American. Its inherent elitism notwithstanding, however, there was no denying the power of the high school to attract students once it was established. In the decades to follow, high school enrollments would climb even faster than they had in the 1800s. After years of struggle and debate the high school had finally arrived, and there was no turning back. Even though these schools served a small fraction of the nation's school-aged population, they had come to be considered indispensable features of the educational landscape (Herbst, 1996; Krug, 1964).

THE AGE OF THE COLLEGE

The 19th century also was a time of rapid expansion among the nation's higher-education institutions. The period prior to the Civil War, in fact, is sometimes referred to as the "age of the college," although only a tiny fraction of the nation's population engaged in college-level studies. Instead, it was a time when many collegiate institutions were established, most with high hopes for the future but little else in the way of either students or resources. These colleges generally prepared students for careers in the ministry or as educators. Other professions usually did not require a college education in the 19th century, although some students did attend college before studying medicine or law. Horace Mann, for instance, graduated from Brown University before standing for the bar. It was not until the closing decades of the century that modern universities began to develop with a focus on science and research, dedicated to preparing students for a wide range of careers. Even then, however, the collegiate sector of the nation's educational system was tiny, enrolling less than 5% of the relevant age cohort. Despite their rapid proliferation, 19th-century colleges were concerned only with a small fraction of the nation's students, something of an academic elite, even if not necessarily the best or brightest students.

As noted in the previous chapter, the United States had a handful of collegiate institutions at the close of the 18th century. In the next 50 years, several hundred others were established, most of them by religious denominations interested in training candidates for the ministry. These institutions fought for survival, competing bitterly over students and financial contributions, and some were eventually forced to close their doors. Many enrolled only a fraction of their students in college-level courses, with the rest taking "prepatory" classes equivalent to those offered in academies or high schools. Even the early state universities were small and religious in character, and they too had sizable preparatory departments. Because the higher-education system was not clearly linked to the nation's changing occupational structure, and because there were relatively few secondary schools to send them students, the colleges struggled through much of the 19th century. They proliferated because of religious zeal and the idealism of pioneering founders, but few prospered until well after the Civil War. By then the fundamental purposes of higher education had started to change (Burke, 1982; Rudolph, 1962).

Through much of the 19th century American collegiate institutions were dominated by a classical curriculum and an academic culture shaped by traditions handed down from the colonial period. These institutions were influenced by English models of higher education, particularly the colleges of Cambridge University, which emphasized classical preparation as the foundation of higher learning. Latin and Greek represented the core of the curriculum, and most classes were conducted by recitation. There were efforts to introduce more scientific, historical, and literary studies. Francis Wayland, for example, advocated such innovations at Brown, but the Yale Report of 1828, a faculty document defending classical studies, helped to slow widespread change during the antebellum period. Simply put, tradition held that a classical emphasis was indispensable; without it no course of study could be said to represent collegiate standards. This, of course, helped to ensure that most of what was taught in the colleges would be irrelevant to developments in the economy, or in society at large. It was a powerful means of transmitting cultural capital, but collegiate education had few practical uses outside of that (Hofstadter, 1955a; Rudolph, 1978).

Things began to change, however, in the closing decades of the century. Passage of the first Land Grant College Act in 1862 was a harbinger of the future. Drafted by Vermont congressman Justin Smith Morrill, this legislation set aside federal lands for the support of institutions devoted to practical and scientific courses of study, particularly in the fields of agriculture and "mechanics." A second Morrill act in 1890 provided even more support for "A & M" state universities, including many that had been founded in earlier decades. Meanwhile, visionary leaders such as Harvard's Charles Eliot broke the stranglehold of tradition in the collegiate curriculum. Eliot introduced a liberal elective system that allowed students to choose courses themselves, with few requirements—a reform that was later modified to feature a required core. Scientific research institutes had been opened at Harvard, Yale, and other institutions even before Eliot's reforms, and new research-oriented universities were established afterward, with Johns Hopkins, Cornell, and Chicago leading the way. As a matter of principle, the leaders of these institutions were influenced by the German model of higher education, which emphasized research-based learning instead of classical training. Flagship state universities, such as Michigan, Wisconsin, and California, also exhibited German influences, and attracted leading professors dedicated to social and technological advancement through scholarship and research. The result was a newfound degree of social relevance in higher education, and enrollments began to climb sharply (Eddy, 1957; Hawkins, 1972; Veysey, 1965).

Of course, rising high school graduation levels also helped to fuel collegiate enrollment, but the brightest students clearly were drawn to the leading centers of innovation. Many other institutions, especially those with strong religious ties, were slow to change, and classical studies continued to be a staple of collegiate study for decades to come. Traditions rarely die easily, but the direction of change ultimately would prove impossible to resist. Colleges were gaining new currency, and there was excitement in the air. A stronger connection had been made between collegiate life and the larger social and economic world, and that would bode well for the future of American higher education (Goldin & Katz, 1999b; Lucas, 1994).

THE SHAPING OF A NATIONAL SYSTEM
OF EDUCATION

The 19th century was a time of profound transformation in American life, and important changes in the nation's educational system. Industrialization and the market revolution helped to expand the economy, raising standards of living at the same time that employment was transfigured for thousands of workers. Rapid urbanization brought a host of new problems to the nation's cities, along with fresh waves of immigrants from other lands. Reformers puzzled over the best ways to respond to these developments, and devised a host of new institutions to address the challenges posed by the emerging urban industrial order. Not the least of these were the schools, which were supposed to inculcate proper middle-class values and work habits at the same time they helped to forge a new national identity. In particular, the common school reform movement aimed to make education the linchpin of social, political, and economic development. It was a means of sustaining republican values in an age of considerable ferment. If society was changing rapidly, schools would help to ease the passage to a better future.

School reform brought many changes to the educational system, most of which reformers would count as progress. Common schools were improved, and high schools were established, most of them open to all members of a community—although many still required an entrance exam. Following the Civil War, many schools outside of the South conducted annual sessions of 160 days or longer, close to today's standards, with the longest terms being in urban areas. And professional standards had been established for much of the nation's teaching force, with normal schools and teacher training departments existing in hundreds of high schools, colleges, and freestanding institutional forms. Hundreds of colleges and universities beckoned to students finishing secondary schools, and even if only a small minority attempted collegiate study, the capacity for higher education to become a normal step in the process of American education was clearly in place (Cremin, 1980).

Of course the United States remained a largely rural nation at the end of the 19th century, and most Americans did not even attend a secondary school, much less graduate from one and enter college. But the basic elements of the national system of education had been established. Corporal punishment and traditional views of childhood and adult authority prevailed everywhere—although probably most clearly in the countryside—but there were voices of dissent, and new perspectives on children and pedagogy were slowly gaining favor. The process of change, however quick in many respects, was also painfully slow in terms of its dispersion to all corners of American society. With some 75 million people stretched across thousands of square miles, the United States was a vast land, with great unevenness in social and economic development, and considerable cultural and social diversity. As significant as the reforms started in the 19th century were, the process of shaping the modern educational system clearly had just started.

What about the direction of change—the question posed at the start of the book? In the 19th century, there can be little doubt that industrialization was the driving force in the transformation of the economy and society at large. One can say the same thing about its impact on education. Clearly, the general thrust of reform in education was dictated by industrial development and urbanization. The basic organizational form of schooling was shaped by the central institution of the industrial era: the factory. Schools were organized to increase efficiency, to raise the quality of a standardized product, and to produce more compliant and dependable workers. This was most clearly evident in reforms such as the Lancastrian schools, but was apparent in other aspects of common school reform as well.

Industrialization also produced a growing commercial middle class, whose members clamored for secondary institutions, especially the public high school. These schools made secondary curricula more practical, bringing education in line with the requirements of the economy and the expectations of the newly emerging capitalistic middling classes. The same could be said of higher education, although it took somewhat longer for these changes to be realized. By the end of the century, however, a clear hierarchy of educational credentials had become available to aspiring youth interested in finding a secure niche in the modern social order.

By and large, changes in the larger economy and society drove the process of change and development in American education during the 19th century. As in the colonial period, the schools appear to have responded to the changing demands of the rapidly evolving social and economic system. In a certain sense, this is what one would expect: Schools, after all, must provide society with people prepared to address the ever-changing needs of economic and social life. On the other hand, education clearly worked to the advantage of some social groups and not to others. Examining the question of how the nation's schools may have helped certain social groups, and effected social change in new ways, the story turns in the next chapter to the issue of education for the nation's "outsider" groups .

CHAPTER FOUR

Ethnicity, Gender, and Race: Contours of Social Change in the 19th Century

Previous chapters have demonstrated some of the ways that education was shaped by larger social forces during the 1800s. There can be little question that industrialization, urbanization, and other broad processes of social change historically influenced the development of schooling in the United States. But what about the opposite relationship? How was the evolution of schooling affecting the process of social development?

As it turns out, this is a complicated question. As noted earlier, the connection between education and the larger society is multifaceted and subject to a wide range of factors and conditions. Some lines of influence were fairly straightforward. Rising literacy rates, for instance, generally have been attributed to the growth of formal education. Greater skill levels of this sort in the nation's population, moreover, have been thought to be linked historically with economic growth. This is a part of what economists refer to as *human capital,* the productive capacities of a given populace. Consequently, schooling is generally considered to represent a direct contribution to improved human capital, and hence to general social advancement. But in other respects the contribution of education to social change is more difficult to discern. There is the question, for example, of how schooling affected the social structure, or the relative standing of various groups in American history. Clearly it helped some to advance, but were its benefits available to everyone? Did the general contributions of schooling to economic growth sustain some groups more than others? This question addresses a particularly sensitive feature of the social change process: who succeeded in history and who did not. Expressed a little differently, it speaks to a key issue in the history of education: Has schooling help to change the prevailing social structure, or did it reinforce existing patterns of inequality?

   This chapter considers some of the most basic elements of inequality in American history. To address these issues, it is necessary to examine several different social groups, and the impact of education on their social status during the 19th century. In many respects, the members of these groups lived at the margins of society during much of American history. The groups to be considered include immigrants (mainly from Europe), White (native-born) women, African Americans (slaves and freedmen), and Native Americans (or American Indians). As noted earlier, these groups all occupied positions of dependency or inferiority in North American society at large. Each was subject to discrimination and exclusion in various forms, justified by an ideology defined and fostered largely by native-born White males, although even its victims sometimes propagated these ideas too. And all of these groups came to attach differing degrees of importance to education in challenging the terms of their subordinate social status. The successes and disappointments they experienced speak to the transformative power of education as an instrument of social change, and to its limitations.

   There are many other stories to tell in assessing the contributions of schooling to social change in the United States during these years. But for these groups the question of education was especially poignant. For some, schooling proved to be a potent vehicle of reformation and social mobility, and for others it ultimately became a grim reminder of failure and a source of frustration. Taken together, these stories point to some of the contours of education, or its boundaries, as an instrument of social change during the 19th century.

CASE: CONFLICT OVER RELIGION AND CULTURE IN EDUCATION

   The late-afternoon meeting of New York's Common Council on October 29, 1840, was a momentous occasion. Attended by a standing-room-only crowd in the Council's City Hall chambers, this gathering was convened to consider a petition by the city's Catholics to receive public funds for the support of schools linked to their churches. Emotions ran high on both sides of the debate that ensued. The Catholic position was presented by Bishop John Hughes, a fervid and articulate champion of New York's Irish community. Opposed to Hughes stood the Public School Society, the semiprivate corporate entity that had managed the city's charity schools for decades (and successor to the Free School Society mentioned in chap. 3), represented in this case by two well-known New York lawyers. In the course of the dispute that unfolded over almost 15 hours in two evenings, practically all of the 19th-century arguments regarding the development of common schools were heard, pro and con. Of particular importance, however, were the Bishop's pointed objections to the idea that a common, nonsectarian form of education was desirable, or even possible to attain. The Catholic petition represented a serious assault on the principle of public education as espoused by Horace Mann and other champions of public schooling. Even though it ultimately was unsuccessful, this challenge revealed much about the tensions that underlay 19th-century American society. In this instance, cultural conflict threatened to overturn public education just as it had barely started. Ethnicity, and all of its varied cultural and religious complications, made the task of defining a common school experience in the United States especially difficult.

Hughes and his Catholic followers objected to the Public School Society's institutions on a number of grounds. The first, and most important in Hughes's eyes, concerned the question of religion. Nonsectarianism, according to the Catholics, was simply another form of religion, and in the case of the city's public schools it took the shape of a general distillation of Protestant precepts and maxims, along with readings from the King James Bible. This, declared Hughes, posed the danger of Catholic children turning against their own faith, while gradually being captivated by the inveiglement of Protestant culture that prevailed in both the schools and American society at large. Even worse was the threat of students losing religion altogether. "To make an infidel, what is it necessary to do?" demanded Hughes. "Cage him up in a room, give him a secular education from the age of five years to twenty one, and I ask you what he will not come out, if not an infidel?" (Ravitch, 1974). To the minds of Hughes and other Catholics, this was a most pernicious sectarianism.

Added to this were numerous slights and slanders against Catholicism and the Irish that marked the popular textbooks and readers of the day, and reportedly characterized the conduct of many teachers in the public schools. It was little wonder, reasoned Hughes, that New York's Catholic children were so poorly represented on the rolls of the Public School Society's institutions. These schools were deemed hostile to the beliefs and cultural heritage of the immigrant Catholic population, and particularly the Irish. Textbooks related appalling accounts of the Inquisition, equating "papists" with intolerance and oppression. Other accounts praised Martin Luther, the founder of the Protestant Reformation, as a heroic figure, leading "mankind" away from the "ignorance and superstition" of the Catholic Church (Lannie, 1968). Another book declared that immigration would make the United States the "common sewer of Ireland" (Kaestle, 1983). Instances such as these confirmed the belief of Hughes and other Catholics that the Church's parochial schools were entitled to tax monies to support their operations. The existing public schools were discriminatory and culturally intolerant, and fairness demanded that Catholics be allowed to run their own public institutions.

Bishop John Hughes was an unusually ardent champion of Catholic and Irish causes, and he quickly rose to a position of national prominence among American Catholics. In this instance, however, he did not succeed in winning public support for the parochial schools. Instead, the controversy over religion in the schools of the Public School Society was resolved by establishing New York's first publicly elected Board of Education in 1842, and within a decade virtually all of the city's tax-supported schools were brought under its control. Offensive passages in textbooks gradually were expunged, and eventually new books were purchased that were more evenhanded in their references to religious themes and immigrants. For his part, Hughes became a champion of separate Catholic schools, and spearheaded the development of parochial school systems in cities across the country. These institutions were especially popular in certain larger cities with significant immigrant populations. For members of these groups, the parochial schools offered a way to maintain the religious traditions of their various nationalities and subcultures, and also a safeguard for native languages and other traditional values and social practices. In short, they represented a means for the preservation of culture, long-observed beliefs, and customs that were threatened by the prospect of assimilation into a larger, assertive American society (Lannie, 1968; Ravitch, 1974).

A part of Hughes's fervor can be explained by the circumstances of his immigrant, largely Irish constituency in the mid-19th century. Most immigrants were quite poor, and they often were subjected to blatant discrimination at the hands of native-born Whites. This was especially true of the Irish, who often arrived almost directly from the impoverished countryside of their native counties, with all of the rough-and-tumble mannerisms and proclivities of their traditional folkways. In the years following 1845, when the infamous potato famine drove more than 2 million Irish abroad, tens of thousands of destitute and desperate immigrants poured into New York and other large coastal cities each year. Crime rates went up dramatically, as did the numbers of individuals and families applying for poor relief (financial assistance) and other forms of public aid. Overcrowded and dirty, the Irish wards of the cities often were rife with sickness and disease. Many native-born Americans reacted quite negatively to these newcomers, labeling them heathens, criminals, and drunkards. Anti-Catholic sentiments were inflamed also, especially in light of the rapid growth of the Catholic Church in the wake of immigration. Nativist (anti-immigrant) fears were fueled by the perception of growing immigrant voting power as their numbers swelled in certain cities. Cognizant of these unfriendly sentiments, leaders of local Irish communities, especially the priests and bishops, recurrently felt embattled. Even though the numbers of immigrants were increasing, they still were a relatively isolated community in a land that frequently appeared to be quite hostile (Archdeacon, 1983; Kenny, 2000).

Often the threats were more than the loss of culture and religious traditions. In the mid 1840s nativist mobs in Boston, Philadelphia, and other cities attacked Catholic establishments, burning churches and other buildings to the ground in fits of anti-Catholic and anti-immigrant hysteria. These episodes were fueled by anxieties about competition for jobs and political influence that the foreigners often represented, and by the growing problems of crime and public disorder that many associated with immigrants in general and the Irish in particular. Violence also was linked to a deeply rooted hostility to Catholicism in American culture, which held the Pope to be a despotic foreign authority who threatened to undermine native traditions of democracy and local self-government. The growth of the Catholic Church, with the spread of parochial schooling and other institutional forms of Catholicism, sometimes was seen as a direct challenge to traditional American institutions.

Incidents of mob violence certainly did not make members of immigrant communities feel very welcome. Indeed, such events tended to reinforce the idea that the foreign-born needed to develop their own institutions and other sources of support, and to actively resist efforts to bring them into the mainstream of American society. For many immigrants in the 19th century, assimilation was scarcely a cheerful thought. The United States seemed an antagonistic land, one that posed particularly great dangers to their children (Archdeacon, 1983; Jacobson, 1998).

Given these facts of life in the 19th century, it is hardly surprising that relatively few Irish children attended school, especially those students from the poorest families. In his comments before New York's Common Council, Hughes estimated that fewer than half of the city's Catholic children were enrolled. He cast the blame for this at the intractability of the Public School Society, and the hostility of its wealthy, Protestant patrons toward poor, Catholic immigrant students. Even though Hughes did not succeed in getting tax monies for his own schools, he did manage to impair the reputation of his principal adversaries. Eventually, the imperious Public School Society was displaced, and the public schools became somewhat more hospitable establishments for the city's Irish students, along with other immigrants. Hughes's expanding system of parochial schools also offered greater educational opportunities to Catholics. But the question of whether significant numbers of indigent foreign children would be educated remained a critical one throughout the 19th century. These students posed a telling challenge to the schools, especially those of the newly formed Board of Education. Could the children's diverse cultural and social backgrounds be accommodated by institutions dedicated to assimilation? Or would ethnic groups stand apart from the educational system, creating a parallel community replete with their own institutions and separate from the rest of American society?

IMMIGRANT STRUGGLES AND SUCCESS STORIES

The ultimate fate of European immigrant communities, of course, is well known. The descendants of the Irish and other groups eventually came into the mainstream of American civilization, and it appears that schooling played an important role in this long process of assimilation. It was not accomplished easily, however, and the ethnic struggle for success in the United States unfolded over several generations for members of the various groups that came to the United States in the 19th century. For the Catholics that Bishop Hughes represented, this was an interval marked by considerable conflict, but one also ultimately characterized by progress. Faced with daunting obstacles when they first arrived in North America, even the poorest European immigrants could look hopefully toward the future, especially as it concerned their children.

The Irish represent an interesting case in point. As noted already, most of these immigrants arrived destitute in the years following the 1845 potato famine. Crowding into eastern coastal cities, particularly New York and Boston, they had few marketable skills and little cultural capital to help secure a foothold in the local economy. Consequently, many were unemployed, whereas others worked as unskilled laborers, living in abject poverty, and fueling stereotypes about Irish shiftlessness and irresponsibility. Irish women worked as household domestics, cleaning the homes of middle-class urbanites and further reinforcing popular impressions of their servile standing. As Bishop Hughes noted, Irish children were less likely than others to attend school; most ceased formal education before their teens in order to find jobs and help support their families. The Irish were more likely than any other major group in New York to land in the city's jails, and they constituted a disproportionate share of the homeless. Theirs was hardly a plight that offered promise of redemption (Kenny, 2000).

With time and much hard work, however, the living conditions and social status of the Irish improved. Although most of the famine generation was unskilled and impoverished, their children often were able to find opportunities for advancement. The second generation moved into the skilled trades in the larger cities, becoming bricklayers and carpenters, plumbers and masons. These were jobs featuring skills acquired at work, or in an apprenticeship, and did not require schooling or knowledge derived from books. The same could be said of posts as factory foremen or skilled operatives. They afforded a higher standard of living, however, and entry into the lower reaches of the middle class. For the enterprising Irish lad who was willing to work hard and learn from experience, it was possible to get ahead. This was the first step in a much broader process of social mobility and adaptation (Archdeacon, 1983; Thernstrom, 1973).

The Irish also benefited when they left the crowded cities of the East, as did other immigrant groups. In the mid-19th century, New York newspaperman Horace Greeley advised his readers to escape the congested urban areas, famously declaring, "Go west young man!" Those heeding his admonition often did quite well; historians have determined that the Irish and other immigrants tended to do better in the cities and communities to the west. These were rapidly growing areas where opportunity abounded, and immigrants and their offspring were less likely to encounter discriminatory stereotypes where large ethnic enclaves did not exist. Accordingly, it was not long before the social profile of the Irish in places such as Chicago, Detroit, and St. Louis came to closely resemble that of the native-born population. Economic fortune contributed to social and cultural integration (Sanders, 1977; Vinyard, 1976).

The gradual success of the Irish eventually led to higher school attendance patterns for their children, and further occupational mobility as a result. By the end of the 19th century, rates of enrollment for students of Irish heritage were practically the same as for those of long-term American natives. The sons and daughters of Irish Americans often attended parochial schools, including Catholic high schools, but the scholastic standards and moral tone of these institutions typically were quite similar to their public counterparts. As a consequence of higher educational attainment, second- and third-generation Irish Americans began to achieve a general level of occupational comparability with the larger American population. This was evident in the reduced numbers of Irish Americans employed in manual labor with each new generation. In the cities, they took positions in the growing civil service, as policemen, and in the rapidly expanding field of office employment. By the beginning of the 20th century, nearly 30% of all public school teachers in New York were of Irish descent, making them the largest single European ethnic group among Board of Education employees. The teaching forces in other large cities exhibited similar ethnic profiles. The Irish, once noted for their poor school attendance, had come to oversee many urban schools and classrooms. This was a telling measure of attainment (Kenny, 2000; Perlmann, 1988).

The Irish possessed a number of advantages that no doubt helped them to succeed in 19th-century America. They spoke English on arrival, and were rapidly integrated into the domestic political system. New York's first Irish mayor was elected in the 1880s, and Irish politicians were successful elsewhere. They also were the first major immigrant group to arrive in the United States, starting in the 1840s, placing them in a position to benefit from the decades of rapid industrialization and urban development at the close of the century. Even though they clung closely to the Catholic Church and established their own schools, hospitals, and other institutions, economic success eventually helped them to feel comfortable in their new homeland (Archdeacon, 1983; Kenny, 2000).

Other groups faced similar challenges, and some of them took considerably longer to achieve the success realized by the Irish. But all of the major European immigrant groups followed a path at least somewhat similar to that marked by the Irish and their offspring. In a careful analysis of the experience of several different ethnic groups, historian Joel Perlmann has argued that some exhibited a greater proclivity toward schooling than others. Russian Jews, for instance, sent their children to school in unusually high numbers, and experienced considerable occupational mobility as a

consequence. Italians and Poles, on the other hand, had lower rates of enrollment, and manifested slower advancements in social status. Over time,
however, school attendance increased for all such groups, and this ultimately contributed to their acclimation to American life. In some cases this
was a painstaking, step-by-step process, but the march of progress was inexorable as the years and decades passed (Hogan, 1985; Perlmann, 1988).

The gradual but eventually successful assimilation of European immigrants into the mainstream of society is the centerpiece to one of the nation's great parables. It is widely known today as the *American Dream*, a
story of success against great odds. As in the case of the Irish, most of these
foreigners arrived with little more than their capacity for hard physical labor. As they slowly made their way in the booming industrial economy of
the time, their children attended school in ever greater numbers. There
was considerable variation in these trends, but the fruits of growing school
attendance inevitably became evident in the changing occupational profile
of successive generations. Schools also helped to accommodate the offspring of immigrants to their new American identities, inculcating national
pride and loyalty along with local community values. These institutions
augmented the human capital of these groups, conveying new skills and
knowledge, at the same time that they imparted valuable cultural capital.
In this respect it is possible to say that the educational system contributed
directly to the process of social change. In many ways the schools were integral to the grand process of social, economic, and cultural integration
that marked the growth of American society in this era. It is a legacy that
continues to the present.

GENDER AND EDUCATION: A QUIET TRANSFORMATION

As noted in earlier chapters, American women had a mixed educational
legacy at the start of the 19th century. In most parts of the new nation they
historically had been excluded from the usual forms of formal education.
Female literacy rates lagged far behind those for men, even in New England,
where girls probably had received more education than in other regions.
The period following the Revolutionary War saw a flurry of activity in female education, but it is not clear just how many women were affected by
these developments. Although some female academies may have been established, no colleges admitted women in the 18th century. In 1800, despite evidence of growing female enrollment in common schools, at least
in the North, most American women were poorly educated compared to
the men of their age (Sklar, 1993; Vinovskis & Bernard, 1978).

All of this changed profoundly in the next hundred years. By the end of
the 19th century, female literacy rates exceeded those of males, women
outnumbered men in high schools, and they gradually were gaining on

them in the nation's colleges and universities. Even if it was a process largely restricted to White women, the magnitude of change was striking. At one time excluded altogether from the higher branches of education, women now threatened to dominate them—causing alarm among some educators. As seen in the previous chapter, the majority of the nation's teachers were women by the end of the 19th century, and other educated job categories were becoming feminized as well. Altogether, a revolution of sorts had occurred in American education, at least as regarded gender, a process of change that is no less remarkable when viewed from the perspective of today (Rury, 1991; Tyack & Hansot, 1990).

A shift of such proportions raises a host of questions for historical consideration. What were the implications of this change? How did it affect women's status? Did it signal a diminishing of sexism, or did it delimit the effect of patriarchy in the larger society? Just how did the rapid growth of female education change the ideological construction of gender in North American society? To answer these questions and others, it is necessary to examine the growth of 19th-century women's education a bit more closely.

The process of change in women's schooling occurred in fits and starts, and was marked by a series of struggles by visionary leaders, both women and men. Perhaps the best known early figure was Emma Willard, founder of the Troy Female Academy, near Albany, New York, today known as the Emma Willard School. In 1819 Willard wrote a treatise on female education to help persuade legislators in New York to support her planned school. She was not successful, but did raise money elsewhere. Decrying the poor state of female schooling, especially at the secondary level, Willard argued that women deserved and needed an education similar in quality—if not exact content—to that provided for "young gentlemen." She called for schools established with endowments—hence her plea for support—so tuition charges would be moderate, and such institutions would not be overly dependent on students for income (Scott, 1979).

Willard did not envision training young women for work or careers outside the home. Rather, she argued that higher quality education was necessary "to form the character of the next generation, by controlling that of the females who are to be their mothers." In other words, she subscribed to a form of the ideology of "republican motherhood," first articulated in the years following the Revolution and discussed in chapter 2. Willard was among the first women to espouse this position publicly, however, marking an important step in the development of female education. Historian Anne Firor Scott argued that this was an early expression of feminism, an effort to create a sphere within which women could grow intellectually and develop their capacities without threatening male roles. Other scholars described this impulse as "domestic feminism." The label was apt, given the concerns expressed by Willard and other educators, and this position became the underlying rationale for the development of White women's education in the remainder of the 19th century (Scott, 1978; Sklar, 1973).

Domestic feminism, premised on the proposition that educated women made better wives and mothers, was the entering wedge for a generation of reformers championing the advancement of women's schooling. It was an argument closely tied to the idea that women made good teachers. Figures such as Mary Lyon and Catharine Beecher also made careers in founding schools, training teachers, and writing about improving women's education. Their cause was abetted by common school reformers like Horace Mann, whose efforts on behalf of women teachers helped to promote the idea of extended schooling for women too. Mann later pioneered collegiate coeducation as the first president of Antioch College. All of this helped to create an atmosphere conducive to higher levels of female education. As public high schools were opened, in that case, they typically were coeducational. In some larger cities separate schools were established for girls, to maintain a certain decorum in segregating the sexes. But even in the most conservative settings, few arguments were offered to challenge the logic of domestic feminism. In opening the city's female high school in 1854, the Boston School Committee declared that women have "the most fearfully responsible duties which can be assigned to human beings: to form and give direction to human character." The purpose of the school, in that case, was to prepare young women to become "competent mothers and teachers," as well as "fit companion(s) of high minded and intelligent men." If American civilization was to prevail, according to this line of reasoning, the nation's women needed the best possible preparation for marriage and motherhood (Clinton, 1984; Rury, 1991; Welter, 1966).

Once the door was open to female enrollment in secondary education, the nation's high school population soon was marked by a preponderance of young women. By 1870 women were a majority in public high schools, and at the century's end there were almost twice as many girls as boys in these schools. The large number of female students was due both to relatively low male enrollment rates and the fact that young middle-class women liked school. Boys could get jobs more easily and at younger ages, leading many not to enroll. On the other hand, being students got the young women out of the house and into a setting where they could make friends and learn about the larger world. It also helped many of them prepare for jobs teaching, working in an office, or even going on to college. About a fifth of the collegiate student population was female by 1900. The high school, in that case, proved quite alluring to teenage girls, especially those from "middling" households, and this represented a major shift in American culture. Given the growth of high school enrollments, and the gender-neutral character of many other educational institutions, White, native-born women probably were better educated than their male counterparts in the 1890s, a notable shift in American history (Tyack & Hansot, 1990).

Not everyone participated equally in this process of change. As might be expected, women from certain backgrounds were better represented in the high schools at this time. By and large, the teenage daughters of white-collar workers, the emerging middle class, were more likely to enroll in school than other girls their age, and young women with parents born in the United States outnumbered those from immigrant families. In this pattern of participation it is possible to see once again the effects of social and cultural capital at play. Young White women from fairly long-established communities, and with relatively well-educated parents, possessed clear advantages when it came to availing themselves of advanced forms of education. Other women also enrolled in high schools, including some from immigrant and working-class backgrounds, but they faced obstacles that their middle-class counterparts did not. Typically, they were required to work to help support their families, and they often married at earlier ages. Domestic feminism, it seems, favored the education of the women most disposed to pursue schooling beyond the primary grades, and those comfortable with the role of transmitting American cultural traditions to the succeeding generations. In this respect, the growth of women's education was the very embodiment of cultural capital, a means of transferring valuable skills and knowledge within customary family roles and structures (Rury, 1988a, 1991).

The expansion of women's education, consequently, was a quiet revolution. The ideology of domestic feminism held that the new skills and knowledge acquired by educated women were not a threat to their traditional roles. Higher levels of education did not mean that women were going to compete with men for positions of authority and leadership in society at large. Women's education, in that case, posed little challenge to patriarchy. Because the numbers of women attending high schools and colleges were still relatively small, less than 10% of the relevant age cohort, female educational attainment hardly jeopardized the status of most men. Although there was some debate over women's education in this period, it generally did not concern a change in women's standing. The success of women's schooling, after all, may have hinged on educators' inability—or unwillingness—to seriously challenge the status quo in gender relations.

CASE: EDWARD CLARKE AND THE DANGERS OF FEMALE EDUCATION

Not everyone was pleased with the development of female secondary and higher education in the late 19th century. Some conservatives were troubled by the prospect of coeducation, which seemed to imply that young men and women should receive precisely the same education. Others worried about the morality of teenage male and female students even mixing in the same building, and feared an epidemic of promiscuity. Catholic leaders, for example, denounced coeducation on these grounds. But perhaps the biggest uproar was occasioned by the publication of a slim volume in 1873 by physician Edward Clarke, titled *Sex in Education, or a Fair Chance for the Girls*. This book, which went through some 11 printings in just 6 years, claimed that extended academic and physical exertion was dangerous to young women, and that schooling during the teenage years threatened their health and prospects of fertility. The controversy that Clarke's book spawned revealed much both about Victorian beliefs concerning women and sexuality, and about popular attitudes regarding female education. And it underscored the magnitude of change in women's education at the time (Zschoche, 1989).

Clarke was a one-time member of the Harvard medical faculty, and this modest academic pedigree added to his book's notoriety. The fact that he was from Boston, a place where conservative morality often predominated in public discourse and in institutional policies, no doubt contributed to the national debate that followed the book's publication. But Clarke did not ground his arguments in tradition and morality. Instead, he maintained that scientific evidence clearly indicated that exertion of the kind associated with school often presented the danger of infertility—or sterility—in young women. He argued that adolescence was a critical time in the physical development of women, when their reproductive organs took shape. During that period, he wrote, a young woman "accomplishes an amount of physiological cell change and growth which nature does not require of a boy in less than twice the number of years." The book featured a series of cases that Clarke claimed to know firsthand, discussed in a clinical fashion, which described high school-aged girls suffering from anemia due to overstrenuous study. Such accounts were no doubt shocking to the sensibilities of most Victorian parents, and the aura of scientific respectability that Clarke lent to them gave the book credibility. To many families, the mere possibility of young women losing their ability to beget children was a specter too terrible to contemplate. It was this question that lay behind the book's considerable public appeal (Rosenberg, 1982).

The threat of infertility struck at the very heart of women's education, particularly as it was supported by the ideological formulation of domestic feminism. If education promised to compromise a woman's capacity to bear children, after all, what was the point of being educated in the first place? The very object of female education was to become better mothers. If schooling somehow put motherhood itself in jeopardy, the logic of domestic feminism would seem to obviate the need or desire for education. Clarke's argument thus appeared to pose a dire hazard to the prospect of reform and growth in women's schooling (Rothman, 1978).

The challenge to women's education represented by Clarke and his book, it turned out, was a rather empty one. The response to his argument was swift and compelling. Within a year of its publication at least three other volumes appeared in print, challenging the idea that schooling was a danger to women's health. Educators across the country clamored to protest Clarke's suggestion that women should be discouraged from pursuing higher education. Several argued that women's health problems were the result of poor exercise and too much confinement indoors at home. Young women, they maintained, needed to get away from the house during the day, and to be stimulated intellectually and physically. They were able to cite dozens of cases of women flourishing at school, instances that seemed to directly contradict the evidence in Clarke's book. Echoing the arguments of others, former normal school principal Anna Brackett argued that young women needed intellectual stimulation to thrive, and that boys and girls were "wonderfully alike" in their search for knowledge and understanding. To deny women the opportunity for education, she reasoned, would leave them "dwarfed and crippled," physically developed but "mentally a child." Statements such as these left little doubt where most of the nation's educators stood on the question. Although some conservatives rallied to Clarke's defense, his argument found relatively little support within the educational community. Despite the book's many editions and the attending public outcry, it ultimately did not exert much influence on the development of women's schooling (Rury, 1991; Tyack & Hansot, 1990).

This episode is telling, however, on a number of counts. Clarke's book sparked controversy because it touched on Victorian anxieties about female fragility and sexuality. At the same time that domestic feminism opened the door for greater female education, it also put women on pedestals in the name of virtue, morality, and motherhood. As suggested in the previous chapter, the idea of a revered but highly delimited role for women was an important component of 19th-century common school ideology. Middle-class Americans thus often harbored contradictory feelings about women's education. Although they welcomed the growing opportunity for girls represented in the coeducational high schools and colleges, they also worried that new patterns of schooling might serve to compromise traditional gender roles. This partly accounted for the great public interest that Clarke's book provoked. In addition to this, 19th-century medical theories placed inordinate emphasis on the reproductive organs in explaining women's health, a by-product of the Victorian preoccupation with sexuality and motherhood as the preeminent female role. Consequently, the very fact that Clarke suggested schooling was linked to illness and hence to infertility was bound to draw attention to women's education (Degler, 1980).

Nevertheless, in the end there were too many factors in support of women's education for critics like Clarke to stem its development. Among the many responses engendered by *Sex in Education* in the year following its publication was a thoughtful critique by William Torrey Harris, then superintendent of the St. Louis public schools (he eventually became U.S. Commissioner of Education). Harris noted that teaching boys and girls together seemed to be a natural arrangement, similar in practice to the ways they worked together in other settings, like the family and church. "It is in accordance with the spirit of institutions," he declared, "to treat women as self determining beings, and less in want of those external artificial barriers that were built ... in past times." In addition to this, Harris suggested that the girls exerted a positive influence on the boys, making them less unruly and providing models of good behavior. "The rudeness and abandon which prevails among boys," he wrote, "at once gives place to self restraint in the presence of girls." Of course, Harris also appreciated the value of women teachers, and the importance of educated mothers, the major tenets of domestic feminism. But his principal motivations may have been quite practical, if not somewhat penurious. Harris realized that without young women, high schools like the ones his own district had spent so much money to build and maintain probably would not have been feasible. Female enrollments made these institutions viable; male students were too few in number and they also tended to have lower graduation rates. Female high school graduates also provided a supply of new teachers for the burgeoning urban districts. Given these considerations, it is little wonder that educators across the country vociferously rejected Clarke's arguments. Women's education was a key component of the emerging public school system, especially the rapidly expanding secondary schools (Reese, 1995; Rury, 1991).

Perhaps the most important element in the debate, however, was the experience young women and their families encountered in the schools. For the most part, American parents who permitted their daughters to go to high school and college did not see them get sick or become sterile. Indeed, there is little systematic evidence that women's experiences in this regard were any different than those of young men. In an analysis of daily attendance records, my own research found that female students in St. Louis averaged only 2 percentage points less than boys over a 15-year period (94% vs. 96%). Clearly, large numbers of girls were not missing school because of illness, and female students also had lower dropout rates. If Clarke's book was intended to give the parents of teenage girls pause about schooling, the experiences of their daughters were cause for reassurance. The vast majority of American high school students were quite healthy, and the girls apparently were no more sickly than their male counterparts (Rury, 1991).

Still, the old Victorian anxieties did not die easily. Popular beliefs about inherent differences between men and women were deeply ingrained, and were reinforced by the professional utterances of ministers, physicians, and a host of other pundits. Even if educators believed in the virtues of coeducation, they also took pains to ensure that female students would not become overexerted, nor find themselves exposed to any unseemly influences. Consequently, it was commonplace for schools

built in this era to feature separate doors and staircases for male and female students. Some educators warned against scheduling too many
classes on higher floors for young women, as repeated stair-climbing requirements might prove a danger to them. Others urged regular programs of exercise for female students, to help build stamina and combat
anemia. Even the most outspoken advocates of coeducation continued
to see women as frail, and in need of special attention to guarantee their
health and vitality. The ideology of domestic feminism was pervasive, and
it linked schooling inexorably to female roles of domesticity and motherhood. The very same ideas that served to expand women's education
also defined the limits to which it might develop. This was the contradiction inherent in the controversy over Edward Clarke's otherwise unre-
markable little book (Tyack & Hansot, 1990).

Coeducation and women's higher education continued to be points of
contention for decades in the United States—and they still manage to
get into the news today. Clarke's book, after all, was published just as the
rapid expansion of female secondary and higher education began in the
later 19th century. At the turn of the century, Teddy Roosevelt and other
national leaders expressed concern about the low rate of marriage
among college-educated women. Others worried about morality, especially as greater numbers of women began appearing on college campuses and images of "flappers" and dating began to appear in the
twenties. Such concerns, like Clarke's, represented the push of women's
education against the boundaries of patriarchy and the ideology of domesticity that had defined women's lives through much of the history of
American civilization. It was a tradition and set of cultural expectations
that would change only slowly (Gordon, 1990; Solomon, 1985).

EDUCATION AND WOMEN'S ROLES

So what was the effect of these changes? If the quiet revolution in women's
education did not challenge traditional gender roles, and the purpose of
women's education was to prepare better wives and mothers, how did
changing patterns of female schooling affect social change? This is a complex question, and a difficult one to answer. One way to assess the impact
of changes in women's education, however, is to consider its relationship
to other areas of women's lives, such as work and social activism. Another
way of posing the question, then, might be this: How did shifts in female
education affect women's engagement with the larger world outside their
immediate families? Did the revolution in women's education stimulate
any appreciable change in other areas of women's lives?

There is a widespread consensus among historians that gender roles
were shifting significantly in the latter part of the 19th century. This was the
era of the early women's rights movement, of course, and activists such as
Susan B. Anthony and Elizabeth Cady Stanton became nationally promi-

nent. Much attention has been focused on this group of women, especially in light of their campaigns for women's suffrage. There can be little doubt that expanding options for women's schooling contributed to the growth of this movement, as its most active members usually were themselves rather well educated. But the women's rights campaign was relatively small in spite of its notoriety. More significant were the thousands of women, most of them middle class, who became involved in other reform activities at this time. On issues ranging from temperance to universal peace and ending child labor, these middle-class women became immersed in a wide array of social reform activities. They were in the forefront of the social settlement movement in the cities. Jane Addams's work at Hull House in Chicago is perhaps the best-known example, but there were scores of other women who worked in similar settings. They became active in local politics, and some even were elected to school boards and other offices in western states, where liberal voting requirements permitted female participation. Women's clubs flourished across the country, and became vehicles for local reform campaigns on a host of issues. Female readers supported the first mass circulation magazines focusing on social issues, and helped to make "muckraking" a potent political influence in the 1890s. In all of these respects, women contributed to the moral leadership for the nation, even if they were denied formal political power at the national ballot box. This also was a new development in American history, and by and large it was educated women who provided the leadership and the most active participants in these endeavors (Rendell, 1985; Rosenberg, 1982; Sklar, 1995).

Cultural historian Ann Douglas has suggested that the cumulative effect of the many changes that occurred in the latter part of the 19th century marked a "feminization of American culture." As middle-class women became more involved in social reform, they wielded a form of moral power that drew on their delimited but nevertheless exalted status as mothers and wives. If they were supposed to be inherently nurturing and virtuous in personal and family matters, after all, it followed that women should also represent a high ethical standard in social affairs. In the public mind, consequently, female reform activities became associated with the amelioration of social ills. But intrinsic virtue, real or imagined, was only a part of the story. To function as effective reformers, these women needed highly developed organizational skills, advanced literacy and analytical capacities, and a refined sense of history and social change. Given this, it is little wonder that educated women played such a prominent part in the development of social reform. Schooling provided women with the skills and the expansive viewpoint necessary to become effective agents of social improvement. They became capable speakers, good writers, and sharp-eyed social critics, examining a wide range of public problems and advocating any number of reforms. And at the same time they were denied conventional careers, more than a few women became outspoken reform figures and leaders of informal advocacy groups. In this regard, education contributed materially to the process of social change, even if female schooling was delimited and tended to reinforce traditional gender roles (Douglas, 1977; Harris, 1978).

Social activism was only one area of change in White women's lives during the latter part of the 19th century; yet another quiet revolution was just getting under way in women's work. As noted earlier, girls and young women had been employed in factories since the early 19th century, and women teachers were commonplace in New England and elsewhere. But beginning in the 1880s and 1890s, women started finding employment in offices and on the sales floors of large retail establishments—the first department stores. The invention of the typewriter in the 1880s spurred this development, as its manufacturers suggested that women were inherently skilled in its use. They compared it to piano playing, a feminine talent in the public mind. Even more important, however, was the rapid growth of office employment, stimulated by the development of large-scale industrial and retail enterprises serving national markets, and the governmental agencies created to supervise them. These new, massive firms required extensive correspondence and record-keeping, functions that called for legions of skilled workers. High school-educated women provided a ready pool of recruits for these positions, usually at a lower cost than men. The same tendency existed in the employment practices of the big department stores and catalogue houses then beginning to appear, such as Sears Roebuck and Montgomery Ward. The result was a new field of work for educated women: employment in a store or office. This was a respectable alternative to the factory, one that generally was clean, well lit, and provided contact with reputable members of the public at large. Without the changes in women's education, however, it is questionable whether the transition to female employment in these jobs would have occurred so quickly and easily (Davies, 1982; Kessler-Harris, 1982; Powers, 1992; Rotella, 1981).

Women moved into a number of other professions in the closing decades of the 19th century, most of them requiring one form or another of advanced education. The new research-oriented universities and professional schools admitted women, and eventually trained some of them to be professors, medical doctors, and lawyers. Although their numbers were tiny at the start, it marked the beginning of a gradual transformation of women's work that would continue through the 20th century and to the present. At the same time, the teaching profession underwent rapid feminization, and thousands of educated women found employment in the nation's schools. Even though the educational backgrounds of these women varied, a growing minority had attended colleges and normal schools. Thus, as the 19th century drew to a close, women began to appear in the ranks of professional employment—another new development in

American history. A key step in this process, of course, was women gaining access to higher education, and enrolling in colleges and professional schools, including normal schools, in ever larger numbers. Here too, shifts in female education were a prelude to changes in women's work (Goldin, 1990; Rothman, 1978; Solomon, 1985).

Changes in women's education, in that case, led to a number of subtle but important alterations in female roles in the closing decades of the 19th century. It is important to recognize that only a minority of women participated in these developments, and for many others traditional role expectations and outright sexism continued to delimit their life opportunities. Most of the women who benefited from education were White and from middle- or upper-class backgrounds. But for those who had access to schooling, change was an option. Women became active in public affairs and moved into new, higher-status fields of employment. Higher levels of education made these changes possible. And they would continue well into the next century, especially in the area of employment. In this regard, it is possible to say that education contributed directly to the process of social change, at least as regarded gender roles. In providing White, largely middle-class women with skills, knowledge, and credentials, it enabled them to challenge many of the restrictions their mothers had faced. It did not spell the end of patriarchy, and it marked only another step in a long and continuing struggle over gender roles. But it was significant nonetheless. It was a telling process of change, one that appears even more significant in light of the experiences of others (Blackwelder, 1997).

AFRICAN AMERICAN EDUCATION: HOPE AND DESPAIR

If White middle-class women benefited from their commitment to education, other groups were not so fortunate. Like women, African Americans also have been subject to discrimination and exploitation in American history. As noted in chapter 2, the very first schools for Blacks were intended to teach them morality and proper behavior, attributes White leaders thought they lacked. Of course, such schools served only a tiny fraction of the nation's African American population; the vast majority of them were slaves in the 18th and early 19th centuries. This meant that opportunities for education were extremely limited, although it would be wrong to assume that a significant degree of learning did not occur in slave communities. During slavery, Black children were taught valuable lessons about the importance of their families and immediate communities, and they learned about their status within Southern society. But they generally were not allowed to become literate. This created a great thirst for knowledge within the slave community, and helped to make education an important priority for African Americans.

Slavery ended with the Civil War, and the period that followed saw a revolution of sorts in Southern Black education. Aided by sympathetic Whites, schools were established across the South and African American literacy rates began to climb sharply. This was accompanied by a political and social revolution, one that saw Blacks gain the right to vote and hold political office for the first time in Southern history. Before long, however, reaction set in, and the gains of the Civil War era were halted abruptly. Even though African American schooling had advanced significantly, little lasting change occurred in American race relations. Regardless of their education, Blacks found themselves subject to virulent discrimination and a continuing legacy of servitude. As regarded the question of race, education does not appear to have been a significant instrument of social change, at least during the 19th century.

EDUCATION AND SUBJUGATION

Education has long been a major theme in African American culture. Dating from the early 19th century, Black leaders emphasized the significance of schooling as an instrument of social uplift. Even in slavery, when most African Americans were denied access to all forms of formal education, enterprising individuals made valiant efforts to acquire literacy and other skills. Virtually all Blacks recognized that lack of education was a mark of inferiority, one that seemed to legitimate their servile status and ensure their political impotence. It is little wonder, in that case, that when slavery was formally abolished during the Civil War, African Americans rushed to educate their children in the schools opened during the conflict's aftermath. Schooling was seen as the road out of Canaan, the way to salvation.

Themes of resistance and redemption predominate in the history of Black education in the United States. During the slavery era and afterward, Blacks worked to maintain a cohesive cultural identity in the face of racist oppression. Formal education typically was denied to slaves, except for training afforded by masters interested owning skilled workers, or lessons learned in church or from friendly Whites, often children. However, after the bloody and much sensationalized rebellion by the messianic slave preacher Nat Turner and his followers in 1832, and the rise of the abolitionist movement at about the same time, many states outlawed instruction of any sort for slaves. To be caught even in possession of a book was cause for severe, even cruel, punishment (Bond, 1966; Bullock, 1967).

But laws and brute coercion could not halt the process of acculturation within the slave community. Important lessons were passed from one generation to another, representing a rich cultural tradition that has left a lasting imprint on the South. Storytelling was an honored tradition, and a highly refined craft in the quarters. Slave children were taught from an early age to honor and respect their elders and to preserve family and community traditions, and at the same time they had to resist the efforts of Whites to exploit and abuse them. Many managed to gain literacy illegally, and passed these skills along to others. They struggled to assert their humanity in spite of Whites' efforts to rationalize slavery by comparing them to animals. In doing this, they cultivated a set of beliefs asserting the moral superiority of African Americans over their crass oppressors, and a tradition emphasizing the exceptional resourcefulness and prowess Blacks demonstrated as a result of persecution. Above all, they expressed the desire for freedom, and the ability to determine their own destinies. Education—with self-improvement—was a central element of this endeavor, and hence a major theme in African American culture (Blassingame, 1972; Webber, 1978).

In the Northern states, where slavery had been ended earlier in the century, free Blacks worked assiduously to establish schools for their struggling communities, or to modify those handed down from philanthropic Whites who had founded them, such as New York's Manumission Society. They often were supported in these efforts by the growing abolitionist movement, with Whites and free Blacks seeking an immediate end to slavery. In the larger cities, these schools—the legacy of the Manumission Society's African Free Schools—eventually became vital Black community institutions. A generation of Black leaders received their formal education in them, and they provided a foundation for higher levels of schooling for African Americans chartered by White abolitionists and other philanthropists. By midcentury the basic elements of an educational system for Blacks were being assembled in the North, with separate colleges and manual training schools just being founded or planned, although some African Americans were educated at White colleges too. These institutions, along with a tiny but earnest cadre of well-educated Blacks, became models for the development of an educational system to serve the much larger African American population of the South after the Civil War (Curry, 1981; Litwack, 1961).

Despite these positive developments, 19th-century African American education was quite different from that provided for other groups. In this respect it reflected the powerful influence of racist ideology during this era. First, it was almost always segregated, and it often encountered fierce resistance from Whites, who recurrently felt threatened by the prospect of a skilled and knowledgeable African American population. Although school leaders argued that boys and girls should attend the same schools, even the most liberal reformers shrank from the suggestion that Blacks and Whites should be educated together. Horace Mann, champion of the common school and an outspoken opponent of slavery, did not support it. Popular reactions sometimes were violent; schools for Blacks were burned and their teachers run out of town. This was a contrast to the response to women's ed-

ucation, which prompted bitter debates but never led to such violent out-
bursts. Second, when Black schooling was provided, it usually had strong
moralistic or vocational overtones. This was a tendency evident from the beginning, as in the Manumission Society's school in the latter part of the 18th
century. Generally speaking, few Whites believed that African Americans
could benefit from advanced academic study. Instead, they usually were
given a curriculum that emphasized good behavior and preparation for a life
of manual labor. From the very start, then, Black schooling was separate and
unequal (Horsman, 1981; Rury, 1983, 1985; Schultz, 1973).

Soon after the Civil War ended in 1865, the victorious North set about to
change the social and political order of the South, a process referred to as
Reconstruction. This was no small task, and there was much debate and
conflict about just how to accomplish it. Even before hostilities had ended,
however, the federal government created the Freedman's Bureau, an
agency charged with supervising the transition of former slaves to their
new status as free citizens. A major part of the new agency's task was to provide schools for the freedmen, to give them critical literacy skills and citizenship education. Over the next several years thousands of these schools
were established, staffed by idealistic teachers recruited from the North,
along with some White Southerners and a growing number of Blacks. Local
African American communities donated hard-earned cash and labor to establish still more schools, and to expand upon the government contributions. Tens of thousands of Black families eagerly enrolled their children in
these institutions, delighted at the opportunity to receive even a modicum
of formal education. Throughout much of the South, enrollment of African
American students matched or exceeded those of Whites, eventually reaching a quarter-million students of all ages. Although the circumstances of
these schools were not always stable, and attendance fluctuated as African
Americans struggled to survive in the new Southern economy, Black literacy rates began to improve significantly. In 1860 only a small fraction of the
region's then mostly slave Black population could read, but by 1890 more
than two thirds were literate. Reconstruction truly marked a revolution in
the lives of former slaves, and education was an important aspect of this
process of change (Butchart, 1980; Foner, 1988; Morris, 1981).

The rise of Black schooling was accompanied by a remarkable period of
political empowerment and activism for the former slave population of the
South. With their basic rights affirmed by passage of the 14th and 15th
Amendments to the U.S. Constitution, and enfranchised by new, liberal
state constitutions, required for reentry to the union, African Americans in
the South found themselves able to vote and hold office for the first time in
American history. The result was a glorious moment of political potency,
when former slaves came to occupy critical positions of leadership across
the region. Black leaders led a movement to form new, liberalized state

governments. Education provisions were written into new constitutional documents, and additional support for public schools was extended. Such changes were especially galling to Southern Whites, who complained bitterly about occasional improprieties or excesses in the wake of these events. The most die-hard racists plotted a counterrevolution, and waged a violent war against the Reconstruction regimes in various states (DuBois, 1935; Foner, 1988; Franklin, 1961).

Unfortunately, the progress made during the decade or so of Reconstruction was not enduring. When Northern Whites lost interest in reforming the South in the wake of an economic recession in 1873, and the federal military occupation of Southern states ended, a resurgence of White supremacist rule swept across the region. This change was not as abrupt as it sounds, for the Ku Klux Klan and other White racist groups had rained terror on Blacks and reform-minded Whites all during Reconstruction. But by the late 1870s there were abundant signs of the old order returning to power. With the great compromise of 1877, when presidential candidate Rutherford B. Hayes agreed to withdraw the last federal troops from the South in exchange for political support in a disputed national election, an arrangement that got him "elected," Reconstruction finally came to a close. This meant changes in many areas of life, but it also marked an end to the rapid expansion of Black schooling experienced in the years immediately following the war (Foner & Mahoney, 1995).

Without the protection of federal soldiers, Blacks were gradually stripped of many basic rights. More importantly, African American political power was dramatically curtailed. At the end of Reconstruction more than 300 Blacks had been elected to state legislatures or to Congress. There was one U.S. senator and a governor too. It was these leaders who had spearheaded the development of Southern school systems, and they played key roles in drafting new state constitutions to support public education. By 1880, however, their numbers had dropped by two thirds and shrank even further in the years that followed. The result was an abrupt change in the region's political culture, with liberal influences sharply circumscribed. Black community leaders, especially those who sought political power, and the Northern Whites who had assisted them, came under pointed attack from the traditional White Southern power structure. From the earliest days of Reconstruction, Northern Whites were called "carpetbaggers" and sympathetic Southern Whites "scallywags." It was after these struggles, during the 1890s, that Southern states initiated poll taxes or other devices to limit Black voting rights, and the region's African American population was reduced once again to a state of dependency on the local White power structure. It was not a historical situation that held much promise for advancing the cause of Black rights, and schooling, at least in the realm of public education, suffered accordingly (Ayers, 1992; Williamson, 1984; Woodward, 1974).

Southern Whites were never enamored of Black education, and even if they did not dismantle the schools established for African Americans, they were not about to provide them with anything more than the most basic support. As a number of historians have documented, the decades following Reconstruction marked a time of widening disparities in Black and White education throughout the South, largely because of differences in state funding. Although there is evidence that Black schooling continued to flourish for a time, disparities began to grow when Southern Whites finally became interested in education. Term lengths in Black schools had stagnated by the 1890s, whereas those in the White schools began to increase, even approaching the standard of the Northern states, 100 days or more per year. Black teachers were paid much smaller salaries than their White counterparts, and were permitted only tiny budgets for textbooks and other supplies. Where there had been some measure of parity in the past, school districts came to spend as little on a typical Black student as a fifth of the amount they expended for an average White student. Public high schools for African Americans were relatively scarce in the South in the latter part of the 19th century, the very time when secondary schools were starting to be built in large numbers elsewhere –and for Southern Whites. Consequently, Black schooling was generally limited to the most rudimentary forms of elementary education, with short sessions and paltry support. Except for a tiny group of middle-class African Americans who could afford to send their children to a handful of private Black high schools and colleges in the region, the vast majority of the Black population was provided with no more than basic skills in reading and calculation. Even if this helped to boost overall rates of literacy among Blacks, it did little to assist their political or economic advancement (Anderson, 1988; Harlan, 1958).

As historian James D. Anderson has pointed out, the underlying problem facing African Americans was their role of servitude in the political economy of the South. In a region still dependent on a cash-crop agricultural economy, the Black population's arduous physical labor was essential to the wealth of the White elite. African Americans no longer were slaves, but they still had to make a living within the existing economic order. Radical proposals to give the freedmen land after the war, expressed in the slogan "forty acres and a mule," were never supported by the federal authorities, so Blacks were forced to return to the plantations many of them had abandoned upon attaining freedom. Various forms of indentured servitude replaced slavery, usually under the guise of "sharecropping." For African Americans who tried to escape to the cities, as many did, new forms of occupational segregation were devised, relegating them to the most menial forms of unskilled labor at the lowest wages. For women in the towns and cities, domestic service became a near universal form of employment, as they kept the homes of middle- and upper-class Whites throughout the South. In short, the old order was restored, albeit in a somewhat new bearing. After the heady experience of Reconstruction had passed, the familiar Southern status hierarchy reemerged in a different form, with Blacks on the bottom rung and wealthy landowners and other Whites on the top (Anderson, 1988; Margo, 1990).

It is important to acknowledge the critical role of racist ideology in providing a set of justifications for these changes. Racism reinforced the servile status of African Americans, and helped to mobilize poor Whites against political challenges to the old order. Theories and myths of Black inferiority abounded, often in even more virulent form than during slavery. Still smarting from the experience of Reconstruction, when Blacks enjoyed basic rights and a modicum of political power, many Whites were determined to prevent any such changes from occurring again. As a consequence, Southern Whites rarely were proponents of Black schooling. Rather, their interests lay in maintaining the abject status of African Americans, as it ensured a ready source of labor for harvesting cotton and tobacco. Schooling, it was said, only ruined a good field hand or servant, making him or her less willing to perform menial tasks and endure long hours of labor. Because many Southern Whites wanted a compliant and tractable Black workforce, they resisted efforts to improve African American education (Fredrickson, 1971; Higgs, 1977).

By and large, education remained underdeveloped throughout the region. Schools of any kind had never been a priority of most Southern states, and plantation owners generally were inherently suspicious of the idea that common folk—White or Black—should be educated. Many found the very idea of popular democracy to be abhorrent, and believed that the spread of education threatened to undermine the region's traditional economic and political order. Even during the common school era, reformers waged uphill struggles to establish even the most basic rudiments of statewide school systems—and they were far less developed than in the North and West. This changed somewhat after the Civil War, as Southerners were forced to adhere to Northern expectations in order to regain admission to the union. In the period when African Americans enjoyed a brief period of political potency during Reconstruction, they led the movement to create systems of public education in Southern states. But with the end of Reconstruction, most states cut back drastically on spending for education, and provided much smaller subsidies for Black schools than for White ones. African American education, despite the ferment and accomplishments of the Reconstruction period, was stillborn. It would not be until the 20th century that new advances would be evident (Bullock, 1967; Harlan, 1958; Leloudis, 1996).

CASE: THE GREAT DEBATE ABOUT BLACK EDUCATION

In the decades following the Civil War there was much discussion and conflict over the direction and role of African American education. As indicated earlier, there was a long-standing tradition in the United States of focusing Black schooling on issues of moral development and vocational education. These were important themes in schooling for Whites too, but for them there also was an emphasis on intellectual development, citizenship education, and the cultivation of future leaders. Proposals for Black schooling often downplayed these latter considerations, because either Whites found such ideas threatening, or racist ideology dictated that African Americans were unlikely to benefit from them. Whatever the rationale, avenues for advanced intellectual training remained severely limited for Blacks throughout much of the 19th century, even after other educational opportunities—such as common schooling and manual training—had started to expand significantly. Still, new prospects for advanced academic preparation did begin to appear in the South just before the close of the period, with many of them started and financed by African American communities. Through these efforts, an articulate class of well-educated Blacks gradually emerged on the national stage, offering new ways of thinking about African American education. As a consequence of this development, one of the great educational debates of American history began to unfold.

The principal antagonists in this conflict were two of the towering African American figures of the age: Booker T. Washington and W. E. B. DuBois. Washington was the older of the two, and without doubt the more prominent at the close of the century. Raised as a slave during his childhood in Virginia, he had been educated in the 1870s at Hampton Institute under the tutelage of its first director, General Samuel Armstrong. Reflecting the singular influence of his mentor, Washington was an avid proponent of the virtues of manual and industrial training for African Americans. In his own experience at Hampton, he had been deeply impressed by the power of physical labor to impart self-discipline and a spirit of self-improvement in students, and in himself in particular. When he became principal at Alabama's Tuskegee Training Institute in 1881, Washington had acquired a vehicle to develop his own educational philosophy, and a platform from which he could proclaim it to the world. Within a decade he was the nation's leading proponent of industrial education for African Americans. It was an idea that was hardly new, but one that was to receive fresh prominence as a result of his influence (Harlan, 1972, 1983).

DuBois's experience could hardly have been more different from that of Washington. Born free in the North to economically stable parents, DuBois was educated in the Great Barrington, Massachusetts, public schools before attending Fisk University in Nashville and pursuing graduate studies in Europe. He also studied at Harvard, earning a B.A. degree and becoming the first African American in that university's history to receive the Ph.D. in 1895. Himself the beneficiary of a classical education, DuBois was an advocate of advanced academic training for African Americans. He felt that Blacks needed thoughtful and articulate leaders to assess and articulate the injustices they had suffered and to formulate strategies to improve their status. To his mind, the traditional emphasis on manual training in African American education was an anathema, an obstacle preventing Blacks from realizing meaningful gains in their political and economic standing. Accordingly, DuBois recommended the education of a "talented tenth" to provide an inspired and socially conscious leadership for the nation's African American population. These individuals would constitute an intellectual vanguard, challenging racist oppression with the ideals of democracy, legal principles of equity and fairness, and appeals to the nation's moral conscience. It was a visionary and in some respects a naive proposal, but DuBois believed it absolutely critical to the future (Lewis, 1993; Meier, 1963).

Between the two men, Washington was more widely recognized and celebrated during his time. This was partly due to the accommodating quality of his public utterances, which made him especially popular among influential Whites. In his most famous public address, at the opening session of the Atlanta Exposition in 1895, Washington invoked the metaphor of a ship searching for fresh water when he called upon African Americans to "cast down your bucket where you are—cast it down in making friends in every manly way of the people of all races by whom we are surrounded." He called on Blacks to look to Southern Whites for economic opportunity, and to accept their place in society, seeking improvement though honest hard work. He emphasized the loyalty and familiarity of Blacks over immigrant workers, and endorsed acceptance of Jim Crow segregation, declaring, "in all things that are purely social we can be separate as the fingers, yet one as the hand in all things essential to mutual progress." Characteristically, Washington poured ridicule on African Americans who sought higher learning. "No race can prosper," he declared in Atlanta, "till it learns that there is as much dignity in tilling a field as in writing a poem," adding, "it is at the bottom of life that we must begin and not at the top." Elsewhere he offered biting caricatures of lazy Blacks seeking education as a way of avoiding hard labor, or educated African Americans who lacked the character imparted by work of any kind. In discussing Reconstruction, for instance, in his widely read autobiography, *Up From Slavery*, Washington noted the high level of interest in education at the time, commenting that "the idea, however, was too prevalent that, as soon as one secured a little education, in some unexplainable way he would be free from most of the hardships of the world, and, at any rate, could live without manual labor" (Harlan, 1972; Luker, 1991).

Washington could not voice too much opposition to education, however, as he ran a school himself and was known internationally as an educator. But he represented a certain kind of schooling. In describing his own institution, Washington emphasized the practical lessons imparted through manual labor, declaring, "We wanted to teach them to study actual things instead of mere books alone." In this respect, the Tuskegee model of African American education conformed closely to that advocated by prominent Whites for decades, one intended to teach Blacks good work habits and sound moral principles. Interestingly, Washington's critique of educated Blacks also echoed the sentiments of many other Whites, who believed that schooling only made African Americans less willing to perform menial labor. Perhaps to avoid this, he always was careful to point out the centrality of work to every aspect of his educational philosophy. It is little wonder, in that case, that Washington was so popular among the nation's White leaders; his stature among African Americans, however, was another matter (Anderson, 1988; Kliebard, 1999).

DuBois was finishing his Harvard training at the time of Washington's famous address in Atlanta. He spent the next decade teaching at various Black colleges in the South and conducting research on the conditions of African American life in the United States. In 1903 he published *The Souls of Black Folks*, in many respects a response to the appearance of Washington's autobiography just 2 years earlier. In direct opposition to the views expressed by Washington, DuBois argued that higher education was the most pressing task facing African Americans. Without the broadest and most intellectually challenging academic preparation, he asked, how would Black leaders be prepared to provide guidance and raise up their brethren? With no colleges and universities, he wondered, where would the faculty for Black secondary schools—or even Washington's Tuskegee—come from? No educational system, DuBois declared, "ever has rested or can rest on any other basis than that of a well equipped college and university." Without higher education, in other words, there would be no genuine education, and no general improvement of the South's Black population (Lewis, 1993).

To DuBois's mind, the time to focus attention on industrial training of the sort practiced at Tuskegee had long past. Sharply critical of Washington, DuBois described his views as "a gospel of Work and Money to such an extent as apparently almost completely to overshadow the higher aims of life." If the African American population was to change its status of servitude and political impotence, a new form of education would be necessary. "The foundations of knowledge in this race, as in others," he wrote, "must be sunk deep in the college and university if we would build a solid, permanent structure." This, of course, was a direct contradiction of Washington's oft-repeated view that higher education for Blacks was a waste of time and resources. But it was only through the leadership of university-trained Black men and women that DuBois thought real advancement was possible (Meier, 1963).

As DuBois noted in *The Souls of Black Folk*, Washington's most outspoken critics were members of his own race, particularly those who had been trained in universities and were involved in Black higher education. His most glowing admirers were wealthy Whites, especially philanthropists eager to help advance the cause of education in the South. As a consequence, Tuskegee and other institutions representing Washington's philosophy of industrial education received a steady stream of contributions from wealthy Northerners, amounting to millions of dollars in the years following Washington's ascendancy. Other African American institutions also received assistance, but it was often accompanied by explicit pressures to conform to the Tuskegee model of manual training. In time this became an important source of resentment among African American educators across the region. There also was a perception that Washington was widely hailed as a Black leader even though he did not represent any particular African American constituency, apart from his own institution. When Washington was extolled in the White press, many Blacks naturally felt pride that a fellow African American was being praised, but others came to resent his statements advocating a delimited form of education and accommodation to the existing Jim Crow social order. Even if Booker T. Washington was held up as a role model, he hardly was universally admired (Anderson, 1988; Anderson & Moss, 1999; Hawkins, 1962; Moss, 1981).

In terms of the educational system of the day, there is no question about the winner of this debate over the future of Black education. Tuskegee was the most widely emulated and influential African American institution of its time. Until his death in 1915, Washington was the most famous and powerful Black man in the United States. Tuskegee-trained teachers fanned out across the region, spreading the gospel of industrial education through Black high school and teacher training institutes for the next several decades. This was dubbed the "Tuskegee Machine" by DuBois—but it was not enduring. Instead, another legacy eventually came to shape the future of African American education and Black social and political aspirations. Frustrated by the impotent political vision of Washington and accommodationist Black leaders of the time, DuBois and other reform-minded African Americans formed the Niagara Movement in 1909—a series of meetings to discuss the problems of race and inequality in the United States and potential solutions. Within a few years, these forums gave birth to a new civil rights organization, the National Association for the Advancement of Colored People (NAACP). DuBois served as the first editor of its magazine, *The Crisis*. Though not as well known nor as influential as Washington's "Tuskegee Machine" at the time, this new association would eventually hold the keys to advancement for African American social and political status in the 20th century. And this made the question of who "won" the great debate over Black education a complex one indeed (Harlan, 1983; Lewis, 1993).

THE DEGRADATION OF BLACK EDUCATION

At the end of the 19th century the lives of most African Americans in the South had reached a low point. The gains they had made during reconstruction were largely wiped out. The majority were poor agricultural workers living in a state of virtual serfdom. The educational advances of the 1860s and 1870s had been rolled back. Even more important, they had been stripped of even the most basic of civil rights. The 1890s were a time of political turmoil in the South, as the populist movement, an alliance of poor farmers and sharecroppers, challenged the established regime. In the wake of these tumultuous events, thousands of African Americans were murdered—most of them publicly lynched—for a variety of purported reasons, ranging from the petty to the profane. Lynching was a practice that dated back to the days of Reconstruction, but it reached new levels of severity as the century drew to a close, and it continued in the South for several decades in the 20th century. Whatever the pretext, this was a powerful lesson in political education, viciously affirming the region's doctrine of White supremacy. And it helped to create an ideological milieu that hardly boded well for the development of African American education (Ayers, 1992; Williamson, 1984).

As historian Louis Harlan has documented, the period around 1900 and immediately afterward witnessed a dramatic expansion of White education in the South, much of it accomplished at the expense of the region's Black population. Disparities between the schooling of children from the two races reached historic highs, with White children receiving as much as 10 times the local expenditures on Black education. In the most heavily populated Black areas of the region, the so-called "Black-belt" where big plantations and the cotton economy still held sway, White education was subsidized by Black taxpayers. More high schools were established, but by 1910 just 65 such institutions had been established for a Black population numbering more than 10 million, and most of them were small. Aside from school teaching and the ministry, there were few professional jobs that young African Americans could aspire to. By and large, the education system for Southern Blacks was designed to enforce their servile status and to ensure their political and economic impotence. Apart from a handful of private or otherwise elite institutions largely supported by Northern philanthropy, it largely offered education for degradation (Anderson, 1988; Anderson & Moss, 1999; Harlan, 1958).

The relatively small Black population of the North, only a 10th of all African Americans, had access to considerably better educational opportunities. Studies indicate that African American school enrollment was equivalent to that of most Whites, and often higher than that of recent immigrants. Their school terms were as long as those for Whites, probably longer on average because most Northern Blacks lived in cities, where the most advanced school systems existed. And in a growing number of places, public schools were formally integrated, even if residential segregation made racially diverse schools difficult to find. But despite their relatively elevated levels of educational attainment, African Americans encountered great difficulties in gaining employment commensurate with their credentials. In his intensive study of social mobility in a Northern city during this period, Joel Perlmann discovered that Blacks benefited the least from education, even though their overall levels of enrollment were higher than those of the Irish, Italians, and a number of other European immigrant groups. Racism permeated the job market, and served to dramatically counteract the benefits of schooling for African Americans. And if this was true in the urban North, it was especially pernicious in the South, where White supremacy was even more thoroughly ingrained in the popular consciousness (Franklin, 1979; Mohraz, 1979; Perlmann, 1988).

All things considered, the educational experiences of African Americans in the latter part of the 19th century were accompanied by frustration and disappointment. Blacks flocked to schools in the years following the Civil War, only to see their educational opportunities circumscribed after Reconstruction. They fought to establish modern educational systems across the South, and then witnessed a resurgence of White supremacy that denied them basic civil rights and elevated White education over their own. They encountered racism at almost every turn, but especially in the labor market, where their schooling was often considered irrelevant, if not an impairment. Where Black education did succeed, it was often designed to train students for menial employment, or to provide preparation for a very narrow range of professional positions. Altogether, it was not a happy story. African American schooling in the latter part of the 19th century provides an instance when hard work and investment in education did not result in meaningful social change. In the end, the school could not materially improve the status—nor change the basic social roles—of most of the nation's Black population. A considerably more prolonged process of social and political change would be necessary to accomplish that end.

SCHOOLING NATIVE AMERICANS

If African Americans were subject to servitude, the Native Americans (or American Indians) were a conquered people, driven from their land and forced to adapt their cultures and traditions to radically new circumstances. Perhaps the central series of educational events for this diverse assortment of groups in the 19th century was their collective experience of loss at the hands of Whites (or European Americans), who defeated them in a series of wars and forcibly relocated them to isolated reservations. This was accompanied by a string of campaigns by Whites to change the lifestyles and beliefs of Native Americans, to eradicate their traditional culture and replace it with the Christian and capitalist values of the nation's dominant groups. The principal vehicle used to accomplish this was the school. The story of Native American education in the 19th century involves a deliberate crusade to fundamentally alter an indigenous way of life, utilizing instruction as a means of instilling new values and behavior on a scale not exercised with other groups. As historian David Wallace Adams poignantly observed, it was "education for extinction" (Adams, 1995).

By the end of the 19th century the era of open warfare against the American Indians had drawn to a close. Battered by almost constant conflict with European settlers, and steadily losing land and resources, the American Indian population in the United States had dropped from perhaps 2 million in 1800 to about 250,000—its lowest point in modern history. In the meantime, the countryside had been settled by Whites, who eventually came to outnumber the indigenous peoples by more than a fifty to one ratio. Once the period of active conflict on the frontier had started to wind down, and the bulk of the Native American population was settled on reservations, sympathetic Whites began to comment on what became widely termed "the Indian Problem." As they saw it, American Indians were not adjusting well to their future roles as potential citizens, and as parents of upright, responsible offspring. Instead, they were seen as living in "filth" and "squalor," without appreciation of the virtues of private property, individual responsibility, and decent standards of cleanliness and personal hygiene. The answer was an aggressive campaign of education to teach American Indians the advantages of modern civilization (Hoxie, 1984; Prucha, 1976).

Native Americans had long practiced their own forms of education, of course, a process of acculturation that varied from one tribal group to another. American Indian children typically learned while working alongside adults, accompanying them to the fields and hunting grounds, and being allowed progressively greater responsibilities in adult tasks. Given the rather sharp division of labor along gender lines in most tribal societies, education also usually differed for males and females. Children were told stories of their ancestors and learned legends about the history of their tribes. Elderly members of the tribal group often served as great reposito-ries of wisdom, providing explanations for complex natural phenomena and suggesting solutions to difficult social and political dilemmas. Native Americans, however, rarely organized separate, formal institutions to edu-cate the young, and illiteracy was usually a norm. Instead, education was a largely informal process, conducted within the everyday events that de-fined life, and was not intended to impart such academic skills as reading and writing (Axtell, 1985; Fuchs & Havighurst, 1972).

The earliest schools for Native Americans were established by Protestant and Catholic missionaries, intent on converting them to Christianity and introducing basic literacy and commercial skills. As noted in chapter 2, a number of experiments in education for American Indians were con-ducted in the 18th century, most with only limited success. These efforts gradually intensified in the next century. The Bureau of Indian Affairs (or BIA) was established as a branch of the War Department in 1824, and helped to supervise efforts to provide education to the Native American population, most of which were conducted by religious groups. By the mid-19th century dozens of missionary schools had been started, but they reached only a tiny fraction of the American Indian school-aged popula-tion, less than a couple thousand per year. It was not until the period after the Civil War, however, when hostilities between Native Americans and the federal government reached a peak, that interest in broadening American Indian education began to take hold (Berkhofer, 1965; Szasz, 1988).

Starting with the presidency of Ulysses S. Grant in the 1880s, educa-tional programs were run directly by the BIA, rather than through mission-ary groups, as a part of the federal government's "Peace Policy" toward American Indians. Thereafter, appropriations increased rapidly, climbing from $20,000 in 1870 to nearly $3 million in 1900. Schools and enroll-ments multiplied quickly too. In the mid-1870s there were about 150 schools enrolling several thousand students, but by the end of the century the number of institutions had more than doubled and enrollments ex-ceeded 20,000. This represented roughly half of the age-eligible Native American population. These changes in federal policy constituted a mas-sive intervention into the lives of American Indian children (Coleman, 1993; Hoxie, 1984).

The statistical growth of these schools, however, was only part of the story. The goals of this educational program were even more ambitious than previous reform ventures, including the schools for African Ameri-cans established during Reconstruction. The vast majority of these Ameri-can Indian students, more than 80%, attended special boarding schools intended to separate them from the influence of their families and tribal customs. Others attended day schools. The first boarding institution, and most famous, was in Carlisle, Pennsylvania. Established in 1879 in an abandoned military barracks by Richard Henry Pratt, a former army officer and veteran of the Indian Wars, the Carlisle school became a model for similar institutions across the country. It eventually became quite famous for its football teams, which competed successfully against top colleges (Adams, 1995; Coleman, 1993).

Pratt fervently believed in the superiority of modern civilization over American Indian culture, and predicted that Native American children could be changed for the better if placed in the right environment. "Transfer the savage-born infant to the surroundings of civilization," he declared, "and he will grow to possess a civilized language and habit." The goal of the government-funded boarding schools, in that case, was to obliterate any traces of Native American culture and identity in their students, and to inculcate the virtues of patriotism and Christian propriety. In the words of Pratt, they were to "kill the Indian in him and save the man" (Adams, 1995).

Clearly, one intention of this new direction in federal policy toward American Indians was the pacification of a potentially hostile indigenous population. A major problem, however, was devising ways to get their children into the schools. As suggested by the early enrollment figures, not many Native American parents initially were eager to send their children to Carlisle or other boarding schools. But large numbers eventually were convinced to give the schools a try. Some of these parents wanted their children to learn the ways of Whites, while others felt pressured to conform to what they believed to be a government policy of mandatory schooling. Through a combination of active recruitment, mild coercion, and personal persuasion, thousands of American Indian students eventually did attend these institutions, most of them for terms restricted to less than a few years. Despite its limited appeal, the federal network of American Indian boarding schools became one of the largest experiments in deliberate cultural exchange in the nation's history (Szasz, 1977).

While on campus, Native American students were offered a course of study focused on manual training and moral development, not dissimilar to the curriculum at Booker T. Washington's Tuskegee Institute. Pratt even initiated a program that allowed Carlisle students to live with White families for a period of months, gaining work experience while learning firsthand mainstream American standards of living. The reaction of students was mixed. Many learned to read and calculate, while gaining valuable insight into traditional American civilization, and even recalled their experiences with pleasure. Others rebelled and returned as soon as possible to the reservation, some of them running away in the middle of the night. But whether they graduated or not, and regardless of how they felt about their experiences, very few American Indian students became assimilated into the larger Euro-American society as a result of their boarding school education. The duration of schooling was too brief, and barriers to assimilation too great, for education alone to accomplish such a purpose (Adams, 1995).

The failure of assimilationist goals was only partly the result of the short-sighted policies of the BIA. Apart from the narrowly vocational quality of the schools, and their strong moralistic overtone, White attitudes toward American Indians proved to be perhaps the greatest barrier to acclimation. Although they did occasionally encounter hostility, Native Americans often were treated as aliens and objects of curiosity. Most had not yet been granted citizenship. Many were exploited by ruthless or racist Whites, forced to work long hours in demeaning jobs with little pay. Not feeling welcome in the larger society, the vast majority after leaving school returned to the reservations, where they assumed the lifestyle of their families and neighbors. In this respect the boarding school experiment was a failure, and Richard Pratt's vision of a "civilized" American Indian was ultimately unfulfilled. The cultural identity of Native American children, it turned out, was considerably stronger than Pratt and other educators had imagined. And most other Americans were not interested in making them comfortable as participants in the nation's mainstream culture. It would take more than a few years of schooling aimed at intentional assimilation to affect change on this scale (Coleman, 1993).

The boarding school movement eventually lost its momentum, shortly after Pratt's generation of educators passed from the scene, and ultimately a more comprehensive and culturally sensitive set of policies was adopted. This occurred after the famous Merriam Report of 1928, which marked a major shift in thinking about American Indians. It was clear that the boarding schools had done little to acculturate Native Americans to traditional Protestant culture in the United States. BIA education expenditures also did not change the social and political standing of American Indians. In the hands of overbearing and misguided reformers like Pratt, and backed by the political will and resources of the federal government, schooling was intended to change the values and behavior of a significant element of the nation's population. Of course, many such measures were undertaken in good will, with the belief that assimilation represented a distinct improvement in the lives of most Native Americans. But unlike the case of African Americans during Reconstruction, reformers did not take account of the wishes of the proposed subjects of this educational experiment. Native Americans were not clamoring for schools, and they attached relatively little value to the formal instruction offered in the institutions established for them. Consequently, the effect of education on the values and social standing of this group was minimal (Szasz, 1974, 1977).

The case of American Indian education provides one of history's clearest examples of schooling being used consciously to affect social change—indeed, to affect dramatic cultural adaptation. But in this case education did little to alter the role or status of a marginal group in American society—in this instance yet another racial minority. As regarded Native American education, reformers had clearly overestimated the power of schooling to affect change. But it is not clear that they ever seriously recognized the possibility of failure; nor did they understand the limits of education as an agent of social change. Cultural chauvinism, abetted by racism and nationalism, blinded them to the enormity of the task they had undertaken and the larger problems associated with assimilation in American life. In the end, social change of this magnitude was more than schools alone could achieve, even under the most enlightened circumstances. Given the paternalistic and intolerant quality of the BIA schools in the 19th century, it is little wonder that they did not prevail.

SCHOOLING AND THE CONTOURS OF SOCIAL CHANGE

The latter part of the 19th century was a time of accelerating change in American life. Guided by the principles of the common school era, educational reformers proposed to use education as a means of social amelioration and assimilation. This idea certainly applied to the destitute immigrants then beginning to fill the cities of the eastern seaboard. During Reconstruction these sentiments led to a massive campaign to educate recently freed African Americans, driven largely by Black aspirations for schooling, and a little later they contributed to a government-led crusade to "educate" American Indians. At about the same time, the offspring of European immigrants started entering the schools in greater numbers, pursuing the promise of success in their new homeland. White women began attending public high schools in ever larger numbers, buoyed by common school ideals of inclusiveness and a political ideology that assigned women a special role in rearing future generations of citizens. Each of these episodes in educational history imparts a lesson about schooling and social change in the American experience. Together they demonstrate the limits and possibilities of education as an agent of societal transformation, revealing some of the contours of social change.

To begin, these examples of educational change allow comparison of the effects of schooling on different groups of people. This is one of the insights afforded by historical analysis, permitting one to discern patterns of inequality in the past that may not be evident today. For instance, during the 19th century, European immigrants and White women benefited substantially from the increased educational opportunities available to them, whereas other groups did not. True, the pace of progress that various ethnic groups and women experienced in entering many professional fields and in assuming larger roles in public life often was quite slow. But school enrollment rates for immigrant children gradually increased, and tens of thousands of young White women graduated from high school in the decades following the Civil War. Over time, a growing number of both groups continued on to college. The educational advance of women was especially dramatic. Before long, they outnumbered the boys in high schools, out-graduating them by nearly a two to one ratio in the 1890s. As noted already, middle-class women came to be better educated as a group by the end of the century than their male counterparts, an attribute that provided them with considerable cultural capital, a degree of social standing and credibility not available to other groups. Even if they lacked formal economic and political power, in that case, White women received tangible benefits from formal schooling, advantages that would eventually help them to advance in other areas of social life. For the descendants of the major European immigrant groups of the 19th century, the school also became a potent instrument of social and economic integration. It was a part of the "American Dream," the idea that upward mobility was possible in American society.

The story was quite different for the other groups discussed earlier. African Americans flocked to schools in the period after the Civil War, supporting them with hard-earned cash and donations of materials and service. They exhibited a high degree of social capital, cohesive community values in support of formal education, and this contributed to rapid enrollment growth and dramatically improved literacy rates. After a brief period of expansive enthusiasm, however, Blacks entered a time of frustration and despair in their educational history. Once freed from federal oversight, Southern states reduced their support for Black schools, and sharply curtailed African American power in other spheres of life. The Southern economy depended on a servile labor force, and Whites were not ready to allow Black education to threaten the existing social structure. Consequently, most African American students were provided a bare-bones curriculum, with meager resources for learning. This was hardly a recipe for social advancement.

The problem of race and social status went far beyond schooling. African Americans who did manage to acquire an advanced education faced severe discrimination in the labor market. Even someone as distinguished as Harvard-educated W. E. B. DuBois, acknowledged today as one of the great social scientists and writers of his time, was unable to gain an appointment at a White university. Indeed, he would not have been even considered for a position in Southern White high school. But plain discrimination was only part of the story. By the end of the century Black education in the South was under attack, and as scores of African Americans were lynched each year, the prospects for further advances in the social standing of this group looked quite bleak indeed. Even in the North, educated Blacks were rarely able to find work commensurate with their credentials. Although African Americans clearly valued schooling, and made education an important priority in their communities, the effect was quite limited. Apart from a very small minority, Black Americans did not benefit materially from schooling in this period. In this case, the promise of education to affect social change went largely unrealized.

The experiences of American Indians were similar to those of African Americans, at least as regards the effect of education on their social standing. Even though the federal campaign to educate Native Americans eventually reached a large number of them, the effects on their social standing and assimilation in American life were negligible. American Indians did not lobby for the educational opportunities they were offered, and many of them doubtless sent their children off to the government schools grudgingly. But even if Native Americans had wanted to use the school as a vehicle of social advancement, it is unlikely that they would have succeeded. The institutions they were provided were not intended to encourage social mobility, and most Americans were not willing to accept American Indians as their equals. For groups such as these, assimilation and social improvement required more than schooling alone.

These historical episodes point to the pervasive power of race as a factor in American life in the 19th century. Racist ideology, which held non-White peoples to be socially and morally inferior, prevented most White Americans from even contemplating the premise of social equity for Blacks and Native Americans. Discrimination against European immigrants, although often expressed in racial terms at first, turned out to be quite different. Even if the Irish were despised when they first arrived, for instance, the fact that they were White eventually served to ease their assimilation. As the offspring of European immigrants became economically successful, learned to speak English properly, and began to intermingle with the native White populace, the old ethnic antagonisms gradually began to fade away. Indeed, as some historians have suggested, the Irish and other foreigners "became White," partly by exhibiting virulently anti-Black behavior themselves (Ignatiev, 1995; Jacobson, 1998). In the case of European immigrants, racist ideology may have hastened the process of social integration by helping to identify a shared set of physical and cultural characteristics.

For non-European minorities, on the other hand, the story was quite different. Distinguished by physical appearance, assimilation was not an option for these groups. Despite the experience of the Civil War, and the antislavery campaigns of the abolitionist movement, racism remained a potent ideological force in American culture. It made the idea that simple vocational education was appropriate for children from these groups appear to be natural and logical. It also was used to justify the gross inequalities in funding levels and the quality of materials used in Black and White education throughout the South, and in much of the North also. Most Americans simply accepted such inequities as unavoidable facts of life, dictated by the social and biological differences that they felt distinguished the country's various racial groups. Many decades would pass before a significant number of American Whites would even begin to question assumptions such as these (Takaki, 1979).

Gender, of course, was an important factor in the nation's social life as well. Sexist ideology, which dictated a subservient status for women, was also quite prevalent at this time. Sexism led most Americans, including many women, to assume it quite extraordinary that women would even dream of seeking social equality, or aspire to careers other than motherhood. The sexual division of labor was pervasive, and it restricted women to a relatively narrow range of work roles in society at large. Despite the pernicious effects and omnipresent quality of sexist ideology, however, Americans generally accepted the idea that White women should go to school, and that they should study more or less the same subjects as men. These views had deep roots in the idea of republican motherhood, mentioned in earlier chapters. There were those who took exception to this, of course, as the controversy over Edward Clarke's book demonstrated. But such views were in a minority by the latter part of the 19th century. The vast majority of American schools were coeducational, and most people found it quite natural that boys and girls would attend classes together on a daily basis, with proper supervision, of course. Despite its baneful influence in other spheres of life, in that case, sexist ideology appears to have left much of the educational system open to women, at least among Whites.

Even if women could go to school, sexist discrimination remained an important fact of life in the United States, and change in women's status occurred incrementally. The fact that thousands of women did receive an education did not necessarily mean that they could compete with men for higher status jobs, or choose to be socially and economically independent. Conservative social conventions continued to dictate well-proscribed roles for women, despite the level of their education. Still, as noted earlier, the range of jobs open to women did begin to expand in this period, at least partly in direct response to the growing numbers of highly educated women ready and willing to fill them. Historians have pointed to the development of clerical work and female positions as sales clerks as evidence of such a shift, and small numbers of women began to make inroads into the professions as well. On top of this, hundreds of thousands of White women became schoolteachers, constituting some 80% of the profession by the end of the century. Even if their social roles were circumscribed, in that case, women do seem to have realized certain benefits from their rising levels of educational attainment. This was one case where schooling does appear to have been a lever of social change, even if a modest one.

Gender and race, therefore, appear to have differed in their impact on education, and the ways that groups and individuals were able to make use of schooling in society at large varied as well. Racism was an especially virulent obstacle to the aspirations of African Americans and to the prospects of Native Americans. Blacks in particular exhibited very high levels of social capital, which ultimately proved to be of limited value to their collective social and economic advancement. Native Americans may not have possessed quite the same set of values, but they too were given few opportunities to utilize their education in the larger society. Race proved to be an especially formidable barrier to advancement, a telling contour of social change. Sexism, on the other hand, limited the opportunities of White women considerably, but left certain avenues of advancement open to those who dared to utilize them. Progress was slow, and the sexual division of labor proved quite formidable, as it continues to be today, but enterprising women were able to realize gains that were largely unavailable to other groups in the 19th century, even if these advances were exacted with a struggle. Gender was a different sort of contour, robust yet also permeable, allowing women to advance in the face of hostility and to contribute in important ways to the shape of social evolution.

Differences such as these, products of historical vagaries affecting the American ideological landscape of the time, clearly shaped the effects of American education on the larger society during the 19th century. There were some groups that found education to be a vehicle of social advancement, such as the European immigrant groups mentioned earlier, and others who encountered discrimination similar to that experienced by Blacks and Native Americans, such as Mexican or Chinese immigrants. For some Americans, consequently, the school was a potent instrument of improvement and opportunity, and a source of hope for a better life. For others it was a false hope, a chimera that ultimately failed to deliver on its promises. In this respect it was, as Henry Perkinson (1968) suggested, an "imperfect panacea." Ideological constructs such as racism and sexism clearly affected the ability of schools to alter the social standing of the people they served. But as time passed, the circumstances of the schools' impact on society would change also, and education would prove to be a powerful instrument of social change in the future. The relationship of education and society would itself change as history moved ahead.

The Progressive Era:
Reform, Growth, and Differentiation

On January 1, 1901, Americans enthusiastically greeted the 20th century, proclaiming that it would be a time of dramatic transformation. Although many of the predictions made at the time proved to be far-fetched, the general sentiment was well founded. From the standpoint of social change, the opening decades of the new era were among the most momentous in American history. It was a time of massive societal development and widespread reform. The modern, urban civilization that came to characterize the 20th-century United States decisively burst into view, bringing with it a host of new social problems. And it was then that many elements of today's public institutions and governmental policies were established, including the modern school system.

The years between 1890 and 1920 are often referred to as the Progressive Era in American history. This term is probably best known in reference to the reform activities of political figures such as Teddy Roosevelt and Woodrow Wilson, and the muckraking journalism of Ida Tarbell, Jacob Riis, and Lincoln Steffens, among others. But it also has been used to characterize a wide range of other reform campaigns, touching on virtually all facets of life at the time. Among the more important aspects of progressivism was educational reform, and the period was marked by many different educational ideas and innovations. In fact, a major current of reform propositions and practices in schools has been self-consciously labeled "progressive education" in the last century or so. As explored later, this broad reform impulse has also been a source of abundant controversy and debate, and it continues to exert considerable influence today. Understanding progressivism in education thus is an important reason to study this period in the history of American education (Goldman, 1952; Hofstadter, 1955b; May, 1964).

The basic tenor of the historical period, however, was not rendered by education or political reform. Rather, it was defined by the forces of industrialization and urban growth, the very same factors that had shaped the course of social development in the age of the common school. The difference between the two periods was largely a matter of magnitude and pace. By the start of the 20th century, the degree of industrial development and the rate of urbanization in the United States had reached a point scarcely imaginable just a few decades earlier. Business enterprises were organized on a mammoth scale, serving far-flung national and international markets, and utilizing new technologies for mass production and the rapid deployment of resources. Cities grew at a dizzying rate, as millions of immigrants arrived to seek jobs in the booming industrial economy. Cultural diversity, a matter of growing concern in the antebellum period, became a fact of life in the largest cities by 1900, where dozens of languages could be heard on downtown streets on any given day. American society was becoming more complex, and it seemed at the time to be subject to forces that were difficult to understand or control (Hays, 1957/1995; Higgs, 1971; Rodgers, 1998).

The disjunction posed by large-scale industrialization and urbanization proved quite disconcerting, to say the least. After all, the newly emerging metropolitan society of the 20th century was a far cry from the bucolic and relatively uncomplicated farm life that previous generations of Americans had lived. This discontinuity became a source of new anxieties, and eventually was the focal point of innumerable campaigns for social amelioration. As noted by Robert Wiebe, it was an era marked by a "search for order," and this more than anything else characterized it as a new stage in American history (Wiebe, 1967).

Progressivism, in short, represented an effort to respond to the hardy new world of dramatic industrial development and urban growth. In the words of Lawrence Cremin, it was "a vast humanitarian effort to apply the promise of American life ... to the puzzling new urban-industrial civilization that came into being during the latter half of the nineteenth century" (Cremin, 1961). Whether or not it was entirely humane is open to question, but there can be little doubt that education was an integral part of this reform impulse. It was an age that called for new forms of schooling, designed to serve a multitude of different purposes. As society became more complex and variegated, so did its educational system. Much of what is discussed here examines the response of education and schools to the dynamic social forces shaping this historical era. But first it is important to consider some of the challenges of growing up in this new urban industrial milieu.

CASE: COMING OF AGE IN URBAN AMERICA

As one might expect, the social environment of big cities had a profound effect on American children. Among other things, contemporaries believed that it loosened traditional sources of authority and mechanisms of control that adults had used to manage the behavior of youth. The growth of cities was seen as ushering in a time of greater freedom and open-mindedness, when the young were allowed a new measure of latitude in how they chose to conduct themselves. These changes were hardly abrupt, as most children and youth continued to be deeply affected by prevailing social and cultural norms. But novelty was definitely coming into fashion, and it was especially palpable in the most populous urban areas.

Anzia Yezierska (1889–1970) was an immigrant to the United States in the early 20th century. She was Jewish, and came with her family from Poland to New York, where she lived on Manhattan's bustling Lower East Side. Like thousands of other young women in her circumstances, she struggled to understand the strange, complicated, and often contradictory world she found herself in. She eventually became a writer, and her work focused on the immigrant experience; she also was a social activist, and had a brief but intense relationship with the educational reformer John Dewey. In 1925 she published a partly autobiographical novel titled *Bread Givers, A Struggle between a Father of the Old World and a Daughter of the New World*, which vividly portrayed several of the biggest challenges she faced. It is a moving work, one that captures the dilemmas many immigrant women encountered as they came of age in the new urban world of the 20th century (Henriksen, 1988; Westbrook, 1994; Yezierska, 1925).

The central character of Yezierska's book is Sarah Smolinsky, the youngest daughter of a rabbi who was dedicated to studying the Torah. Even though her father had little income, and the family lived in dire poverty, Sarah and her sisters found themselves subjected to his paternal domination. A man of tradition, he expected the women of the house to respect his every whim and to provide most of the family's livelihood. This was a way of life for many Orthodox Jewish families in the immigrant ghetto. As Yezierska noted sardonically, "Only if they cooked for men, and washed for men, and didn't nag and curse the men out of their homes: only if they let the men study the Torah in peace, then, maybe, they could push themselves into heaven with the men, to wait on them there."

In the book Yezierska described the miserable, crowded conditions of her family's life in New York. They shared a tiny apartment, with poor lighting and ventilation and barely adequate plumbing. They rarely left lower Manhattan, where they inhabited a world of towering tenements and buzzing streets. There was precious little beauty in their daily existence, and there were few prospects for hope in the future. Sarah was a bright student, but in the view of her Orthodox father, women were not supposed to be scholars. She was expected to help support the family and to obey her parents, particularly her father. As Sarah grew older, however, it became more difficult to conform to her father's demands.

A turning point came when young Sarah saw her three older sisters pushed into marriages arranged by their father, to men they neither loved nor much admired. Even though her father received cash payments for agreeing to these unions, a traditional practice known as a "bride's price," the prospective husbands were hardly well-to-do. They too were poor, and expected their wives to abide by conventional expectations for women. Indeed, Sarah became gradually more horrified as she watched her sisters enter into lives with little hope of improvement, subject to the dominance of their seemingly cloddish husbands. "I began to feel I was different than my sisters," she announces. "If they ever had times they hated Father, they were too frightened of themselves to confess.... But could I help it what was inside me? I had to feel what I felt even it killed me." She became determined to avoid the fate of her sisters, and to escape her father's authority.

The closing chapters of the book describe Sarah's flight from both the control of her family and the cultural and physical confines of the ghetto. Fed up with her father's hypocritical and self-serving pronouncements about wanting only the best for his family, and frightened by the prospect of an experience like those of her sisters, Sarah left home abruptly. She found a job ironing clothes at a cleaning establishment and rented a room of her own. Even though the space was small and her furnishings quite modest, she felt a new sense of independence and self-esteem. In examining the room, she remarked on the fact that it had a door, a feature missing in the rooms of her family's apartment. "This door was life," she declared. "It was air. The bottom starting-point of becoming a person. I simply must have this room with the shut door." Thus Sarah Smolinsky began to define herself anew, with the ability to shut out those parts of her world she no longer wanted to identify with, and to define herself with a modicum of personal control over her destiny.

Education was a powerful agent of change in Yezierska's book. Always bright and enterprising, the newly independent Sarah found that she was able to qualify for a college scholarship. Winning it, she decided to go away to study, an option that would have been unthinkable for a woman in the patriarchal tradition of her father's Orthodox Jewish beliefs. She found college exhilarating, even if she was painfully aware of her status as a cultural outsider in a collegiate world dominated by Protestant and middle-class sensibilities. Moved by her own experience of growth, Sarah decided to focus her studies on education, to prepare to become a teacher. Eventually she graduated, and took up the life of an educated, independent woman, dedicated to her profession and finally able to look dispassionately at her family's experiences. It was a tale of success against great odds, and redemption from the trials of challenging tradition and finding one's own way in the world. It also was a story that captured many themes of immigrant achievement in the United States during the early years of the 20th century. In this respect it was a continuation of the parable of uplift and assimilation derived from the experience of the Irish and other groups in earlier decades.

Anzia Yezierska was an astute observer and a compelling writer. She experienced many of the events described in *Bread Givers*, but also shaped the story to represent the lives of other young women like her. Millions of immigrant children grew up in the teeming ethnic ghettos of New York and other Northern cities. Even though their parents often clung to traditional values and Old World customs, the younger generation was unavoidably exposed to the rapidly evolving mores of the city, and to the ever-changing fashion of youth. They lived hard lives under crushing conditions. Crowded tenement apartments, similar to the one Yezierska described in *Bread Givers*, were a fact of life for many families. But the dynamism of the city, with its atmosphere of continuing change, always seemed to offer the prospect of a better future. As long as the urban industrial economy continued to expand rapidly, there would be opportunities for improvement (Binder & Reimers, 1995; Kessner, 1977).

As a work of historical fiction, *Bread Givers* captures the theme of conflict between different generations within immigrant families, but it also highlights the difficulties facing immigrant women who found themselves caught between old and new value systems. These women loved their families, but often felt constrained by traditional expectations that sharply restricted their options in life. Of course, many of them willingly conformed to the wishes of their parents, marrying within their immediate ethnic communities and striving to pass traditional values onto the next generation, their children. But others, like Sarah Smolinsky, rebelled in one way or another, making a break with the older generation and defining a new way of life for themselves. Most of these women probably did not experience as sharp a rupture with tradition as Yezierska's Sarah, but the rapidly evolving culture of the urban environment made it difficult not to challenge at least some of the tenets of parental authority. There was a big, bright world outside of the teeming ghetto communities, and the new generation of immigrant children was bound to discover it sooner or later. And for immigrant women, the lights often shone even more brightly and alluringly (Gabaccia, 1994; Harzig, 1997).

Education was an important part of this story as well. It is no accident that Yezierska's principal character found college to be an effectual vehicle of escape from the prisons of her past life. For thousands of immigrants and their children, formal education turned out to be a potent means of social improvement. This was especially true for Jewish immigrants, as their children attended schools in unusually high numbers. Schooling provided skills that they could utilize in the job market, and it also gave them a better command of English and other aspects of mainstream American culture. In other words, education provided access to better employment opportunities and it served as an agency of assimilation. For bright young immigrant women like Sarah Smolinsky or Yezierska herself, various forms of higher education—whether in normal schools, colleges, or specialized training institutes of one kind or another—proved a means to professional status and a degree of independence unimaginable to their mothers' generation. By 1920 the daughters of immigrants represented the largest single group of teachers in New York City, and they comprised a similarly large fraction of the teaching force in other

Northern cities as well. To be educated meant that assimilation was well under way, and it also suggested a greater degree of independence for American women. In this respect, schooling helped to break the chains of tradition (Markowitz, 1993; Rousmaniere, 1997).

The emergence of a dynamic urban civilization during the early 20th century signaled a new era in the history of American childhood. The rapid growth of cities, greater ease of transportation, and seemingly boundless opportunities made many young people impatient to leave home and start life on their own. It was harder for parents to exert strict controls over their children in these circumstances, even if many continued to attempt it. Other changes also affected family life in these years. The average size of American households became smaller, and an atmosphere of greater tolerance and compassion progressively came to characterize familial relations (Mintz & Kellogg, 1988). This is discussed in the next chapter, but such developments marked the advent of greater independence and freedom of expression for children and youth in the United States. As one historian has suggested, teenagers especially began to move to "the beat of different drummers" in this era (Graff, 1995). Expanded educational opportunities, with new forms of schooling, also were a part of this story. It was a time of rapid change and exciting possibilities; it was the 20th century.

GROWTH AND DIFFERENTIATION: AN AGE OF UNCERTAINTY

As noted in chapter 3, the closing decades of the 19th century were a time of unprecedented economic growth in the United States. It was the height of the industrial revolution, a period when manufacturing output, urban development, and immigration from abroad all expanded at a faster pace than in any other time in the nation's history, including the present. It was also a moment of great societal and political turbulence, much of it stimulated by rapid shifts in the nation's economy and its social structure. New scientific developments changed the way people lived, and revolutionary theories about nature and society challenged the precepts of religion and traditional ideology. International contacts grew also, and ideas from abroad influenced the way that Americans thought about the new social order. As suggested earlier, it is probably safe to say that there was a greater degree of social change at that point than during any other, simply because of the volume of economic expansion and population movement. Even from today's perspective, when the pace of innovation seems ever faster, it is difficult to comprehend the scale of change experienced by people who lived at the turn of the 20th century (Crunden, 1982; Hays, 1957/1995; Rodgers, 1998).

This is evident in examining basic social and economic indicators. In the three decades between 1870 and 1900, for instance, the size of the nation's rail system grew fourfold, from 50,000 to more than 200,000 miles, sharply reducing the time of travel and transport of goods for the vast majority of the nation's population. At the same time, the proportion of the labor force engaged in nonagricultural employment approached 60%, a sharp difference from the farm economy of the early 1800s. As industrial output grew, some cities expanded almost exponentially. Chicago, one of the boom towns of the era, roughly doubled its population every decade between 1870 and 1910, until it finally exceeded 2 million people, second only to New York among U.S. cities. Other metropolises grew at a similar, if somewhat less frenetic, pace. Altogether, the proportion of Americans living in urban areas reached 40% by 1900, and it became a majority by 1920. The time when the typical American experience was growing up on a farm had clearly passed. The social milieu of the 20th century was decidedly urban, and this represented a new stage in the nation's development (Brownlee, 1979; Chudacoff, 1975; Higgs, 1971).

With the growth of cities came a subtle but important series of changes in the social order. The increasing volume of trade and a widening division of labor led to ever greater tendencies toward specialization in the production of goods and services. This became a well-known and widely studied process among social scientists, and has been described through use of the term *differentiation*. Because of this general pattern of development, as urban settlements grew ever larger, a wider range of roles was available for people to play in the local economy and in the social order. In very large cities, highly specialized economic functions appeared, and there was a number of new social and cultural groups for individuals to identify with. For instance, it was possible for young women to find employment in a wide array of jobs in these places, from laundries to hat shops to dance halls, depending on their backgrounds and preferences. New professions developed for men also, from specialized engineering fields (such as civil or industrial) to streetcar operators and police detectives. These were social and economic roles that did not exist in smaller communities, simply because such specialized economic capacities and positions could not develop there. This extensive array of new opportunities provided city dwellers a measure of freedom and choice in their work and careers that had been unavailable to earlier generations (Hershberg, 1981; Schnore, 1974; Zunz, 1982).

This was the good news, but there was another side to these changes. Rapid population growth and social differentiation also loosened social bonds and weakened the modes of identification that gave smaller communities social cohesion. Chicago sociologist Louis Wirth noted that life in the biggest cities was characterized by a loss of community. People no longer knew their neighbors and other community members. Social relations became more impersonal. Given this, it is conceivable to say that social capital was dissipated. In highly urbanized areas people were known by their so-cial roles rather than as individuals. Although urban growth offered greater liberty and options, it also entailed a degree of social detachment and isola-tion that was a new feature of American life. This was a critical dimension of societal change in the United States: As the cities expanded, it was possible for individual persons to become lost in a sea of humanity (Hogan, 1985; Reiss, 1964).

There were yet other features of social change that marked this era as distinctive. Fueled by demand for industrial workers, immigration surged, peaking at more than a million per year by the early 20th century. The vast majority of these newcomers were drawn to the industrial cities, where they often formed distinctive residential enclaves, conspicuous for their social and cultural links to the various homelands. This was yet another di-mension of differentiation: The urban landscape became a patchwork of culturally unique communities. The new urban geography often was high-lighted by distinctive religious districts, each with its own traditions and ethnic-based neighborhood organizations. And the numbers were monu-mental. By the time of the First World War, when immigration began to sub-side, about a quarter of the nation's population was immigrants or their children. In the urbanized states of the northeast and upper Midwest, the foreign-born and their children represented an even larger segment of the populace (Archdeacon, 1983; Bulmer, 1984).

The first waves of immigrants were from such western European coun-tries as Germany, Ireland, and England; by the turn of the century large numbers arrived from poorer areas in Southern and eastern Europe, espe-cially Italy, Poland, and Russia. Most of these new immigrants were Roman Catholic, and a significant minority was Jewish, two religions historically viewed with suspicion in the United States. In cities with populations over 100,000, immigrants and their children represented two thirds of the resi-dents, defining a variegated cultural milieu that was altogether unprece-dented in American experience. For once, native-born Protestants found themselves in the minority in these settings, even if they continued to com-mand considerable prestige and cultural capital. This new, culturally di-verse urban scene had emerged in a span of just several decades, and it made traditional relationships of status and authority suddenly appear a little topsy-turvy (Barton, 1975; Gleason, 1992).

In addition to cultural diversity, there also was a problem of widening in-equality in the nation's major industrial areas. Industrialism and the fac-tory system brought thousands of workers together under harsh conditions, often for meager pay and little job security or other benefits. A 60-hour workweek was commonplace, and workers had no recourse if they were injured or laid off. Understandably, these conditions contrib-uted to a festering resentment and a series of mounting protests against the industrial system. There was a mounting prospect of class warfare in the face of inequity and exploitation. Treated like pawns in a gigantic competition for industrial riches, industrial workers eventually revolted in massive strikes that were met by violence from capitalists and state authorities. During industrial downturns, when large numbers of workers found themselves unemployed, such labor clashes peaked in dramatic episodes of conflict, sometimes pitting thousands against the police or the military (Stowell, 1999).

Beginning in the mid-1870s, the nation witnessed a series of such confrontations each decade. For instance, national attention was drawn to labor conflict in 1886 following a riot at Haymarket Square in Chicago that resulted in 10 deaths, and in 1894, when the federal agents arrested labor leader Eugene Debs to forestall a national railway workers strike. These widely publicized events contributed to public anxiety about the pace and direction of change in American life. Even relatively small instances of disorder over these issues were seen as cause for concern, adding to fears that labor conflict could pose a threat to the nation's social and political stability. To many middle-class Americans, unaccustomed to civil strife on this scale, such thoughts were hardly comforting (Babson, 1999; von Waltershausen, 1999).

At the same time that labor battled for basic rights and better pay, wealth became ever more concentrated in the hands of a relatively small group of industrialists and bankers. This was the age of the "robber barons," men such as Andrew Carnegie, Henry P. Morgan, and John D. Rockefeller. Many people today associate such names with philanthropy and culture because of their support for famous libraries, museums, and schools. In fact, these men did establish such institutions, along with sizable foundations that eventually came to play a prominent role in education and other arenas. But at the turn of century these individuals were widely considered notorious for ruthlessly amassing huge fortunes through monopolistic business practices, brutally stamping out competition in their respective industries, and rejecting the pleas of reformers for regulation of markets and improved working conditions (Wiebe, 1967).

Such criticisms did not account for the success of this new breed of big business leaders. Their financial accomplishments were largely a by-product of the logic of large-scale industrial production: big enterprises serving national markets and wielding economic power to overcome local competition. These achievements reflected the advantages of capital, technology, and economies of scale possessed by monopolistic national firms. In the eyes of many, however, these companies and the upstart millionaires who ran them were embodiments of greed and unbridled hegemony. To contemporaries, they threatened to become a source of power even stronger than the federal government. The idea of seemingly amoral business tycoons running the country also helped to make many people quite anxious about the future (Crunden, 1982; Goldman, 1952; Hofstadter, 1955b).

It was an age of unrest, and political turbulence extended beyond the cities. Farmers in the Midwest and South were buffeted by dramatic swings in prices for the crops and other products they brought to market, much of which was caused by the ups and downs of the new urban industrial economy. Increasingly, they felt themselves at the mercy of railroads, commodity brokers, packing companies, and a host of other middlemen who took large shares of the revenue from agricultural products. During the industrial depression of the 1880s, when farming prices were severely undervalued, farmers began to organize. A radically new organization emerged from this experience, the Farmers Alliance, and it grew rapidly in the following decade. Eventually, the populists, as these farmers and their supporters were called, became the political foundation for the presidential candidacy of William Jennings Bryant in 1896. Although Bryant failed to win, this episode demonstrated that farmers were not immune to problems engendered by the new urban industrial civilization. To many middle-class Americans, this too was very unsettling, and contributed to the sense that reform of the social and political order was inevitable (Goodwyn, 1978).

The closing decades of the 19th century also marked a time of dramatic technological and scientific advancement. A host of inventions and scientific discoveries began to transform everyday life, beginning with electric lights, the telephone, gas furnaces, and the internal combustion engine. Figures such as Alexander Graham Bell and Thomas Edison became national heroes, and their laboratories produced a host of technological innovations to make life easier and communication faster. Eventually the development of the automobile, and the advent of mass-production techniques to make autos widely available, would mark the dawn of a new era in transportation and in American popular culture. Henry Ford became yet another national icon in the early 20th century. Each one of these technical achievements was important; taken together, they marked a sharp break with the past. Technology was no longer confined to the factory, nor was it limited to simply making goods less expensive. Now inventions had an immediate and palpable impact on daily existence, and this too contributed to a public perception that change was accelerating rapidly (Cowan, 1997).

Yet other scientific developments contributed to the climate of change. The most significant intellectual events of the era followed from Charles Darwin's promulgation of evolutionary theory in 1859. Grounded in careful field studies and the development of an imaginative hypothesis about the origins of species, Darwin's work revolutionized biological thinking by suggesting that living organisms were shaped by their immediate environment. Taken at face value, Darwin's theory of natural selection appeared to challenge traditional religious explanations for the beginnings of life and the position of humans in the natural order. As a consequence, it profoundly changed the way that many people viewed the world and their place in it, lending even greater significance to the realm of science and higher education (Moore, 1979; Russett, 1976).

The influence of Darwin's ideas extended far beyond the natural sciences and religion. It also led to the development of a host of parallel explanations for other phenomena, especially human behavior. Perhaps the best-known instance of such influence was the rise of *social Darwinism*, a variant of mainstream ideology that held that attempts to assist the poor were misguided and contrary to the laws of nature. The social Darwinists reasoned that if the poor suffered harsh working and living conditions, it was a natural outcome of their inferior abilities and poorly developed work ethic. Thus the logic of natural selection was used to justify the advantages of wealth and social and cultural capital: The superior status of the rich was depicted as inevitable. Although Darwin's ideas challenged some aspects of the dominant ideology, they also reinforced or augmented others. In this and many other ways, the dramatic impact of new ideas contributed to the sense that the traditional world of the 19th century was rapidly giving way to a new one, where new scientific discoveries about both nature and society promised to change the way people viewed themselves. To use a term Aldous Huxley later made popular, it was a brave new world indeed, one that created a good deal of uncertainty about the future (Bannister, 1979; Hawkins, 1997).

Change abounded as the 19th century drew to a close and the 20th began. For Americans who had grown up on the farm and moved to the city, whether literally or figuratively, the pace of shifts in the economy, politics, technology, and social mores was almost too much to comprehend. It led many Americans to question the future of traditional values, and to wonder about the prospects for the next generation. This was the making of a wide range of reforms, most of which can be grouped together under the banner of *progressivism*. For those concerned with the broadest array of changes, however, one reform stood out among all the others. Following a proud and long-established American tradition, the people concerned with saving modern industrial society from its own worst excesses turned naturally to the schools.

PROGRESSIVISM IN EDUCATION

Reform touched on many aspects of life in the opening years of the 20th century, but few issues were affected by it as much as schooling. It was a characteristically American response to the tidal wave of change then washing over the country: inventing new institutional mechanisms to mediate the impact of social transformation. In this case the institution was the school, and the response was an explosion of new ideas and programmatic innovations aimed at making education better attuned to the needs of society. Of course, there were many ways of defining social needs at the turn of the century, just as there are today, so it should hardly be surprising that progressive school reform included many different types of innovation, some of them quite contradictory in spirit and intent. Consequently, there was considerable debate and disagreement about school reform during this era, as there had been in earlier periods. In fact, the volume of argument about educational issues increased audibly, as schooling became an ever bigger public concern. Such conflicts notwithstanding, there can be little doubt that progressive education, in all of its various guises, left an indelible imprint on American schools. Like progressivism writ large, it was a broad and diverse movement, embracing many different viewpoints as it sought to make education a central element of the new social order (Cremin, 1961).

As a general principle, historians have identified two broad impulses that characterized educational reform during this period. The first was a humanitarian disposition toward making education more responsive to the needs of children, and integrating the school more closely with its immediate community. Identified with such renowned reform figures as John Dewey, Francis Parker, and William Heard Kilpatrick, this movement has influenced a relatively small but highly visible cadre of educational reformers throughout the 20th century. Historian David Tyack has described this band of educators as "pedagogical progressives," an apt title for a group of men and women who historically were primarily interested in changing instructional practice. A second group of educational reformers dating from this era were less idealistic by temperament and more concerned with issues of efficiency and carefully aligning the purposes of schooling with the needs of the economy. Tyack named these individuals "administrative progressives," because they were especially interested in improving the organizational arrangement of educational institutions. Historically, even though they did not produce heroic reform figures to point to, the administrative progressives came to exert enormous influence on the development of American schools. Accordingly, terms such as *efficiency, management,* and *vocationalism* have become important watchwords in education during the 20th century. These too are part of the legacy of progressivism (Tyack, 1974).

As one might imagine, the differences in perspective and basic values embraced by these two wings of progressive educational reform were vast. At various times, representatives from these rather diffuse groups engaged in sharp debates over particular educational issues. For the most part, however, they managed to coexist, largely because they generally were interested in different spheres of the educational enterprise. As suggested earlier, pedagogical progressives were most concerned with matters of instruction, and related issues of how children learn and links between the school and its proximate community. Their primary focus was inside the classroom, and on kindred issues of personal growth and understanding. It also is probably accurate to say that their greatest influence was on primary education, especially for younger children. Theirs was a fundamentally compassionate impetus, one that aimed to make schools better attuned to children's needs and interests.

The administrative progressives, on the other hand, chose to devote most of their attention to matters outside the classroom, on questions related to the organization of schools, the purposes of various curricula, and the large-scale measurement of student learning. Of course, many of these questions can, and did, have a direct bearing on what occurred in classrooms across the country. But the administrative progressives, by and large, did not concern themselves directly with issues of teaching practice, at least not during the first half of the 20th century. Instead, they were content to set the parameters within which most American teachers performed their instructional tasks, whereas the pedagogical progressives tried heroically to inspire teachers to improve their methods of teaching. In this way, the two sides of progressive reform managed to coexist, even if neither could claim complete mastery of the entire field (Kliebard, 1986).

Of course, the lived reality of most educators at the time was considerably more complex than suggested by these widely divergent categories. Many probably took inspiration from both wings of progressivism in education, without seeing them as necessarily at odds with one another. It was a time of frenetic change in schools, and reforms of one stripe or another were considered modern innovations intended to improve education. Consequently, elements from both sides of the reform impulse often were adopted pragmatically to move school systems forward. The result was a rather disjointed process of change, one that pushed and pulled on the educational system in different directions, often producing rather a confusing and contradictory array of outcomes. This was progressive educational reform in all its disparate and paradoxical glory, a process that established many features of the current American school system (Graham, 1974; Zilversmit, 1993).

PEDAGOGICAL PROGRESSIVISM

Like the progressive movement in American politics, historians have linked progressive education to the rhetoric of crusading journalists bent on challenging the nation to recognize the problems it faced. Joseph Meyer Rice was a pediatrician who toured the country in the 1890s examining children and classrooms in big-city school systems. He wrote about his findings in a widely read series of articles in *The Forum,* one of the nation's premier muckraking (or reforming) journals. Rice's discoveries were shocking. He reported children required to recite lessons in machinelike order, complete silence expected of classes containing scores of children in cramped spaces, and administrators who took pride in punishing even the most inconsequential infractions against the prevailing order. As a medical doctor who treated children, he questioned the pedagogical and physiological effects of such approaches to education. Was it possible for children to learn when all of their inborn, natural propensities to exercise their bodies and minds were denied by these repressive school regimes? Was it healthy for children to sit in silence for hours on end in crowded, poorly ventilated school buildings? As big-city school districts scrambled to find classroom space for their rapidly expanding populations of poor, immigrant children, often cutting corners and pressing substandard facilities into use, many other people started asking similar questions. Most importantly, a growing number of reformers became interested in the way children were being asked to learn in schools, and they began to consider alternatives to the prevailing models of memorization and recitation. It seemed to be time for a change, and for a new way of thinking about teaching and learning (Cremin, 1961).

As noted earlier, the reform figures who advocated more humane and child-friendly practices in schools were described as *pedagogical progressives.* These individuals challenged the logic of faculty psychology, which argued that memorizing and reciting school lessons helped to build greater mental capacity and discipline. Instead, pedagogical progressives suggested that children learned best by following their interests, expressing themselves, and actively investigating the world around them. In this regard, they represented the legacy of such well-known 19th-century European educational thinkers as Friedrich Froebel, Heinrich Pestalozzi, and Johann Herbart, men whom Horace Mann and other 19-century American educators had admired from afar. Their ideas also reflected the influence of Edward Sheldon, who trained teachers at the Oswego, New York, normal school and was the chief American proponent of Pestalozzian ideas. Sheldon introduced the use of objects to teach school lessons, the origin of today's widely used phrase "object lesson," and lectured widely on "new" methods of instruction. Pedagogical progressives also were influenced by William James, a Harvard professor and pioneer of modern psychology who emphasized the importance of experience, and who was also the brother of novelist Henry James. These men and like-minded thinkers downplayed the notion that human beings had inborn proclivities and strengths that required isolation to be developed, and instead argued that engagement with the larger realm of human endeavor was the key to individual growth and learning. Education was supposed to be fun, they suggested, as the child eagerly satisfied a natural curiosity to know and understand the world of experience. Schooling did not have to be a matter of drudgery and restraint; it could represent a process of liberation, one that allowed children to express their inherent proclivity to learning. (Cremin, 1961; Curti, 1959; Reese, 2001).

The most famous of the pedagogical progressives was John Dewey, although there certainly were many others. Dewey was born in Vermont in 1859, just a few months after Horace Mann's death. He attended local schools and worked briefly as a teacher until he went to Johns Hopkins University for graduate studies in philosophy during the early 1880s. Gradually embracing a far-reaching philosophy of experiential learning, Dewey eventually went on to become the preeminent American philosopher of his age and perhaps any other. Dewey also became well known for his work with the University of Chicago Laboratory School, which he founded when he joined the university's faculty in the mid-1890s. It was Dewey's work at the Lab School, as it soon became known, that led to his early writings on education and learning (Dykhuizen, 1973; Ryan, 1995).

Unlike more traditional educators, Dewey believed that education was a process of interaction between the child and the curriculum, and between the school and society. But Dewey was not a radical reformer; he did not advocate doing away with traditional subjects altogether, and letting children follow every whim and fancy. Instead, he felt that school matter should be taught differently, utilizing the larger world of experience to impart critical lessons in history, biology, geography, and other subjects. Accordingly, students at the Lab School learned about the past by visiting museums and historical sites, they toured factories to learn about the economy, and they conducted biological experiments in parks and nature preserves. In these ways and many others, Dewey and the Lab School faculty (his wife Alice served as director) experimented to learn more about the process of education and ways of improving the conditions of teaching and learning. Dewey wrote extensively about the insights he and others gained from this experience, providing the intellectual tutelage for a growing movement to transform the school (Cremin, 1961; Kliebard, 1986; Tanner, 1997).

John Dewey eventually came to believe that the school was the central institution in a modern democratic society. It was the school, he reasoned, that provided citizens with the skills and knowledge necessary for political participation, an argument Horace Mann had articulated 70 years earlier, but also with the scientific sensibility necessary for membership in a rapidly changing urban industrial social order. As a result, Dewey's understanding of the school's role in society went far beyond Mann's ideas. For Dewey, the concept of democracy embraced more than simply a well-informed polity;

rather, it was a way of life that allowed for the fullest possible development of every member of society. Democracy, in that case, embraced a range of ideas, such as tolerance, fair play, critical discussion of social issues, and respect for the rights of others. Ultimately, it was nothing less than the highest form of collective intelligence. If a democratic society was to succeed, the school's role was to help cultivate these and similar values, and the key to imparting them was experience. In short, Dewey believed the school should model these values, and should represent itself as a microcosm of community in order to help teach democratic values experientially, in a way that children would be unlikely to forget. The school was the first place where most children encountered the larger world outside of their immediate families on a sustained and intensive basis, and because of this Dewey felt it essential that these institutions exemplify the very best values and practices of democratic society (Westbrook, 1991).

The atmosphere of rapid social transformation that characterized this period also contributed to Dewey's conviction that schools had a critical role to play in sustaining a democratic civilization. Like many others in his time, Dewey was alarmed by the magnitude of the social and economic shifts then evident, especially in places like Chicago and New York, the cities where he spent most of his professional career. He was concerned about the growing social divisions between the rich and poor, about conflict over labor issues, and about the fragmentation of society due to religious and ethnic differentiation. Industrialization, he declared, threatened to turn people into "mere appendages of machines." Because of these tendencies, he suggested that the school had an even more important role to play in teaching democratic principles than during earlier periods of American history. Where Horace Mann had invoked an industrial metaphor in declaring the school a "balance wheel" of society, Dewey saw it as a refuge from the ravages of the factory and commercial life, a place for children to learn essential values of democracy and principles of reasoning (Dykhuizen, 1973).

Unlike Mann, Dewey did not dwell on placing various elements of the population together in a single institution, the central idea of the common school. Although he certainly was in favor of schools bringing people together, Dewey recognized the reality of social and economic differentiation and focused more on the construction of community within the walls of the institution. Consequently, the role of the school was to impart the tenets of democratic life and the principles of scientific thinking, so that democracy could flourish in spite of rapid societal change, even if the schools could not immediately bridge the fast-growing civil divisions. As the social distance between various elements of the nation's population increased, the role of education would become ever more important in sustaining these core elements of American civilization. Dewey's basic concern, in that case, was not simply a more humane and sensible form of pedagogical practice; it was nothing less than the preservation of essential American values in the face of sweeping social change (McCluskey, 1958; Westbrook, 1991).

Dewey was hardly the first pedagogical progressive, and he drew many of his ideas from the work of other educators with similar concerns and interests. Chicago became something of a hotbed for these ideas after Francis Parker arrived in the early 1890s to head the Cook County Normal School, one of the city's teacher-training institutions. Parker had established a national reputation for innovation in education as superintendent of schools in Quincy, Massachusetts. While there, he had done away with traditional drill and memorization approaches to instruction, and emphasized the cultivation of children's natural curiosity and propensity to learn through direct experience. The Quincy schools drew visitors from around the world to see new methods of learning through the study of objects, taking field trips, and allowing children to devise answers to problems they encountered. After leaving Quincy, Parker spent a frustrating period of time as superintendent of the Boston schools before moving to Chicago. Once there, he established a practice school connected to the normal school, one that demonstrated his principles of education in action. It was hardly coincidental that when John Dewey arrived in Chicago, he enrolled his own children in Parker's school. Eventually the two men became collaborators in forging a new approach to schooling. Parker represented an important progressive educational influence, one whose ideas found expression in many of Dewey's writings (Curti, 1959; Ryan, 1995).

Parker's school, however, represented just the early stage of a movement that gradually gained momentum in the opening decades of the 20th century. Inspired by his example and by Dewey's Lab School and writings, and by the work of other educators, dozens of visionary individuals established schools embracing progressive pedagogical principles. In 1915 Dewey and his daughter Evelyn published *Schools of To-Morrow*, a description of a number of exemplary progressive schools in different parts of the country. These cases provided evidence that schools embracing progressive ideals of nurturing individual interests, fostering expression, learning through experience, and upholding democratic values could be established in a wide range of settings and circumstances. Thousands of other like-minded educators took heart from these examples and others, and the ideals they represented found their way into countless schools and classrooms across the country and around the world (Cremin, 1961; Zilversmit, 1993).

While in Chicago, Dewey had been profoundly influenced by his friendship with the famous progressive social reformer Jane Addams, and he was a strong proponent of gender equity in education. Women were especially prominent in this reform movement, founding and leading new schools with progressive principles and occasionally providing leadership to school districts. For example, Caroline Pratt, Marietta Johnson, and Flora Cook were prominent leaders of innovative private institutions, and Chicago's Ella Flagg Young was among the nation's most important progressive superintendents of the era. Perhaps even more important, the principles of pedagogical progressivism proved to be especially significant among teacher-educators, both women and men, who were deeply influenced by Dewey and other progressive intellectuals. In this way, progressive ideas lived on for generations in many of the nation's leading university schools of education, as they do today (Blount, 1998; Lagemann, 1979, 1985; Semel & Sadovnick, 1999).

After Dewey took a position in the philosophy department at Columbia University in New York, his influence became particularly strong at that institution's affiliated education school, known as Teachers College. A number of faculty members at Teachers College became widely known as advocates of curricular reform strategies designed to introduce a stronger experiential and problem-centered approach into traditional schools. Perhaps the most famous was William Heard Kilpatrick, who developed an instructional reform approach known as the "project method" in the early 1920s. Kilpatrick's approach was a way of circumventing traditional curricular structures, such as the disciplines of English, history, and mathematics, by allowing students to undertake projects that were linked to their own experiences. His intention was to devise a way to infuse opportunities for children to study topics of interest to them, often focusing on social issues outside of the school, while developing such traditional skills as reading, writing, and numerical analysis. Defined often without regard for traditional subjects, these "projects" were supposed to be carefully planned and evaluated. Dewey was critical of Kilpatrick for breaking so dramatically from the academic disciplines, but this had little effect on the popularity of his ideas. In a relatively short time, Kilpatrick's techniques were being tried in school districts across the country, spreading the doctrine of progressive education as they proceeded. In addition to this, thousands of students were influenced by Kilpatrick and his progressive-minded colleagues at Teachers College, which soon became the nation's most prominent and influential school of education. Many of these individuals eventually became important educators in communities across the country. These developments, along with the founding of the Progressive Education Association in 1919, helped to give the movement an institutional voice and a stronger identity (Graham, 1967; Kliebard, 1986; Westbrook, 1991).

It was not long, however, before criticisms of the pedagogical progressives began to surface. Traditional educators complained that experiential methods did not teach children basic reading and computational skills. Students who learned history on field trips, critics charged, often did not know essential names and dates from the past. Older English teachers suggested that an aversion to drill and memorization resulted in a marked increase in spelling and punctuation errors in student essays. More perceptive critics noted that progressive methods of instruction seemed to work most easily with affluent children, whose rich resources of cultural and social capital provided a ready stock of educative experiences to draw on. It was a greater challenge, however, to convey essential skills and knowledge to children from impoverished families, especially when their immediate home environments offered relatively little stimulus for intellectual growth. Classes with these students often demanded more direction and control by teachers. It was little wonder, then, that many of the most famous progressive schools were private institutions serving a middle- and upper-class clientele. Critics were quick to point this out, occasionally lampooning progressive education as a trendy fad among the social and intellectual elite (Cremin, 1961; Ravitch, 2000; Zilversmit, 1993).

These and similar comments came to resonate with large segments of the adult public, many of whom equated discipline and traditional forms of achievement with their own experiences in the schools of the 19th century. A majority of American parents probably continued to believe in the importance of controlling children, and were inherently suspicious of educational doctrines that seemed to celebrate self-expression. To many observers, progressive schools appeared to be little more than children running amok. Such perceptions were not always unfounded, of course, and there also was a good deal of criticism of progressive education's excesses within the movement itself. Dewey and other reform figures found themselves struggling to prevent the misrepresentation of their ideas, and attempted to distance themselves from educators who eschewed any links to traditional subjects at all. By 1938, when Dewey published *Experience and Education,* his major corrective statement, the progressive education movement had lost a great deal of its creative energy and originality. Too many educators had come to interpret progressivism as simply the replacement of books with life experience, instead of Dewey's conception of utilizing experience to enrich and extend traditional sources of learning. Despite their early promise and broad appeal, the pedagogical progressives failed to fundamentally transform even a small portion of American education. They left an indelible mark on educational thought and practice, however, one that continues to influence educators right down to the present (Cremin, 1961; Cuban, 1984; Ravitch, 1983).

ADMINISTRATIVE PROGRESSIVISM

At the same time that the pedagogical progressives were seeking ways to bring the assorted elements of American democracy together through education, other educators sought to make the schools better attuned to the widely different social roles demanded by the new urban industrial order. As noted earlier, historians have labeled this group of reformers *administrative progressives,* but it would be wrong to consider them a movement comparable in terms of unity and coherence to the pedagogical progressives. Rather, the term *administrative progressivism* encompasses a wide range of educators, most of whom were simply striving to make the schools function as smoothly and effectively as possible (Tyack, 1974).

By and large, the administrative progressives were not committed to using the school as a vehicle for changing society or overcoming such social problems as inequity or safekeeping democracy. They worked instead to adapt the educational system to the rapidly evolving urban society, especially the increasingly complex labor market. Although the pedagogical progressives included significant numbers of women, educators who fit the administrative profile were mostly men. Their efforts often were supported by business and other fiscally conservative elements in society, and they frequently were opposed by organized labor. The administrative progressives probably greatly outnumbered their pedagogical counterparts, and as such they represented the principal direction of change in American schools at the time. Ideologically, their ideas were shaped by the business ethos of the banks and large corporations than becoming a dominant force in the economy (Tyack & Hansot, 1982).

If one word were to express the principal bearing and object of administrative progressivism, it would be *efficiency.* Most of the nation's leading educators were particularly interested in building an educational system that was both rationally organized and cost effective. This was partly due to the immediate historical experience of the larger school districts, especially those in the leading cities. As noted earlier, this was a period of rapid expansion in the nation's educational systems. Major cities like New York, Chicago, Detroit, and Los Angeles were growing especially rapidly, and their schools received tens of thousands of new children each year. The need to constantly build new schools, train additional teachers, buy textbooks and other supplies, and devise new curricula placed an enormous strain on public school resources. This in turn led to greater public interest in the use of tax funds earmarked for education, and concern about inefficiency and corruption in the disposition of the rather large budgets of urban school systems. In the closing decades of the 19th century, when city schools were often controlled by ward (local or even neighborhood) politicians, it was not unusual for public education funds to find their way into the pockets of political machine bosses, along with money earmarked for many other municipal services. Widely publicized cases of political figures and school administrators being caught at accepting bribes to award jobs, or demanding cash payments in return for construction or textbook contracts, heightened public awareness of the need for greater professionalism in the administration and governance of public education. As urban school systems faced even greater demands, and budgets grew ever larger, such questions loomed significantly for public education (Callahan, 1962; Drost, 1967).

These concerns led to a general movement to create new, centralized, and highly efficient school systems in cities across the country between 1890 and 1920. This was a part of a sweeping reform campaign in municipal government, one that attacked the corruption associated with ward-based political regimes. By 1920 hundreds of municipalities had changed from ward-level school boards and city councils to centralized and bureaucratic forms of governance and administration. It was one of the principal accomplishments of the administrative impulse in progressive educational reform, creating a new ethos of urban educational leadership. Instead of localized directors selected by politicians, urban school systems came to be run by boards elected from across a community or municipality, and administered by superintendents selected for their experience and professional competence. It marked a new era in urban schooling, one that emphasized separation between local political organizations and the supervision of schools. School leaders were supposed to be above corruption, expert at effective management of the resources they were given, and knowledgeable in the educational methods necessary to accomplish their goals. Efficiency was the modern watchword in school leadership, and a growing number of educators were committed to making it a principle that permeated public education (Hays, 1964; Reese, 1986).

As important as these changes were, however, there was more to administrative progressivism than just efficiency. If a second word were to characterize the ethos of this period it would be *differentiation*. This term was encountered earlier in describing the changing social organization of cities during this period. In the larger society, differentiation of roles was associated with the widening division of labor, and with the growth of specialization in the labor market and the professions. Although this process of differentiation was a source of deep concern to pedagogical progressives like Dewey, other educators embraced it as an inevitable feature of modern social organization. Administrative progressives felt that the schools could help to make the general process of specialization and differentiation unfold more rationally and smoothly, by allocating individuals to different social roles based on their natural interests and abilities. To this end they adapted the term *differentiation* itself to represent the school's commitment to distinguishing between different goals for students. This was a departure from earlier generations of educators, who had emphasized themes of commonality and fellowship in public schools. With the arrival of the administrative progressives, specialization and distinction were newly accentuated, making the school a place where students began to work toward their separate destinies (Krug, 1964; Violas, 1978).

The principal arena for these developments was the secondary education system, the network of public high schools that developed rapidly between 1890 and 1920. Basically, administrative progressives sought to make the high school into an instrument for helping young people prepare for the labor market and for the widening array of occupational and social roles available to them. Accordingly, vocational education became more important during this time, including curricular innovations such as home economics, commercial and clerical training, and the manual arts. Programs of study like these were designed to prepare young men and women for strikingly different purposes. The extent to which the educational system was able to perform this function was expressed in the term *social efficiency*. This phrase was perhaps most prominently associated with David Snedden, a one-time Massachusetts education superintendent who eventually became a faculty member at Teachers College. It was intended to represent the ability of schools to provide students with the knowledge and skills needed by the larger society. This was a somewhat different dimension of efficiency than that sought by the new, expert superintendents then running the big-city school systems. It referred to the degree to which the schools aided and abetted the process of social differentiation, and thus contributed to the growing range of roles and economic functions people would play in the social order. Historically, it was a novel role for secondary education, and one that engendered a good deal of controversy and debate at the time (Drost, 1967; Kleibard, 1999).

The development of this new direction in secondary education was not entirely without precedent, but it certainly became more commonplace during the Progressive Era. Differentiation was hardly a new concept in urban education at the turn of the century. In the nation's largest school systems there had been evidence of specialization and marking distinctions for decades before social efficiency became a buzzword for the administrative progressives. In Boston and New York, for instance, manual high schools had been established as early as the 1880s, and they existed elsewhere as well. As suggested in chapter 4, a significant number of cities had long maintained separate schools for male and female students, believing them fundamentally different in interests and aptitude. Many cities also had elite high schools that specialized in preparing students for college or desirable positions in the business world; Philadelphia's Central High School was a well-known example. What was different after the turn of the century, however, was the new weight attached to practices such as these. As the public high school grew in importance, and enrollments mounted quickly, the question of how the schools would prepare students for employment proved impossible to ignore. Consequently, vocational education and related curricula appeared in schools all over the country, not just in the big cities, and the doctrine of social efficiency spread accordingly. It was a sign of the growing complexity of society, and of modern social relations, and the administrative progressives believed it the responsibility of schools to respond in kind (Fisher, 1967; Kantor, 1988; Krug, 1964).

Developments such as these gave rise to a new form of school management and control: *Bureaucracy*. In many respects, this was a historical corollary of differentiation and the drive for greater efficiency. As the social theorist Max Weber noted, bureaucracies developed as systems of rules and regulations, monitored by individuals empowered to allocate resources according to increasingly elaborate codes of behavior. Such forms of organization allocated power and resources in ways that appeared rational and objective, representing values of impartiality and efficiency. In the late 19th century, this was believed necessary to forestall corruption and political interference in the schools. As urban education systems grew larger and more centralized, bureaucratic forms of administration became ubiquitous. When specialized programs and schools appeared, following the dictates of differentiation, they were governed by the new bureaucratic ethic, including rules dictating who was eligible to attend and graduate from different types of programs. Bureaucratic rules also came to govern systemwide purchasing and distribution practices, observing economies of scale and providing uniform and efficient services to schools throughout a given area. The administrative progressives who designed these logical systems of resource allocation and control believed they were creating a model for realizing the greatest possible good from a limited set of assets. In the words of David Tyack, they attempted to build the "one best system" of educational organization, believing that the bureaucratic mode of school administration and governance was the optimal choice for efficient management (Katz, 1971; Tyack, 1974).

Of course, the newly rationalized ethos in education called for measures that would allow judgments to be made about various elements of the school system. This need was answered in part by new systems of bookkeeping and accounting, and by the legions of trained clerks who later became known as bureaucrats. The corollary to this on the instructional side was the development of standardized or mental testing, and a generation of professionals trained in a new subfield of psychology eventually labeled *psychometrics*. This was a natural concomitant to the themes of social efficiency, differentiation, and preparing students for an assortment of social and economic roles. It also was well suited to the bureaucratic impulse for clear criteria on which to base rules and decisions about the disposition of resources. A French researcher named Simon Binet devised the first general test of mental aptitude at around the turn of the century, and after a short time psychologists in the United States had adapted his methods for use with American subjects. Lewis Terman of Stanford University and Edward Thorndike of Teachers College were among the best know proponents of this new technology for measuring abilities, and they quickly gained international reputations for their work in the emerging field of psychometrics (Jonçich, 1968; Lagemann, 2000; Minton, 1988).

In 1917 the practical use of such tests was demonstrated when the U.S. Army administered them to millions of men to help determine their eligibility for various types of training. By the later 1920s thousands of school districts employed standardized tests to judge students' suitability for a particular program, or to justify curricular decisions, or simply as points of information for teachers and parents. Test construction and publication became a burgeoning business, and hundreds of university-trained psychologists were employed in producing and evaluating them. Perhaps most importantly, the use of these various testing instruments lent legitimacy to the idea that the abilities of students differed widely, and that certain roles simply were not appropriate for everyone. Thorndike, Terman, and others provided a seemingly scientific justification to the principle of differentiation, and the new discipline of testing only heightened the allure of the administrative progressive viewpoint (Brown, 1992; Cravens, 1993; Gould, 1981).

The rise of the mental testing movement held especially important implications for the education of children with special needs or learning difficulties. Children who were blind, deaf, or impaired in speech had been educated in special schools since the mid-19th century. Most of these schools were residential and served only a small fraction of the relevant population. Following the Civil War, similar institutions were established by various states for retarded children, often called "imbeciles" at the time. For families unable or unwilling to send their children away, there often was little recourse: These children were educated in the common schools with other students or they simply stayed home. This was not considered a big problem in rural communities, where the incidence of such cases was relatively rare, but in larger cities the numbers of children with these conditions could be quite significant. As urban school systems began to grow rapidly, special courses were established for students with various categories of learning impediments. In 1879, for instance, Cleveland established a special class for "feebleminded" children; Boston followed suit in 1898, as did many other cities at about the same time. By the early 20th century a fairly wide range of such programs existed, supported by the incipient testing movement. This was a new degree of differentiation, and the standardized tests provided an added degree of legitimacy to decisions to place children in these various types of classes (Franklin, 1994; Winzer, 1993).

As it turned out, this was a domain the testers were only too happy to claim. Early psychometricians charged into the field of diagnosing various categories of mental ability, coining such technical terms as *idiot* and *moron* (each representing a different level of mental retardation), and suggesting that such conditions were hereditary in nature. Public concerns were raised about the prospect of children labeled in these ways intermingling with the "normal" population, sentiments fueled by pseudoscientific advocates of *mental hygiene* and *eugenics,* a term for human perfectibility. Zealous proponents of these ideas issued racist bromides against immigration and the assimilation of various minority groups, and even urged the sterilization of "feebleminded" couples. Such concepts led to even greater efforts to segregate children with learning problems, as it was widely believed that they posed a threat to other children and that they could not learn much anyway. This was differentiation taken to an odious extreme, reflecting the influence of racialist ideology in its preoccupation with segregating people based on biologically linked criteria. Given these origins, mental tests would come to cast a long shadow over the subsequent course of American education (Gould, 1981; Lemann, 1999; Selden, 1999; Trent, 1994).

Administrative progressivism thus had a flavor entirely different from that of its pedagogical counterpart. Concerned with efficiency and fitting the educational system to the needs of society, the administrative progressives were preoccupied with finding rational solutions to the various educational and organizational problems they encountered. Unlike the pedagogical progressives, their efforts could hardly be described as an altruistic impulse in school reform. And certain features of the administrative progressive ethos, such as mental testing and bureaucracy, soon proved to be quite controversial. Although there were some urban school regimes that pursued reforms in the name of humanizing the schools, especially in cities like Toledo and Milwaukee with socialist mayors, most others sought to impose a rationality that distanced these institutions from everyday public concerns. What is more, administrative progressives eschewed the idea that education should uplift and transform children, preferring instead to devise school programs that would reproduce the social division of labor (Reese, 1986; Tyack, 1974).

Like their pedagogical counterparts, the administrative progressives managed to stir up opposition to their ideas in the general public. Organized labor was often in the forefront of campaigns to stop certain efficiency measures, especially when such steps threatened the livelihood or working conditions of teachers. Unions, socialist groups, and neighborhood associations resisted reductions in school expenditures when they believed the quality of education was being threatened. And large numbers of working-class Americans remained suspicious of vocational education, fearing that it was a tool that employers would use to undermine trade unions. It would be wrong, in that case, to imagine that the administrative progressive strand of reform swept into prominence by universal acclamation. These ideas were at least as controversial as those of the pedagogical progressives, but unlike other reformers the administrative progressives received the support of powerful political and financial interests. For this reason, it is easy to believe their success was preordained. But at the time it was by no means a certainty that their agenda of efficiency and differentiation would triumph (Kliebard, 1999; Reese, 1986).

The administrative reformers ultimately prevailed, however, and most believed they were improving the ability of the schools to address important social issues. They claimed, for instance, that in helping schools to serve the diverse purposes of an increasingly variegated student population they were upholding the democratic aims of public education. Identifying the differing abilities of students, they argued, allowed the schools to be of the greatest assistance to individuals as they searched to find their roles in the larger society. Although they may have lacked the fervor and messianic vision of a Francis Parker or William Heard Kilpatrick, they believed they were making the schools of the 20th century far better than their 19th-century predecessors. In this regard, administrative progressivism was an important strain of modern school reform. Simply because so many elements of the program it represented continues to inform the administration and governance of public education, it is sometimes difficult to recognize the accomplishments of its adherents. They managed to impose a certain type of order on the entire nation's schools, one that highlighted the bureaucratic norms of efficiency and differentiation. Theirs was a prodigious task, and the fruits and consequences of their many accomplishments are evident as a new century in the history of American education begins today.

THE RISE OF THE MODERN HIGH SCHOOL

As noted earlier, the opening decades of the 20th century were a time of very rapid growth for the American high school. Enrollments had expanded quickly through the latter half of the 19th century, and stood at about 300,000 in 1890 (public and private schools combined). By 1930 the number of high school students had increased more than 10-fold, to nearly 5 million, a figure representing almost half of the nation's eligible teenage population. Much of this expansion was accomplished by a remarkable increase in the number of these institutions: On average, a new secondary school was established nearly every day between 1890 and 1930. By the twenties, in that case, most American communities outside of the South had access to some form of secondary education, typically through a nearby public high school (Goldin & Katz, 1999a; Herbst, 1996).

This was a big change from the 19th century, when common schools represented the universal standard for mass, publicly supported schooling in the United States. Now most Americans had relatively easy entry to an even higher level of academic achievement. Although a slight majority of teenagers still did not attend high school, and many more never graduated, the mere fact that secondary schooling was available to such large numbers of people marked a new stage in the development of the nation's educational system. If the 19th century was the age of the common (or primary) schools, the opening decades of the 20th were the era of the high school.

As one might imagine, the rapid growth of secondary education gave rise to a good deal of controversy about ways it was to be conducted and its larger purpose in American society. Historians traditionally have focused on two public reports about the high school to characterize these debates, both commissioned by the National Education Association, a broad-based professional group for all educators at the time (and today a union). The first of these was the "Report of the Committee of Ten," published in 1893. Comprised mainly of university representatives and national education leaders, this group was chaired by Charles Eliot, president of Harvard University, and included William Torrey Harris, U.S. Commissioner of Education. Their purpose was to establish order and uniformity in a secondary education system that included high schools, academies, private and religious schools, and sundry other institutions providing instruction beyond the primary level. (Angus & Mirel, 1999).

Eliot, Harris, and other members of the committee were traditionalists, and they represented a rather conservative perspective on the question of how secondary education ought to be organized. By and large, they felt that the high school should remain squarely academic in orientation. Although they were open to a degree of flexibility regarding curricular matters and the objectives of high school students, they did not intend to substantially expand the high school's purview. They envisioned little variation in secondary school curricula, regardless of whether students intended to attend college after graduation. Basically, they felt that all students should take a rigorous course of English, history, mathematics, science, and language study, but that the "collegiate" course should include classical languages while the others could substitute modern languages or advanced mathematics and science courses. Vocationalism was not much evident in their thinking. As proponents of a psychology of discipline, the committee's members believed that the powers of concentration, memory, and communication gained from such a program of studies would be appropriate for any career a student may choose. This was a point of view that would be roundly criticized in subsequent years (Cremin 1961; Krug, 1964).

The second famous document in the history of the high school was the "Cardinal Principles of Secondary Education," the report of the Commission on the Reorganization of Secondary Education, often called the "Kingsley Commission," after its chair, Clarence Kingsley. Issued in 1918, the Cardinal Principles report offered a new vision for American secondary education: the comprehensive high school. Unlike the Committee of Ten, the Kingsley Commission advocated a differentiated secondary curriculum, but it also called for bringing students from all backgrounds together within a single institution. In other words, differentiation would be achieved by groups of students pursuing distinct courses of study while attending the same school. Some pupils would follow vocational programs, for instance, while others might pursue a precollegiate course of study, and yet others might opt for a general or commercial diploma. Certain classes, however, would provide an opportunity for these students to mingle, particularly in such courses as citizenship, physical education, and health and hygiene (Angus & Mirel, 1999).

In advocating a comprehensive vision of the high school, the commission hoped to encourage secondary education to follow the logic of differentiation, considered by many to be necessary for the institution's growth, while preserving an element of commonality and shared community among its increasingly diverse constituencies. The Cardinal Principles report attempted to preserve the democratic character of American public education, addressing a major concern of the pedagogical progressives, while acknowledging the importance of differentiation, one of the themes of administrative progressives. Whether the commission succeeded in charting a truly new course for secondary education is an open question, but its formulation of the high school's various purposes clearly reflected the influence of both wings of progressive education. In this regard it was a uniquely American response to the challenges posed by secondary schooling. With such an outlook, the high school remained a distinctive national institution (Cremin, 1961; Herbst, 1996; Krug, 1964).

These two reports provide an interesting contrast, and because of this they have fascinated generations of historians. One perspective advocated a largely academic high school, with only minor differences between the various programs students would take. The other provided for considerably more diversity in curricula, but also emphasized the school's role in socializing young people for their shared future in a democratic society. In reality, the schools of the early 20th century probably did not embody either of the ideal types portrayed in these documents. There certainly was substantial evidence of vocationalism in secondary education at the time of the Committee of Ten; indeed, differentiation was increasingly the order of the day, especially in the major cities. Conversely, there still was a good deal of traditional academic work in high schools following publication of the Cardinal Principles. In fact, the institution's largest constituency continued to be middle-class students interested in academic courses. Comprehensive high schools eventually did become more commonplace, but only after the secondary student population increased even more following 1930. Other developments in the high school's history may have been just as important as these documents, particularly measures establishing universal standards for graduation, accounting for various types of credit, and setting criteria for different curricula. It would be wrong, in that case, to suggest that either of these reports changed the course of American educational history. They do, however, represent telling commentaries on the concerns of the day and the ways that progressivism may have affected the thinking of secondary educators (Angus & Mirel, 1999).

Regardless of its philosophical orientation, perhaps the most striking feature of the high school during this period was its remarkable expansion and its impact on the economy. The high school evolved from a rather elite institution to one open to the vast majority of American adolescents. Economic historian Claudia Goldin has described the rise of secondary schooling as the "second transformation" of U.S. education, placing educational attainment far ahead of other nations for much of the 20th century. The geographic areas that led this secondary school expansion were in the Northern, Midwestern, and Western states, regions with relatively high levels of income and little inequality. Enrollments tended to be higher in communities with fewer jobs in manufacturing and low numbers of immigrants. In other words, homogeneity of economic conditions and social stability of community, given a modicum of income or wealth, seems to have fostered the extension of education to the secondary level. In areas where factory employment did not lure teens away from school, and where investments in additional education seemed reasonable, the high schools flourished (Goldin, 1998).

Goldin and other historians also have argued that the growth of secondary enrollments added significantly to the nation's economic growth after 1920. She suggested that human capital and technological change were to the 20th century what the factory was to the 19th: an engine of development. This was reflected in the rapid increase in white-collar employment in the 20th century, growing from less than a 10th of the national labor force to more than a quarter in the space of a few decades. People in such positions were necessary to coordinate the nation's increasingly complex industrial production and distribution system, which was quickly becoming the most sophisticated in the world. This called for a massive national investment in human capital, achieved through ever higher levels of schooling. Advances at the secondary level accounted for most of the increase in total the nation's educational attainment, a general measure of human capital formation. In other words, the skills that individuals gained in high school contributed to greater productivity and efficiency in the economy, expanding its capacity for growth considerably (Goldin, 2001).

For young men and women in certain areas of the country this meant that there was a substantial economic return (or payoff) to education, especially early in the century, a condition that doubtless affected their decisions to enroll in the first place. Analysis of data that Goldin gathered from the 1920 Iowa census, for instance, indicated that the income of people who attended high school was significantly higher than it was for those who did not. Many found jobs in the rapidly expanding white-collar sector of the economy, as managers, bookkeepers, and clerical workers. Even high-paying, skilled jobs in certain manufacturing industries were reserved for high school graduates. It is not surprising, in that case, that arguments for attending secondary school at the time included the belief that a secondary diploma could improve opportunities for economic security and wealth. The high school was seen as a way to get ahead, and this perhaps more than anything else accounted for its rapid growth (Goldin & Katz, 2000).

The link between secondary education and the economy was a critical element in the evolution of American society. Eventually, a gradual decline in the wage premium to high school graduates appears to have set in, after the initial boom in enrollments in the 1920s and 1930s. With the expansion of the high school, larger numbers of Americans competed for coveted white-collar positions, exerting downward pressure on wages. But during the opening decades of the 20th century, the economic impact of the high school appears to have been quite substantial. Secondary education contributed to an important process of growth and change in the American economy, a gradual shift away from industrial employment to white-collar jobs in management, planning, and record keeping. It was the early glimmering of a postindustrial society, and at the center of this shift lay the development of the nation's educational system. This was indeed tangible evidence of a strong connection between education and social change.

All things considered, the opening decades of the 20th century were a momentous time for American secondary schools. These institutions experienced dramatic expansion, enrolling nearly half of the adolescent population by the 1930s. Although high schools were mostly traditional academic institutions in the latter part of the 19th century, by the 1920s they were slowly evolving into somewhat more comprehensive entities, embracing a variety of different curricula and vocational purposes. Perhaps more important, secondary education was becoming a significant factor in the national economy, contributing to large-scale development of the stock of human capital at the same time that it increased the earning power of its students. In this respect the high school had come to fulfill the purposes that many administrative progressives had expressed for it. High schools became the key link between the nation's education system and the labor market. This was the leading edge of what eventually would become known as the "human capital revolution," and education would never be looked on as inconsequential again.

CASE: INDUSTRIALISM AND PROGRESSIVE REFORM IN GARY, INDIANA

Creating ever-closer links between the economy and the schools was an important theme in progressivism. Of course, this aspect of reform had many sides in the early years of the 20th century, some of which did not conform neatly to the categories historians have devised to describe them. One such instance occurred in the case of the schools in Gary, Indiana. Under the leadership of William Wirt, a charismatic and enterprising superintendent, this city's education system became a famous example of progressive reform at work in an industrial setting. It was seen as a case that demonstrated the possibility of uniting many of the contradictory elements of progressive education reform, and it showed the potential for controversy that schooling engendered during this period. School reform in Gary also provides an interesting lesson about the fate of educational ideas and practices once they were removed from the settings in which they were originally conceived.

Gary, Indiana, was an unusual city. Founded in 1906 by the U.S. Steel Corporation to house the workers for its giant blast furnaces and mills on the southern shore of Lake Michigan, it was named for the company's founder, Judge Elbert H. Gary. Like other industrial company towns at the time, it grew quickly as the population of workers and their families, many of them immigrants, began to settle there. A key part of the new city's planning was the establishment of a school system, and in 1908 William Wirt arrived from nearby Bluffton, Indiana, to begin his tenure as its first superintendent. Wirt was a one-time student of John Dewey and held great admiration for the ideas of pedagogical progressivism, and he had started experimenting with ways of implementing progressive principles while in Bluffton. The call to lead the establishment of a new city's school system in Gary provided him with an opportunity to develop these ideas even further. Within a relatively short time, in fact, Wirt had helped to make Gary a showcase of progressive educational reform (Cohen, 1990).

Like Dewey, William Wirt was a strong believer in the importance of learning from experience about the larger world outside of the everyday experience of children. Like the managers at U.S. Steel, he also aspired to greater efficiency in the enterprise he supervised. Given these predilections, he devised a series of reforms in the organization of schooling, such that both sets of purposes were addressed. Instead of requiring children to remain in one classroom throughout the day, as was common in primary schools of the time, Wirt rotated children between periods of academic instruction and various types of activity learning, including laboratories, gym periods, and assembly sessions. Wirt labeled his system the "work-study-play school" but it quickly became known as the Gary Plan. This approach allowed the schools to accommodate larger numbers of children, as only half the student body required seats in classrooms at a given time. The other children would be in the gymnasiums, the auditoriums, on the playgrounds or in labs. Utilized in this way, no major resource of the school was idle at any time, and children were exposed to a wide variety of different learning situations. Wirt also emphasized learning from the larger community, and he encouraged field trips and visits by various representatives from business and civic life. He made provisions for some schools to be open to the community throughout the year, giving substance to the progressive stipulation that the school should be a center of neighborhood life. His was a practical and energetic brand of progressive reform, and it was not long before it achieved wide acclaim (Cohen & Mohl, 1979).

As one might imagine, the Gary Plan proved appealing to both wings of the progressive impulse in education. Dewey praised it for the emphasis on activity learning outside of class and the imaginative ways the Gary teachers utilized instructional time in the schools. He and other pedagogical progressives were impressed by the degree of public involvement in the schools, and the willingness of Wirt and his teachers to embrace the local community. Administrative progressives, on the other hand, were struck by the system's efficient use of resources. School leaders in other rapidly expanding urban districts marveled at the idea that schools could serve as many as twice the number of children contained in classrooms simply by utilizing other spaces for different types of activity learning. With enthusiastic endorsements from educators on both sides of the great divide in American education at the time, the Gary Plan was widely seen as the best example of progressive ideas put to practical use. After Dewey featured several Gary schools in his book *Schools of To-Morrow*, and other writers commented on the system's efficiency, Wirt became an important figure in educational reform (Callahan, 1962; Cremin, 1961).

A key element of the success of Wirt's plan in Gary was his own commitment to the principles of progressive pedagogy. Teachers who supervised children outside of classrooms had to be carefully selected and trained in activity learning. Wirt recognized the dangers of these periods becoming little more than supervised play, or expensive baby-sitting sessions. Even though it was a rapidly growing city, Gary was small enough so that responsible and well-trained teachers could be recruited for such duties, at least in the beginning. Making field trips, lab experiments, and other activities a regular part of the curriculum required a good deal of coordination, and considerable cooperation from local businesses, government offices, and a host of other agencies. Wirt strove to provide the resources necessary to make such planning possible, and his personal magnetism and reputation helped to assure good will toward the schools. As the system grew larger, however, and Wirt's personal attention was diverted to other matters, the details of such preparation increasingly were left to others. Eventually, the educative value of these alternative forms of learning became open to question. Despite the emphasis Wirt and others placed on progressive pedagogy in the system's early years, as time passed it seemed that educators were most intrigued by the Gary Plan because of the potential it held for cost savings. Even if the great appeal of Wirt's system was its ability to combine the different aspects of progressive reform, it eventually became clear that one side or the other would predominate (Cohen & Mohl, 1979).

In 1914 Wirt was called to New York City, where the mayor and local school officials asked him to help implement a variant of the Gary Plan, also called the "platoon" system, into the city's schools. Wirt came into town with great fanfare, declaring that he could save the city thousands of dollars by organizing the schools to use their resources more efficiently. After setting up a small number of demonstration projects, Wirt claimed to be ready to implement his ideas on a wider scale when he found himself in the middle of a controversy. The platoon school became an issue in the city's mayoral election, with labor and teacher groups protesting the movement of children from one activity to another, declaring that quality education was being sacrificed in the name of cost savings. As a result of this uproar, Wirt's plan eventually was rejected by the New York schools, and he returned to Gary chastened but unapologetic. Even though the Gary schools continued to be the subject of considerable attention well into the 1920s, Wirt focused his energies on matters closer to home. The New York experience had taught him just how difficult it was to transplant a complex set of educational ideas and practices into a new and different social and political context (Cohen, 1990; Ravitch, 1974).

The basic concept of the platoon school, however, proved very appealing to district administrators faced with rapidly expanding enrollments and a fixed stock of classroom spaces. Eventually more than 200 cities adopted some form or another of this method of school organization. Much of the platoon school's popularity can be attributed to the work of Alice Barrows, Wirt's idealistic and enthusiastic assistant in the ill-fated New York experiment. Barrows subsequently took a position in the U.S. education office and became an untiring advocate of Wirt's ideas. It is open to question, however, whether school administrators agreed with the progressive pedagogical predilections of Barrows as much as they were interested in the greater efficiency the platoon plan afforded their districts. Children moving around the school to use laboratories, art rooms, and gymnasiums eventually would become a staple of American education, but it is not clear that such activities were linked to a progressive conception of teaching and learning. Like so many other educational ideas, Wirt's platoon system was adapted by local educators to serve their own purposes, and to help the schools achieve their traditional goals in a more efficient manner. As David Tyack and Larry Cuban have noted, most educational reforms have ended up in producing only slight alterations to the existing modes of school organization, as they were adjusted to suit the needs of teachers and principals in particular settings. The Gary Plan, however appealing at the start, was no exception to this general rule (Cohen, 1990; Tyack & Cuban, 1995).

William Wirt's approach to progressive reform was one of dozens of similarly localized efforts to improve schools both in terms of pedagogy and efficiency. The schools of Winnetka, Illinois, under the leadership of

Carlton Washburn, were another prominent example, along with Helen Parkhurst's "Dalton Plan," which originated in the high school at Dalton, Massachusetts. Parkhurst later was associated with a private institution she founded in New York City, the Dalton School. Not all of these of these reform regimes were as schematic as Wirt's; most were located in relatively affluent communities and emphasized individual expression and a break with traditional curricula. By the end of the 1920s, however, many of them were on the defensive. In the case of Gary, a survey of the schools headed by Abraham Flexner, the famous critic of higher and professional education, found that students performed poorly on tests of traditional knowledge and that Wirt's highly touted efficiency was not evident in all of the district's schools. Similar criticisms were leveled at other districts identified with pedagogical reform. Perhaps findings such as these were inevitable, given the hyperbole that often accompanied the work of educational reformers in this era. Despite its great promise, progressive reform seems never to have fulfilled its image of a fundamental transformation in American schooling. Even with visionary leaders, and an abundance of local resources and goodwill, the pace of change in schooling was ultimately quite incremental. This is a lesson from history that most would-be reformers seem all too eager to overlook even today (Semel & Sadovnik, 1999; Zilversmit, 1993).

OUTSIDERS: GENDER, RACE, AND EQUITY IN EDUCATION DURING THE PROGRESSIVE ERA

Progressive school reform was rooted in humanitarian principles, and Dewey and other reformers were concerned about democracy, but the movement's record on questions of race, gender, and social equality was hardly a good reflection of these values. Despite the interest that school leaders expressed in serving all the various elements of society, there is evidence that inequity in education grew worse during the Progressive Era. The benefits of progressive reform were not available to everyone. Large segments of the American population were left untouched by pedagogical progressivism, and administrative reforms—guided by the dictates of efficiency and differentiation—probably served to delimit the educational prospects of students from certain social groups. Even though there was a growing national debate about these questions, ideologies of racism and sexism were widely propagated at this time, even by educators. It was an era of sharp differences in social status, and this was reflected in the nation's schools. Put simply, equity was not a major focus of reform.

One example of this was women's secondary education. In chapter 4 it was noted that the latter part of the 19th century was a time of a remarkable gender equity in American high schools, notwithstanding the efforts of Edward Clarke and other opponents of coeducation. Girls outnumbered boys by a two-to-one margin in secondary schools during the 1890s, and outperformed them on most measures of academic accomplishment. Most important, they appear to have taken generally the same courses as the boys; there was little evident curricular differentiation according to gender. This would change in the early 20th century, partly because some educators became uncomfortable with the idea of relative equality for women. They expressed anxiety that the high school was becoming feminized by all of the young women in attendance, and that the male students were in jeopardy of losing their masculinity. These fears were voiced by the prominent psychologist G. Stanley Hall of Clark University, and echoed widely throughout the educational establishment. Just a few decades after the controversy occasioned by Clarke's attack on women's higher education, it appeared that a new consensus was building to change female schooling once again (Rury, 1991; Tyack & Hansot, 1990).

At the same time that some educators, mostly men, were fretting about the perceived feminization of American schools, others were working to devise new forms of education for young women. Ellen Richards, a chemist and the Massachusetts Institute of Technology's first female faculty member, helped to launch a distinctive academic field called *home economics* in the first decade of the 20th century. The home economics movement eventually sought to define an entire academic discipline around the study of problems related to women and their roles as mothers and housekeepers, embracing everything from nutrition to consumer behavior (often called *family and consumer studies* today). For educators in the high schools, however, home economics became a way of defining women's roles through training in accepted forms of work, and socialization in prescribed standards of conduct. In this regard it represented a way of differentiating the education of young women from that of males, at the same time that it proposed to ready them for their "true" calling in life: preparing to become a wife, mother, and homemaker. In a relatively brief period, home economics would become one pillar of a distinctively female segment of the high school curriculum (Kliebard, 1999; Rury, 1991).

There were other areas of change in women's education too, most of them connected to shifts in female employment. As suggested earlier, thousands of young women took new jobs in stores, offices, and other settings where they performed clerical tasks for the burgeoning corporate and governmental sectors of the economy. This led to a boom in enrollments for programs in commercial education, where women received training in stenography, typing, bookkeeping, and other subjects that could help them obtain clerical positions. It was not long before these classes became dominated by women, helping to typecast such forms of employment and training as feminine. The same tendency was evident in programs to train students in sewing and other skills suitable for the garment trades. The earliest programs of this sort were conducted in private schools that specialized in commercial and vocational education, but eventually most students who wanted such training opted for programs in the public high schools, where they were free and easily accessible. The development of a sizable portion of the public high school curriculum devoted primarily to preparing young women for "female" jobs in the labor force was yet another aspect of gender differentiation in education. As the high school became increasingly concerned with vocational preparation for its students, and young men and women were trained for different careers, the institution's course of study came to be divided along the lines of gender (Powers, 1992).

Although these developments probably did not result in a dramatic change in the schooling of many young men and women, their impact was pervasive. Most schools continued to be coeducational, and girls and boys still took most of their academic classes together. The process of change occurred at the margins, in a relatively small number of vocational subjects, but it would be wrong to underestimate the importance of these events. The very fact that several classes in most large, comprehensive high schools were almost exclusively populated by women—home economics, typing, stenography, sewing, and similar subjects—while others were considered the domain of the boys—shop, drafting, mechanics, and the like—sent a clear message: Gender was still a powerful determinant of a person's ultimate role in society. Unlike the 19th century, when the high school was dominated by academic subjects and there were few differences between the sexes, by the 1920s it was clear that boys and girls were destined to occupy distinct positions in the social division of labor. There is evidence, moreover, that it was about at this time that the academic performance of young women in certain subjects, particularly mathematics and science, began to fall behind that of the men. Just as the labor market dictated that young women were best suited to assume roles as secretaries and filing clerks, many educators came to believe that female students were not as analytically keen as their male classmates, at least in specific classes. A subtle but insidious set of gender distinctions slowly began to take hold, and it would be several decades before they would eventually come to light in public discussions (Rury, 1991; Tyack & Hansot, 1990).

The movement toward gender distinctions in American high schools was embraced enthusiastically by progressive educators of every stripe. For administrative progressives it represented an axiomatic case of curricular differentiation. After all, they reasoned, few areas of life exhibited a more striking set of distinctions than gender, and the urban industrial economy clearly called for men and women to fulfill different occupational roles. For pedagogical progressives, on the other hand, subjects like home economics for girls and shop for boys represented a healthy connection between the school and the wider world of work and living that students were preparing for. What better way to introduce them to their likely future positions in society? Few educators posed questions about the inequities inherent in this pattern of curricular specialization. Instead, the appearance of new courses such as home economics and the commercial subjects was widely hailed as the dawn of a new era in secondary education. Some enthusiastic reformers made fantastic claims: Ellen Richards, for instance, predicted that home economics could save American civilization, as women learned to be better mothers and housekeepers. This was the ideology of "republican motherhood" taken to a new extreme. Such an assertion may seem silly today—David Tyack and Elisabeth Hansot labeled it "social salvation with white sauce"—but it helped obscure the sexist quality of the reforms being proposed. For educators in the early 20th century, the concept of differentiation was too logical to resist, even if it sharply delimited the options their students would have in the future (Powers, 1992; Tyack & Hansot, 1990).

A similar set of issues confronted African Americans in school at this time, but the pattern of discrimination and ideological classification they encountered was even more pronounced. As noted in chapter 4, Black schooling was decidedly inferior to that provided to Whites in the South in the latter part of the 19th century. This pattern of unequal education continued into the Progressive Era, with Black schools hobbled by shorter terms, lower pay for teachers, and fewer supplies than similar institutions for Whites. More than 90% of the African American population lived in the South and were forced to scratch out a meager living in the region's agricultural economy. Although the North experienced large-scale industrialization and urban development, the pace of economic change was considerably slower in the land of Dixie, despite booster claims of a "New South." In the years following 1910, hundreds of thousands of Blacks moved to the rapidly expanding cities of the North, to take industrial jobs and escape the Jim Crow mentality of Southern society. For the vast majority of the African American population that remained, however, life in the South did not improve appreciably. The poor condition of Black education was an important aspect of the region's continuing legacy of servitude (Bond, 1966).

Despite the grotesque inequalities that characterized Southern education, there were some signs of progress. Spurred by the activities of Northern philanthropies, Southern states invested more resources in public education, including Black schools. The vast majority of this new funding for African Americans, however, was spent on primary schooling. New schools were built, additional teachers hired, and supplies purchased, but only to provide education in the elementary grades. This provided Black Southerners with basic literacy skills but little else. In the meantime, it gave Whites political cover when they were accused of depriving Black taxpayers of essential services, and it also helped to mask inequities in other areas of the educational system (Margo, 1990; Werum, 1997).

Perhaps the biggest source of racial disparity in Southern schooling appeared in secondary education. During the Progressive Era fewer than 5% of high school-aged Black students were enrolled at the secondary level, most of them in private schools supported by tuition, local donations, and Northern philanthropy. In the meantime, public high schools were established throughout the South for White children, particularly in the region's larger towns and cities. Even if Southern school systems lagged behind the rest of the country in terms of facilities and attendance patterns, public secondary schools for the White population became available quite rapidly. Between 1905 and 1920 more than 500 of these institutions were established, making secondary schooling widely accessible. By contrast, in 1916 only 58 public high schools for African Americans existed in 14 Southern states, with just 25 in the former Confederate states. Even though the numbers of teenagers in each race were about the same in the states of the "Deep South," White public high schools outnumbered those for African Americans by more than a 10 to 1 ratio. For the Blacks, secondary education remained an elusive goal, a bitter reminder of their subservient status in the regional culture (Anderson, 1988).

Even when public high schools did exist for local Black communities, there were questions about their academic quality. Reflecting the influence of Booker T. Washington, many Black public secondary institutions featured a manual training curriculum. This meant that the male students spent most of the school day in shops and tool rooms, learning carpentry, other trades, or simple handicrafts. For Black women, the largest segment of the manual training program was home economics, with an emphasis on working as domestic servants, the largest category of employment for Black women at the time. These schools offered only a smattering of academic classes, and certainly were not equivalent to the highly scholastic quality of the best White high schools in this period. Not everyone was enamored of manual training, and many Black communities struggled to maintain strong academic secondary institutions for their children. But such efforts often faced an uphill struggle. In the minds of Southern Whites, secondary education was simply not appropriate for most African Americans, and when offered it was most suitably focused on vocational subjects. Southern congressmen led the way in drafting the first federal legislation to support vocational education, the Smith–Hughes Act in 1918, arguing that it would benefit the region's African American population. Like other education funds, most of this money eventually went to White schools, but the link between manual training and Black schooling was firmly established. It would take decades to change (Werum, 1997).

These differences in the availability and quality of secondary schooling held enormous implications for African Americans. If indeed the opening decades of the 20th century were the age of the high school, and secondary education became increasingly important to economic advancement, the nation's Black population missed out on this crucial step in the human capital revolution. It meant that an entire generation—or more—of them were deprived of the skills necessary to compete for employment in the expanding white-collar and managerial sector of the labor market. They could not hope to get jobs as clerks or typists, much less as accountants or office managers, without the critical credential represented by a high school diploma. What is more, they could not pass the knowledge and insights gained from such positions—human and cultural capital—on to their own children. The withholding of secondary education from Black Southerners thus caused this large segment of the American population to fall even farther behind the rest of the nation in educational attainment and everything that accompanied it. As seen in chapter 6, this would prove to be a difficult legacy to overcome.

The experiences of young women and African Americans in this period should be considered a part of the legacy of Progressivism. As suggested earlier, the treatment of these groups in secondary schools can be thought of as yet another aspect of differentiation. Indeed, David Snedden and other devotees of administrative progressivism probably would find little cause for concern in the foregoing account. The schools, after all, were simply supposed to efficiently reproduce the existing social division of labor, not eradicate it—hence the term *social efficiency*. If African Americans occupied a servile position in the social order, it was not the educational system's task to change that. Differences attributable to race and gender often were seen as biologically based, and thus taken to be God-given and not subject to human or institutional intervention. The purpose of schooling, in that case, was to prepare each group for its inevitable social destination, and not to raise thorny questions about equality and fairness along the way (Drost, 1967; Kliebard, 1999).

If it is simple to comprehend the position of a conservative such as Snedden, it is harder to understand the view of the pedagogical progressives on questions of race and gender. John Dewey was a giant among American liberals of his day, yet he was strangely quiet on these issues—especially concerning race. Perhaps the battle against traditional forms of education was all-consuming, and pedagogical progressives feared that addressing yet other questions would jeopardize their fragile movement. It is possible that Dewey and other progressive thinkers did not feel compelled to confront racial issues explicitly, simply because relatively few Blacks lived in the North at the time. Although Columbia University was immediately adjacent to Harlem, a vast Black community, Dewey may have felt that the question of race was part of the larger issue of inequality in American democracy, a matter he devoted much time and energy to addressing in broad terms (Westbrook, 1991). Yet some historians have questioned Dewey's commitment to diversity, suggesting that he was less than tolerant of cultural differences when he encountered certain immigrant groups, such as those from Eastern Europe (Karier, 1972, 1979). Whatever the cause, the question of race and ethnicity appears to have been something of a blind spot in the progressives' humanitarian campaign to transform the school. It was not a set of issues that they devoted very much time and energy to, and the movement—not to mention the nation's education system—was the poorer for it.

THE UNIVERSITY ENTERS AN AGE OF HUMAN CAPITAL

As noted in chapter 3, institutions of higher education underwent an important set of changes in the latter part of the 19th century. The old-time college, with its emphasis on classical study and mental discipline, slowly gave way to the modern research university. These new institutions were governed by an ethic of investigation and discovery, along with engagement with the problems of society. The leaders of this movement were elite eastern private institutions and the flagship state universities of the Midwest and California. By the early 20th century it had become fashionable for middle-class youth, women and men alike, to attend these schools, both for the lively social scene and to gain credentials that would be useful in the labor force. Enrollments mounted quickly, as students found that higher education provided pathways to employment in the large corporations, government, and the professions. Even though overall attendance remained a small fraction of the number of high school students, these developments were a harbinger of the future (Cass, 1977, Veysey, 1965).

The shift from the traditional college of the 19th century to the modern university was a gradual process, even if the differences between the two types of institutions were rather dramatic. Religion had played a prominent role in the colleges, and although it continued to be an important element in the life of the university, its dominance of the cultural ethos in higher education declined markedly with time. A new generation of faculty members was trained in Europe, most of them in Germany, where principles of scientific research held sway over traditional concerns with classics and religious morality. Many of these professors also believed that the university should be more intimately involved in improving society, whether through social reform or simply improving the efficiency of existing institutions and practices. By and large, they found a receptive audience. Increasingly, the classes that students took were grounded in the new research-based academic disciplines, and not classical languages or Biblical scholarship. Although large numbers of the graduates of the old-time college had become ministers in the 19th century, after 1900 more university graduates began to take jobs in business and the professions. All of this contributed to a new atmosphere of secularism and an ethic of individual advancement in higher education. While many students still went to college for purposes of piety and scholarly growth, they were joined by a new type of student, one interested in having fun and getting a good job (Marsden, 1994; Reuben, 1996; Rodgers, 1998).

These changes were correlates of growth. Overall enrollment climbed from about a quarter-million in 1900 to more than a million in 1930, representing more than 10% of the age 18 to 21 population at the time. This was a significant fraction of American youth, even if it still constituted something of a social and cultural elite. Large concentrations of college students at the leading state universities, particularly those in the Midwestern and Western states, began to develop their own cultural identity. Enrollments grew into the thousands at these campuses, and an elaborate social life began to flourish. The number of female students grew even faster than the male collegiate population, expanding from less than 40% of the student body in the 1890s to almost half by the 1920s. These developments infused new energy into campus life. A brisk dating scene sparked an atmosphere of sexual openness and experimentation, the so-called flapper era, characterized by drinking, dances, and "necking." Although only a minority of students participated routinely in such behavior, these students represented a sharp break with the past. Fraternities and sororities also became very popular, especially after 1920, along with spectator sports such as football. All of this marked a new era in campus cultures. College life was emerging as a distinctive phase in the experience of middle- and upper-class youth, even if many still skipped college altogether. For those who participated, the social side of the university often constituted the start of a career in business or the professions: Many students formed friendships and associations that extended well into their adult and professional lives (Bledstein, 1976; Horowitz, 1987).

In case there was any doubt about these shifts, the utilitarian cast of the university was certified with the appearance of a host of new professional schools and institutes. In the 19th century legal and medical training had been conducted by private schools or individuals; around 1900 the universities began acquiring these institutions, or developing their own, and awarding degrees to students who completed professional courses of study. Similar arrangements were made for the preparation of engineers, social workers, and other professionals. It was also in this period that the first university programs to provide training for business were established, offering courses in accounting, finance, management, marketing, and similar subjects. These developments proved to be a substantial boost to enrollments, as students were drawn to the campuses to obtain the credentials they would need for entry into work life. With the advent of professional study, it was harder to cast the university as an isolated academic ivory tower. For better or worse, higher education was being drawn ever closer to the practical worlds of business, government, and the major professions. It was providing human capital, critical knowledge, and skills, for the nation's future leaders (Geiger, 1986; Goldin & Katz, 1999b; Levine, 1986).

The growth of higher education also led to a proliferation of different types of institutions. This was yet a new kind of differentiation, as the demand for various forms of higher learning met with an institutional response. In addition to elite eastern private schools and the big state flagship universities, along with other largely residential institutions, a number of new colleges and universities appeared in this era. Among the most important was a 2-year institution designed to provide the most basic courses as a preparation for higher study, the junior college, later called the community college. These institutions first appeared in the West and the Midwest, numbering some 200 by the latter 1920s but enrolling less than a 10th of all undergraduates. Other more popular forms of higher education also flourished, among them municipal colleges in the larger cities and private urban universities. These institutions served commuter students, providing baccalaureate education along with a variety of professional programs. Career-minded students in New York, Cincinnati, or Detroit thus could attend local public colleges, whereas those in Chicago went to DePaul, Loyola, or the Armour Institute (today's Illinois Institute of Technology). This was higher education for the lower middle class, students who could not afford more elite schools or who were unable or less inclined to live away from home. Producing legions of lawyers, accountants, managers, and teachers, these institutions embodied the new pragmatic ethos of American higher education (Brint & Karabel, 1989; Levine, 1986).

The early 20th century was a time of significant growth and change in higher learning. Responding to the demand for new knowledge and skills, the human capital requirements of the urban industrial age, the nation's colleges and universities shifted their mission to providing students with credentials they could use in the rapidly evolving economy. As enrollments grew steadily, and coeducation became a national norm, a distinctive collegiate culture came to characterize the lives of students at these institutions. These changes highlighted the increased prominence that higher education was coming to assume in American civilization. They also were a portent of the future development of the university as a distinctive and critical feature of the nation's educational system. As striking as these events may have seemed at the time, they were just the beginning of the emergence of the modern system of higher education.

EDUCATION AND SOCIAL CHANGE IN AN URBAN INDUSTRIAL ERA

The Progressive Era was a period of transformation in the United States. The industrial revolution unleashed powerful forces of change. The economy expanded at an unprecedented rate, the nation's transportation and communications systems evolved rapidly, and the cities underwent booming growth. All of this demanded significant changes in the educational system, to provide both basic education to the masses of industrial workers and higher forms of instruction to the emerging white-collar labor force. As the nation's population expanded—a result of both natural increase and immigration—thousands of new schools were needed. With the educational system's growth, more sophisticated forms of management and organization were required to address these conditions. Along with this, fresh educational ideas were debated as educators struggled to fashion a new system of schooling for the 20th century.

As regards the direction of change, it seems clear that the schools responded to shifts in the economic and social organization of the nation. The rational, bureaucratic reforms of the administrative progressives were in part a response to the development of large, complex, urban school systems, and to the problems of maintaining consistent standards of conduct for students and school employees alike, not to mention board members and politicians. High schools proliferated, in large part because of the demand for clerical workers, managers, and other white-collar workers needed to record and process information for the age's new large corporate firms and the governmental agencies established to monitor them. Demand for professional service, from legal advice to accountants and engineers, spurred new levels of interest in higher education, as colleges and universities created degree programs to serve their expanding clientele. If the industrial revolution was transforming American society, the education system was responding in kind. A new age was dawning, and modern schools were developed to meet its varied needs.

Did schools change society in this period as well? Clearly, they provided the skilled and knowledgeable workers needed for the growth of the urban industrial economy. This was not a small matter, as Claudia Goldin and others have argued, for without an educated workforce it is unlikely that the U.S. economy would have developed as rapidly as it did. But what about other types of change? Did the pedagogical progressives succeed in creating a renewed sense of community by making schools more humane and "child-centered"? Did John Dewey and his followers establish an ethic of democracy for the nation's schools, militating against industry's tendency to make people "appendages of machines"? Here the impact of school reform appears to have been considerably more modest. Although the pedagogical progressives did create a number of exemplary schools, and conducted a number of inspired local reform experiments, such as in Gary and Winnetka, their impact on the larger educational system appears to have been modest at best. Driven by the rationalistic and efficiency-minded reforms of the administrative progressives, most teachers and administrators in American schools were not influenced much by the likes of Parker, Kilpatrick, or other pedagogical reformers. Instead, their lives were probably more immediately and deeply affected by the growing educational bureaucracy, by the testing movement, and by the sheer growth of the educational system than by any new ideas about how to improve or humanize instruction. As a result, the legacy of pedagogical reform in this period is an ambiguous one. It produced many zealous reformers, passionate experiments, and idealistic principles, but it is an open question whether it created lasting change in most of the nation's classrooms.

The impulse toward greater differentiation and "social efficiency" in American education is one area where the effect of school reforms does indeed appear to have had a significant impact on social change. As noted earlier, the desire to make the schools respond more effectively to the "needs" of different social groups helped to perpetuate and widen existing patterns of social inequality. Women and African Americans suffered as a consequence of efforts to design schools to fit them to subservient social roles. The development of vocational education, home economics, and manual arts schools was a part of this process. It would take decades before the effect of these "reforms" was recognized and remedied.

Education and social change were thus clearly linked during the progressive period of American history. The schools responded to the demands created by the nation's rapidly developing economy. The "human capital revolution" gave certain forms of schooling new prominence, especially secondary and higher education. This would be a harbinger of developments to come in the future. In other respects, however, educational reform does not seem to have succeeded in accomplishing the lofty aims its spokespersons articulated for it. This was the great disappointment of a period of considerable ferment in American education, a tradition of advocacy for change that continues down to the present.

CHAPTER SIX

Education in Postwar America:
The Human Capital Revolution

There can be little doubt that the decades following World War II marked a time of profound alteration in American life, and in the nation's schools. Just considering transportation, communications, and popular culture, familiar facets of daily life, things have changed a great deal since the 1940s. Equally dramatic shifts have affected social policy issues and the relationships of various groups in American society. This was especially true in major metropolitan areas, where the vast majority of Americans had come to reside in the latter part of the 20th century. Altogether, it was a period of change comparable in significance to the time of the Industrial Revolution. It is against this backdrop that recent events in American education can be best understood.

From the standpoint of this book, however, perhaps the most striking feature of this period was the growing importance attached to formal education, both as a matter of public policy and as a private concern. It was during these years that the human capital revolution finally came to full bloom in the United States. As in earlier times, schools continued to be seen as engines of economic development, but after World War II they also became instruments of federal social policy. In this latter connection, the role of the school expanded significantly, to attempt the redress of seemingly intractable patterns of social inequity. The federal government became a major source of funding and policy initiatives in education, and schooling developed into an important issue in national politics. At the same time, more Americans attended schools than in any previous period. Enrollments climbed at all levels of the educational system, but especially in the nation's high schools and colleges. Everyone, it seemed, was interested in going to school, and educational attainment became a telling public preoccupation.

This also was a time of change in the nation's intellectual life, and in the major ideological currents that shaped thinking about the schools. Progressive education fell out of favor with much of the public. Opposition to these ideas and practices came to a peak in the 1950s, abetted by a conservative ethos fostered by the anti-Communist sentiments of the Cold War. At the same time, however, there was a gradual liberalization of racial ideas, partly influenced by wartime revulsion at Nazi theories of Aryan supremacy. The 1954 Supreme Court decision in *Brown v. Board of Education*, declaring segregated schools to be inherently unequal, was a milestone of national educational policy and in popular thinking about social justice. It also was a defining moment for the modern Civil Rights movement, an event that altered the landscape of public life in the United States. Movements focused on women's equality and students' rights eventually took inspiration from the struggle over racial justice, and these too had an important effect on the schools. As a consequence of these changes, American education would never be the same (Ravitch, 1983).

In addition to these developments, several major social trends in the postwar period had an impact on American schools. The first of these was the changing racial and ethnic composition of the nation's principal metropolitan areas. As noted earlier, most African Americans lived in the South prior to the Second World War. Demand for cheap labor in the war industries, however, combined with the mechanization of agriculture in the South, led to a massive shift in the nation's Black population to urban areas in the North and upper Midwest. With the migration of millions of poorly educated Blacks during the late 1940s, 1950s, and 1960s, big-city public schools systems became differentiated along racial lines. Despite the principles of integration and equity embodied in the 1954 *Brown* decision, and the effort of liberal-minded educators across the country, growing inequalities in the type and quality of education came to characterize metropolitan life (Kantor & Brenzel, 1993). If policymakers and large segments of the public believed that one purpose of the public school was to bring students from different backgrounds and with differing social destinations—together, the process of racial and social/economic differentiation made it less tenable as time passed, something educators quickly came to recognize (Conant, 1961).

Another major event in the postwar era was the appearance of a vibrant, pervasive, and commercially expansive youth culture. This partly was a consequence of demographic numbers. Following the war, birth rates soared, as men (and women) returning from the military began to settle into family life. This was the beginning of the historically large "baby boom" generation, which created a large cohort of teenagers by the later 1950s and the 1960s (Hawes & Hiner, 1985). The new youth culture also shaped the evolution of courtship practices, especially as teenagers became interested in sexuality and relationships, building an elaborate set of rituals and social practices around these concerns (Modell, 1989). With growing high school attendance in the 1950s and 1960s, followed by rising college enrollments, educational institutions became the location in which these emerging forms of adolescent culture could develop most rapidly (Coleman, 1965). This may have been fostered, of course, by the push for ever-larger schools that educators pursued in this period. In doing this, they unwittingly may have contributed to new forms of youth behavior that helped to undermine the academic goals of these institutions.

Finally, there was the evolution of the American economy in the postwar period, particularly the changing occupational structure, and rising educational requirements for different types of jobs. This was perhaps the clearest manifestation of the new significance attached to human capital in American economic life. The high school dramatically expanded its purview, but its economic significance diminished. As the number of jobs requiring a high school education or less declined, particularly in the years following 1980, rates of college enrollments began to increase significantly. American employers raised their educational expectations, and so did students (Buchman, 1989). Consequently, the vocational education programs that educators had devised to serve American high school students were increasingly seen as irrelevant to the demands of the job market. By the later 1980s, a majority of high school graduates were entering college, and the differentiated curriculum of the comprehensive high school was seen as largely unrelated to their interests (Murphy & Welch, 1989).

Each of these issues is examined in greater depth in this chapter. The postwar years marked a time when the relationship between education and social change became quite complex. As a matter of social policy, schools increasingly were called on to address problems of economic and social inequality. At the same time, the nation's educational system was itself profoundly affected by ideological shifts, and by underlying patterns of economic and demographic change. Even as schooling assumed greater importance, the questions of its availability and quality became vital concerns. Given these dynamics, determining the relationship between education and social change in this period is a challenging task. First, however, it is important to consider one of the central issues of this era in American civilization: changing patterns of family life and the emergence of a teenage subculture that eventually swept the nation.

CASE: REBELS IN SEARCH OF THEMSELVES

In many respects the postwar period marked the beginning of the era of the teenager in the United States. Even though the teenage population was comparatively small in the 1950s, due to low birth rates during the Depression and war, changing employment patterns had given teens a great deal more free time, and national prosperity meant that they had money to spend, too. Changing employment trends and labor laws enacted during the 1930s and 1940s sharply reduced the number of factory workers under age 19, and growing high school enrollments meant that large numbers of teens found themselves clustered together in classrooms and hallways for hours on end each day. All of this contributed to the development of a distinctive teenage society, a national subculture marked by particular patterns of behavior, fashion, and values.

Youth cultural identities had existed in earlier decades, but in the postwar years the emerging teenage social world seemed more prevalent and troubling. It was not long before a wide range of commentators began remarking on the problems of American youth, and such terms as *juvenile delinquent* and *high school dropout* began to become commonplace. Teenagers seemed to be rejecting the values of their parents, listening to new music, and experimenting with tobacco, alcohol, and sex. It was a phenomenon that adults struggled to understand, even if many found the problems of the nation's youth quite alarming (Gilbert, 1986).

A series of books, magazine articles, television reports, and movies appeared in the 1950s and 1960s focusing on questions of teenage behavior. Perhaps the most famous of the movies was the 1955 film *Rebel Without a Cause*, best known today for the role of its principal actor, the charismatic James Dean. *Rebel* is widely regarded as one of Dean's best cinematic performances, but it also featured Natalie Wood and Sal Mineo in roles that helped to launch their own careers. What made the film especially interesting, however, was its portrayal of the troubles teenagers experienced, and the role of adults—especially parents—in the creation and resolution of these problems. It was a dramatic story, but not one that exploited public fears by depicting base stereotypes. Unlike other films of the era, it was not a tale of demonic youth, crazed by music, sex, and alcohol, bent on self-destruction. Instead, it offered a portrait of misunderstood teens in search of parental love and guidance, forced into the bizarre social world of their peers by the selfishness and inhibitions of their elders. In these fundamental terms, *Rebel* was something of a morality play about the shortcomings of American civilization and about ways in which the larger society had neglected the nation's youth. As such, it offers a compelling glimpse into many of the concerns of its time, especially the feelings of many about problems related to education and growing up in the modern world (Doherty, 1988).

Rebel Without a Cause was a tale of alienation, violence, and love. Loosely based on the true story of a juvenile criminal, the script was developed from a story line by the film's director, Nicholas Ray. Some critics noted that it bore certain Shakespearian characteristics, and loosely resembled Romeo and Juliet. All three of its central characters, Jim Stark (James Dean), Judy (Natalie Wood), and John or "Plato" (Sal Mineo), were teenagers struggling with different forms of parental neglect or rejection, and coping with this loss in ways that ultimately turned out to be quite self-destructive. In the case of Jim (Dean), his weak father was unable to provide a clear and admirable role model, filling the young man with self-doubt and insecurity. These traits caused him to lash out at adversaries, and to engage in aberrant behavior (such as binge drinking) to get the attention of his parents. Natalie Wood's character, Judy, was a young woman feeling rejected by her father, who is made insecure by his daughter's budding sexuality and her yearning for his approval and affection. And John (Mineo), known mostly by his nickname Plato, was a social misfit whose wealthy parents had abandoned him altogether, leaving him in the care of an African American maid. Judy sought solace in the in the fast company of other young malcontents, while John drifted at the margins of teen society until he met Jim, who became his friend and something of a father figure. It was these conditions that framed the movie's action, and revealed its principal message about the way adult society was disregarding the nation's youth.

Perhaps the most telling relationship in the movie is that between Jim and his father, played by Jim Backus (later the millionaire on the TV show *Gilligan's Island*). Backus's character is morally vacuous, and appeared unable to take a firm stand on anything. He is afraid of his wife, who seems preoccupied with observing social conventions and maintaining appearances. When describing his troubles to a sympathetic police detective, young Jim complains that his parents are always bickering and that his father cannot stand up to his mother. "How can a guy grow up in a circus like that?" he declares. "Boy, if I had one day when I didn't have to be all confused ... if I felt I belonged someplace, you know." Later in the movie, when Jim is faced with a moral dilemma and asks for guidance, the father can only mumble platitudes, urging him to be careful and not to do anything risky. This leads directly to the movie's violent climax, wherein two characters die, one of them Plato. The message was clear: Adults abdicating their responsibility for moral leadership can have dire consequences for the country's teens (Cohen, 1997).

Given the quality of the actors' performances and the story's dramatic impact, the movie painted a telling picture of adolescence at midcentury. It also helped to document changes in the ways that Americans thought about childhood and adolescence. The contrast between the image of Jim's father in *Rebel* and that encountered almost 40 years earlier in Anzia Yezierska's *Bread Givers* could hardly be more striking. As noted in the previous chapter, Sarah Smolinsky's father was domineering and manipulative. He imposed his values onto his daughters, and took payments from men who wanted to marry them. Jim Stark's father, on the other hand, was almost wholly inaccessible to him. Emotionally distant, he offered his son no clear sense of values and little guidance. While young Sarah yearned to escape her father's dominion, Jim hungered to be closer to his father, to have a clear sense of identity that they could share. Like Sarah he took flight, but because he had no distinct set of values to draw on, he drifted into trouble. The two characters reflected differing times and circumstances, and contrasting patterns of youthful experience.

To some extent the differences in these two stories reflect culturally distinctive modes of childrearing and adolescence in 20th-century America.

The families depicted in *Rebel* were decidedly middle and upper class, and the problems depicted in the movie were supposed to be those of the affluent. But childrearing practices had changed in the United States for many families by the 1950s. Several decades of progressive critiques of authority and discipline had contributed to a new regime of parental behavior, at least in the middle class. At the same time, family size had dropped steadily, so that the average number of children among Whites was only around three (it had been as high as eight in the 18th century). Moreover, these families began to offer their children greater freedom. Following progressive models of education, self-expression came to be seen as more critical than obedience and conformity to traditional values. The famous baby doctor Benjamin Spock helped to revolutionize child care by telling mothers to heed and fulfill their infants' needs and desires. Freudian psychology, reaching its popular peak in the 1950s, warned against the dangers of repression and overt control. Like teachers in many "progressive" classrooms, parents were told that they were not supposed to be authority figures. Instead they were to strive to relate to their children as individuals, as friends. In a logical extension of this line of thought, some parents abstained from moral judgments altogether, letting their children freely discover their own point of view. This was the pattern of parental involvement that came under scrutiny *in Rebel Without a Cause*, and it represented a telling break with past traditions in American culture (Engelhardt, 1995; Graff, 1995).

Historians and other social observers have noted this pattern change in family life in the 20th century. Some, like Viviana Zelizar, suggested that middle-class Americans came to view children as extensions of themselves, and not as sources of support for their families—as in the case of Sarah Smolinsky—or as a religious and moral obligation—as Francis Wayland believed. In the new family, children became a form of self-expression, a way for parents to demonstrate and enhance their social status. This is not to say that parents did not care for their children, but it often meant that they placed different obligations or expectations on them, with greater psychological demands. This new outlook raised a host of questions, however, some of them voiced in *Rebel* and other social commentaries. If children were simply manifestations of a consumer ethic, allowed to inherit the materialism of their parents, there remained the issue of how they would learn the lessons of personal and social responsibility. Like many critics of the new progressive mode childrearing, the producers of *Rebel* suggested that a lack of discipline and authority lay at the root of the new problems with American teenagers. Some believed that the fate of the nation hung in the balance (Mintz & Kellogg, 1988; Zelizer, 1985).

The teenage problem, in that case, was a thorny one. If indeed the critics of progressive education were correct in suggesting that it was the lack of traditional values in families and schools that contributed to teen misbehavior, nothing less than a sweeping change in these institutions could suffice to change things. This was precisely the solution that some observers recommended. More realistic voices, however, recognized that the problem was considerably more complicated than suggested by either the makers of *Rebel Without a Cause* or other critics of progressivism. The development of the nation's youth subculture was in fact just getting under way, and would gain even greater force in the decades ahead. James Dean died at age 24, but his memory lived on in a teen society that became ever larger and more pervasive. The rise of this adolescent culture would become one of the major developments of the postwar period (Modell, 1989).

IDEOLOGICAL CURRENTS IN THE POSTWAR ERA

The 1930s and 1940s marked a significant change in the way Americans thought about a number of social issues. The experience of the Great Depression and World War II caused many to question prevailing theories of social superiority, especially those based on race and social class exclusion. During the 1930s, millions of people had lost their jobs, shattering illusions about the stability of social status and the security of a middle-class lifestyle. Socialists and communists were quite active at this time, and helped to spread radical ideas about equity and social justice. More important, the rapid growth of industrial trade unions, particularly those affiliated with the Congress of Industrial Organizations (or CIO), propagated ideals of brotherhood, unity, and fairness, and militated against exclusionary practices and divisiveness. In certain respects, the world was turned topsy-turvy, and many traditional ideas were subject to question. This was the start of an important shift in popular thinking about a range of social issues (Engelhardt, 1995; Patterson, 1996).

The Second World War also left an indelible impact on the United States. The very fact of millions of men and women leaving the country to fight abroad, and the mobilization of millions more to work in the war industry, made a lasting impression on the public mind. It was a good war, fought to save democracy and to turn back the forces of avarice and destruction. The enemies were contemptible, especially the Nazi regime in Germany. It was a war that helped Americans to feel good about themselves and their nation's egalitarian traditions. Many thought of the conflict as a struggle of democracy against totalitarianism, and this lent new significance to pleas for greater equity and social justice in American society. If the United States was opposed to dictatorships abroad, how could it sanction inequity and intolerance at home? And there was a racial dimension to the question. For once, Americans were confronted with an explicit ideology of racial superiority that was used to justify a quest for world domination. This was more than a little ironic, given the long history of racist oppression in this country, and the brutal experience of racial violence in the South. But the battle against Nazism helped to turn the tide of popular thinking against outright theories of racial superiority, perhaps for the first time in American history.

It was the dawn of a new era in American thinking about these questions (Polenberg, 1980; Sitkoff, 1993).

These tendencies were abetted by advances in the thinking of leading social scientists and other prominent social critics. Swedish sociologist Gunner Myrdal published his classic work on American race relations, *An American Dilemma*, in 1944, suggesting that racism was an anachronistic holdover from the 19th century, an ugly remnant of slavery. Myrdal noted that practices of discrimination stood in stark contrast to American ideals of liberty and equality, and predicted that they would eventually be changed for the better. In the same year, President Franklin Roosevelt issued an executive order banning discriminatory behavior in the nation's war industries, opening a wide field of industrial employment to the Black population. The ensuing demand for workers helped to start a new movement of African Americans out of the South, into the large industrial cities of the North and West, where they enjoyed new freedoms. This too represented a new step in race relations (Chafe, 1986; Lemann, 1991).

Such developments helped to set the stage for a rapid shift in American opinion about questions of race and discrimination. The Truman administration's decision to desegregate the armed forces soon after the war reflected this, as did new federal civil rights measures in the areas of housing and employment. Meanwhile, the NAACP, described in chapter 5, undertook a series of legal challenges to segregation in education, most of them at the university level. Its legal team, led by Thurgood Marshall, adopted a stance implicit in Myrdal's analysis of racism: that such discrimination was inherently inconsistent with the basic principles of American life, including the legal system. By the 1950s, the NAACP lawyers were attacking the policy of formally requiring Black children to attend separate schools so that they would not intermingle with their White counterparts, a practice still widespread in the South and certain other parts of the country. This was a difficult legal strategy for the NAACP to implement, as it required an expensive and time-consuming process of challenging individual school districts in the hopes that the federal courts would establish clear precedents against these policies in their rulings. But the judicial challenges pushed forward (Klinker & Smith, 1999; Sitkoff, 1978).

As it turned out, the NAACP approach to attacking discrimination through the judicial system proved dramatically effective. When the case its lawyers had launched against the Board of Education of Topeka, Kansas, was decided by the Supreme Court in 1954, it marked a landmark in American social policy. The Court ruled that policies of formal segregation in public schools were contrary to the equal protection clause of the 14th Amendment of the Constitution, directly challenging prevailing practices in most of the educational systems of the South. There was an immediate outcry against the decision, with political leaders across the South declaring their determination to fight the ruling. But elsewhere in the country there was a broad sentiment of support for the Court's action. Many Americans were ready to end the Jim Crow practices of formal segregation, even if most still were not yet ready to embrace full residential and educational integration in their own communities. In the years that followed, progress in ending the segregation of public education was difficult and halting, and often accompanied by dramatic—even violent—confrontations. But the 1954 *Brown* Supreme Court ruling marked a decisive change in the prevailing ideology of racial exclusion in the United States. The pace of change in years to follow would often be incremental, but once the Supreme Court had ruled, there could be no turning back (Kluger, 1976; Wilkerson, 1979).

Brown also gave added momentum to the development of the civil rights movement, a broad-based, collective effort by opponents of racism and discrimination to confront and end practices of segregation and racist oppression in the South and elsewhere. Although it embraced a wide cross section of Americans, the civil rights campaign was led by African Americans, and it was Blacks who constituted the vast majority of its participants. An expansive and diverse movement, it eventually embraced leaders as disparate as Martin Luther King and Malcolm X, and organizations extending from the NAACP to the Black Panthers. Some hoped to achieve an integrated America, whereas others pursued a separatist agenda, campaigning for Black control of their own neighborhoods and institutions. Although there was a good deal of debate and conflict between these various groups, the common thread that held the movement together was the struggle for equal rights. With an unusually creative and resourceful leadership, and many dedicated volunteers, the civil rights movement eventually succeeded in pointing out the contradiction between American ideals and the ugly reality of racist discrimination. Its impact was monumental (Cook, 1998; Klinkner & Smith, 1999).

Education remained a critical focal point for civil rights agitation during the 1950s and through the following decade. Other issues eventually took over the limelight, such as housing and voting rights, but schooling continued to be a major concern. If the promise of democracy and social equality was to be extended to the nation's Black population, after all, most African Americans believed that equitable access to educational opportunities was an essential step. In this spirit, battles were waged to force school systems to end policies and practices of segregation and educational inequality, first in the South—where compliance with the 1954 *Brown* decision was especially controversial—and later in the North, where de facto patterns of segregation represented the principal barrier to improved schooling for African Americans. Gradually, de jure (or "by law") policies of educational segregation were ended, but de facto ("by fact" of other conditions) segregation proved much harder to change. Despite the success of struggles waged in this period, the problem of racial inequality in education has continued to be a critical problem facing the United States up to the present. Historically, however, the ideological climate in the United States changed dramatically in the postwar years. The civil rights movement placed the question of social and educational equality squarely on the national agenda, and it could no longer be overlooked. Open espousal of racial segregation and discriminatory practices of any kind had ceased to be intellectually acceptable or politically tolerated. And educators everywhere, at least in principle, became conversant with the ideals of equity and social justice. Altogether, it represented a remarkable shift in the nation's intellectual disposition (Eskew, 1997; King, 1996; Orfield, 1983).

At the same time that the quest for civil rights exposed many Americans to more liberal ideas on certain social questions, more conservative tendencies were at play too. One of the issues that garnered the greatest conservative response in these years was education, especially the way schools and classrooms were run by educators. In particular, the ideas and practices of progressive education came under sharp attack.

By the 1940s progressivism had become an important intellectual force in professional thinking about schools and learning, even if it still represented a relatively small segment of the nation's educational system. Although most Americans may have been suspicious of progressive ideas about education, they were rarely openly hostile to them. This changed in the years following 1950, as a number of prominent academics and journalists took aim at progressive education, linking it in the public mind with failure in the schools. This was partly due to the climate of the "cold war" and nativist suspicions that progressive educators were "soft-headed" or left-leaning and therefore susceptible to communist influence. It also reflected widespread concerns about the lack of discipline in American children, particularly teenagers, and fears of juvenile delinquency, sex, and violence. Like the producers of *Rebel Without a Cause,* many critics of progressive ideas believed that a return to authority and traditional values was necessary, especially in the classroom. Consequently, there were calls for a return to traditional teaching methods, and a renewed emphasis on core academic subjects such as history, mathematics (especially algebra and geometry), English, and the sciences. Above all, however, there was an outcry for more order and control in the daily lives of children (Hofstadter, 1963; Ravitch, 1983).

This general tendency was bolstered by widespread public concern about the nation's schools in the wake of the Soviet Union's successful launch of the Sputnik spacecraft in 1957. The first man-made satellite, and the opening event of the much-anticipated "space age," Sputnik's success was a major source of embarrassment for American national pride. The seeming superiority of Russian scientists focused attention on the need for higher standards of academic achievement, especially in mathematics and the sciences, leading to the passage of the National Defense Education Act (NDEA) in 1958. This was a major step in expanding federal aid to schools, although it was focused on math and science programs and programs for teachers (Kaestle, 2001). Meanwhile, the National Science Foundation and other agencies began to support programs to improve instruction and curricular materials, and antiprogressive sentiments reached a peak. The Progressive Education Association, long an advocate of progressive school reform, dissolved itself in 1955, and 2 years later the magazine *Progressive Education* ceased publication. Although proponents of the ideas of Dewey and other progressive educators still existed, especially in colleges of education, the tide of national opinion had clearly turned in a more conservative direction as regarded schooling and childrearing practices. While it is questionable whether these attacks on progressive ideas had any immediate effect on the actual conduct of educators, it does appear that the influence of certain progressive ideas was weakened as a consequence, at least for a time (Cremin, 1961; Spring, 1976).

By the start of the 1960s, in that case, the nation's schools were buffeted by the influence of widely differing ideological trends. Although there was a dramatic liberalizing of attitudes about race and discrimination, there also was a pronounced turn toward traditional ideas concerning instructional practices. In certain respects, both of these tendencies reflected a repudiation of progressive ideas. The civil rights movement, after all, attacked the principle of differentiation so dear to the administrative progressives. The cry for greater integration and equal education was, at least in part, the very antithesis of the Progressive Era preoccupation with highlighting distinctions of background and aptitude in the schools. At the same time, conservative critics assailed the pedagogical progressivism of Dewy and his many disciples. At the very moment that certain matters of educational policy grew more equitable, in principle if not completely in practice, other aspects of educational practice may have marked a return to traditional methods. Such was the state of ideas about education in the decade following the Second World War, an odd legacy of progressivism indeed.

RACE, EQUITY, AND EDUCATION

In the years following the Second World War, race became an overriding issue in the nation's principal urban school districts. This did not happen overnight, but it eventually became an unavoidable question as larger numbers of African Americans moved to the North during and after the war. Because of changes in Southern agriculture and the reduced demand for farm workers, nearly 4 million Blacks moved from the South in the two decades after 1945. Most of these migrants came to the largest urban areas of the northeastern, midwestern, and western states. Once there, they usually settled into existing inner-city ghettos, or working-class neighborhoods being deserted by Whites. By the 1960s, cities such as New York, Chicago, and Los Angeles, and scores of others, had acquired sprawling Black settlements, typically areas marked by higher population density, rates of poverty, and crime than other neighborhoods. The degree of racial segregation in these cities was typically even greater than it had been in the South. As a result of these sharp patterns of residential separation, public school enrollments became highly segregated in the nation's major cities as well (Lemann, 1991; Wilkerson, 1979; Wolters, 1984).

Given these dynamics, race came to affect the spatial organization of cities in ways that other facets of social organization, such as ethnicity or social class, had not in earlier periods. Blacks often were forcefully kept separate from Whites, a feature of urban life that was maintained by violence, as well as with legal and quasi-legal action (Massey & Denton, 1993). African Americans who attempted to leave the ghettos were met with hostility, whereas "red-lining" mortgage-lending practices and legally binding restrictive covenants attached to deeds barred large numbers of them from settling in certain neighborhoods. Educational resources, of course, were also spatially distributed, a point that eventually became a matter of great controversy. The schools in Black neighborhoods tended to be overcrowded, with larger classes and fewer experienced teachers than schools in White areas. Graduation rates were lower in these parts of the city, and fewer students went on to college after graduating. In many respects, there were clear and well-documented differences in the quality of schools along racial lines. This, as critics noted, posed a great challenge to the very principle of public education as a fundamental institution of American civilization. If public schools were supposed to treat children equivalently, how could such disparities be reconciled with national ideals? These concerns led to a great deal of conflict over remedies for inequities in education during the sixties and seventies. In big cities across the country, the question of school desegregation became a major bone of contention, a flash point of political conflict (Rury, 1993, 1999b).

There were other facets of city life that exacerbated these issues. Social and technological trends made the spatial organization of urban areas a major policy question in this period. At the same time that millions of African Americans began pouring into the central cities, other residents had just started to leave. World War II had barely ended when a grand migration to suburbia began in most of the nation's largest cities. Pressured by severe housing shortages in the central cities, and encouraged by public policies that stimulated road building and guaranteed inexpensive private transportation, building interstate highways, and maintaining cheap gas, Americans began flocking to newly opened developments on the fringes of the urban core areas. Between 1940 and 1960, the country's suburban population grew by some 27 million, or more than twice the numerical increase in the population of central cities during the same period. As a result, the share of the urbanized population living in central cities dropped from nearly 63% in 1940, to 59% in 1950, and to 51% in 1960. The decline continued thereafter, and by 1980 only 40% of metropolitan residents lived in these cities, with the rest in surrounding suburbs (Fox, 1985; Jackson, 1985; Teaford, 1990). This was a dramatic change in the spatial organization of the nation's major urban areas.

Migrants from the central cities were disproportionately young, middle class, and upwardly mobile. The availability of Veterans Administration (VA) and Federal Housing Authority (FHA) loans in the decades immediately following the Second World War, along with housing shortages in central cities, made the suburbs especially attractive to new families. The expanding economy provided a stable source of employment, particularly in downtown office complexes but also in rapidly developing suburban retail and manufacturing centers. These families could afford to buy housing in the suburbs, and held jobs that allowed them to spend the time and incur the costs involved in daily commuting. A postwar "marriage boom" added more than 10 million new households within a decade. And the "baby boom" made relatively cheap homes in suburban subdivisions difficult to resist (Fox, 1985; Palen, 1997).

Suburban migrants were also overwhelmingly White. By 1960, when the suburban population exceeded that of the central cities, less than 5% of suburbanites were African American (Goldsmith & Blakely, 1992). Thirty years later they were less than 10%, and suburban Blacks were largely segregated in separate communities. This was partly because of discrimination that discouraged Blacks from buying homes in White suburban areas. As a group, Whites were allowed to move into these new, burgeoning, affluent communities on the edge of the expanding metropolitan area. And as they moved to suburbia, the populations of the country's central cities became older, poorer, and darker in complexion (Jackson, 1985; Massey & Denton, 1993; Teaford, 1990).

These developments changed public perceptions of the big cities dramatically. The proportion of central-city residents that were White diminished each decade after 1950, falling from more than 80% to about a third in the 1990s. The Black population increased rapidly in the 1950s and 1960s, leveling off at about a third of central-city residents, and the number of Hispanics increased significantly after 1970. As sociologist William Julius Wilson noted, poverty levels increased sharply among all groups of city residents in the closing decades of the 20th century, but particularly among Blacks. This was a consequence of discrimination, but it also sprang from what Wilson and other social scientists described as "concentration effects," the fact that Black city residents were crowded into poor ghettos. Although some 11% of central-city residents were impoverished by the mid-1970s, and 18% of central-city Blacks were poor, by 1990 the figures had jumped to almost 20% and 34%, respectively (Goldsmith & Blakely, 1992; Wilson, 1987). This is a large part of what had become known as the "urban crisis" by the latter part of the 1960s, and it has continued up to the present.

It was the early stages of this process of change that educators confronted at the end of the 1950s. The decades following World War II witnessed a profound transformation of American metropolitan areas, creating a new cultural geography defined by race and income. This had a dramatic effect on many aspects of life in the nation's major urban centers. It meant that for large numbers of urban and suburban residents there were few shared public spaces and social experiences. Stereotypical images, increasingly fostered by the development of mass media, created an atmosphere of mistrust and fear (Fox, 1985). It was a situation ripe for escalating conflict and misunderstanding.

In the 1960s and 1970s, these problems grew worse as the Black population of urban school districts approached a majority, particularly in large Northern cities. Despite protests, schools remained highly segregated, closely mirroring patterns of residential segregation in urban areas (Mirel, 1993; Orfield, Eaton, & the Harvard Project on School Desegregation, 1996; Rury, 1999b). Examining the racial composition of Chicago public high schools in 1963, for example, along with a variety of other school characteristics, Robert Havighurst (1964) found in all but four schools the student body was 90% or more Black or White, despite the fact that the district's population was almost evenly divided between these groups. The vast majority of predominantly Black schools, moreover, reported low achievement scores and high dropout rates. This pattern was evident in other large cities in this period (Harrison, 1972). In general, the movement of Blacks into Northern urban school districts was marked by high levels of segregation—or racial isolation—and big Black–White differences in educational outcomes (Mirel, 1993; Stolee, 1993; Wells & Crain, 1997). It was a situation that did not bode well for the traditional vision of the American public school.

Inevitably, questions of equity in Black and White education became major policy issues facing urban school districts. In public education, the question of race came to be a source of great political dissension, a point of differentiation that defined the institution in new ways. The 1954 *Brown* decision had helped to put schools at the very center of the emerging national civil rights movement. In large metropolitan areas this led to conflict over desegregation and equality, initially in the South but eventually in other regions also (Hochschild, 1985). In the major cities, the impact of these issues was decisive. In the late 1950s and 1960s the NAACP and other civil rights organizations began to agitate around the question of equity in urban education. Massive demonstrations and school boycotts were staged against segregated and inferior schools in the nation's major cities. In Chicago, for instance, during the fall of 1963 nearly 300,000 children stayed home from school, and tens of thousands of parents marched to the downtown offices of the Board of Education to protest de facto school segregation. Similar events occurred elsewhere, sometimes focusing on a single school and in other instances an entire district. In California and Texas, Hispanic students and teachers launched their own boycotts and protest marches, demanding curricular reform and improved facilities. It was a time of confrontation and struggle, and tensions over questions of equity and social justice were running very high (Anderson & Pickering, 1986; Donato, 1997).

One of the principal civil rights strategies was to issue legal challenges to de facto patterns of school segregation, most of them charging urban school districts with upholding segregation to avoid aggravating Whites. This, of course, was a continuation of the tradition of activist litigation that had led to the *Brown* decision. As a result of this, a series of federal court decisions in the late 1960s and early 1970s established a new legal doctrine in barring de facto segregation as a cause of segregated schooling, the root of educational inequities in many urban districts outside the South. This was a major extension of the logic employed in *Brown,* which had focused mainly on de jure practices of segregation. In the 1971 landmark *Swan v. Charlotte-Mecklenburg* case, a federal district court established mandatory bussing of students as a legitimate remedy to entrenched patterns of residential segregation. With this, school districts could be expected to redress inequalities due to segregation by moving children from one part of the city to another (Orfield et al., 1996). As parent groups on both sides of the issue began to organize in response to these developments, an already tense situation became even more politically explosive.

The controversy, in fact, had been smoldering for some time, and drew national attention to the dilemma of urban education. In 1961 former Harvard president James Conant published the book *Slums and Suburbs.* He was hardly a proponent of desegregation, and when he visited Chicago to collect data he avoided the question of racial inequities in the schools (Hampel, 1986). The contrasting conditions Conant observed in writing *Slums and Suburbs*, however, gave him pause in advocating the comprehensive high school, the secondary vision of the common school ideal, as a model for big-city school districts. Like others, he had no answer to the dilemma posed by the disparities in educational and social resources on either side of the urban–suburban divide. And the differences would grow even more stark in the years to come (Kozol, 1991; Wells & Crain, 1997).

Chicago offers a telling example. By the late 1960s massive "White flight" to the suburbs and to private schools had led the city's public school system to be populated largely by minority students. When the district was ordered by a federal judge to implement a desegregation plan in the 1970s, there were hardly enough White students in the system to make such a proposal viable. Non-Hispanic Whites were less than 20% of the public schools' student body by 1980, and in 1990 they were barely a 10th. This made meaningful integration, particularly in the system's 60 large high schools, a virtual impossibility (Kleppner, 1984; Rury, 1999b). The ideal of the public school functioning as a microcosm of American society was inconceivable in these circumstances.

The story elsewhere was similar. By the time the 1973 *Keyes* decision finally established the principle of federally mandated desegregation in Northern and Western urban school districts, the term "White flight" had already become a part of the national vocabulary. The *Milliken I* decision just a year later, blocking a massive interdistrict integration plan in Detroit, foreclosed the possibility of legally mandated desegregation plans across urban–suburban boundaries. As a result, the racial profile of schools on either side of the big-city district lines became increasingly stark, and segregation became even more entrenched in many places. In the 1980s only a small minority of public school students were White in the nation's largest cities, and an even smaller—although growing—portion of suburban students was Black (Orfield et al., 1996). Meanwhile, the portion of the nation's population living outside metropolitan areas continued to decline (Goldsmith & Blakely, 1992). If some observers had hoped that schools in nonmetropolitan communities would provide the model for others to follow, this ideal became less tenable with time.

These changes had a particularly big impact on the culture of American high schools. As secondary education in major metropolitan areas became characterized by a sharp pattern of racial segregation, it was closely associated in the public mind with perceptions about the quality of education (Wells & Crain, 1997). This was evident in the early 1960s in large Northern cities, and became ever more pronounced as the desegregation struggles in public education reached a peak in the 1970s (Hochschild, 1985; Orfield, 1978). Of course, Conant had examined extant patterns of segregation in the early 1960s, but the differences between urban and suburban high schools grew even more striking in the decades that followed. By the end of the 1980s there were relatively few public high schools in large cities with a significant number of White students, and few schools that could be classified as academically excellent. Location came to be a significant factor in the life chances of children (Bettis, 1996; Mora, 1997; Sexton & Nickel, 1992). Schooling, of course, was a big part of this. Urban and suburban school districts became ever more dissimilar in the years following the protracted struggle over desegregation (Stone, 1998). In the realm of public perception, urban education became linked to poor academic performance and the problems of crime and violence. These images inevitably were influenced by questions of race.

In the decades since 1950, the ideal of a common school experience for American youth appears to have become increasingly elusive, at least as regards questions of equity. Residential segregation, which changed little with the growth of large minority populations in American cities, has led to even less heterogeneity in many urban high schools' student bodies (Rumberger & Wilms, 1992). As metropolitan areas have grown in size and complexity, these patterns of differentiation have maintained their salience, despite the effort of generations of civil rights agitation. If the public school system was supposed to bring students from different backgrounds together, it has not succeeded in accomplishing this goal in the nation's major metropolitan areas, at least as concerns the issues of race and social class (Mora, 1997; Wells & Crain, 1997). In this respect, and in these settings, the traditional vision of American education certainly has not been fulfilled. At the start of the 21st century, this remains a vital question for future generations of American educators.

SCHOOLS AS AGENTS OF SOCIAL CHANGE

As already suggested, when the nation grappled with questions of inequality and social justice, many looked to the schools as a means of overcoming these problems. Earlier generations of reformers had called on the schools to address social problems too, but this time the impetus came from the highest levels of the nation's political system. For the first time since Reconstruction, the federal government adopted policies to utilize public schools to resolve long-standing patterns of inequality. This was a sign of both the added significance that was assigned to education in the wake of the human capital revolution, and the increasingly popular idea that education alone would be sufficient to end poverty and discrimination. As the United States struggled with ways to address the growing crisis over social inequality, and race discrimination in particular, schooling of one sort or another appeared to be a handy and appropriate policy mechanism. This reasoning would eventually lead to the schools becoming even more embroiled in the new politics of inequality that came to dominate the closing decades of the twentieth century (Kantor & Lowe, 1995).

In certain respects, this new thinking about education was a logical outgrowth of the arguments made by Thurgood Marshall and his associates in the 1954 *Brown* Supreme Court case. Marshall maintained that education was a vital resource, critical to the future success of African Americans, both individually and as a group. Segregated schooling was inherently unequal, he argued, and therefore constitutionally questionable. This was an argument the Supreme Court accepted. But if schooling was an indispensable public service, segregation was not the only problem; there were other sources of inequality in the way it was distributed to different social groups. Perhaps the most telling cause of educational inequity was the nation's historic commitment to local control and funding of public schools. This geographical approach to school finance meant that institutional resources varied enormously from one community to the next, depending on the general wealth of the population and taxation levels. As many observers quickly came to realize, this was a source of school inequality nearly as great as formal systems of segregation, even if disparities were considerably less than had existed in the past (Wise, 1968).

The financial inequality between urban and suburban school districts was a major theme of Conant's *Slums and Suburbs*, and of many other studies in the years that followed. The relative fiscal standing of the urban school districts actually declined in the 1960s and 1970s, as thousands of middle- and working-class Whites left for the suburbs. This great departure helped to erode the local tax base at the same time that it proved a tremendous boon to the suburban schools. As the numbers of poor city dwellers increased, the condition of public schools in many of the larger cities deteriorated significantly. By the end of the 1960s it was commonplace for observers of city schools to refer to a growing financial crisis in urban education (Katzman, 1971).

It did not take long for the federal government to recognize this problem, led by Commissioner of Education Francis Keppell and other activists in the Democratic Party. In 1965, following enactment of sweeping civil rights and antipoverty legislation, President Lyndon Johnson oversaw passage of the nation's most comprehensive federal education bill to date, the Elementary and Secondary Education Act (ESEA). This was an integral part of Johnson's "War on Poverty" campaign, a defining policy initiative of his presidency. The ESEA went far beyond other measures defining federal involvement in the schools, such as the NDEA with its focus on science, mathematics, and related issues. (Kaestle, 2001). In supporting this legislation, many Democrats were seeking ways to provide assistance for the cities, long a stronghold of support for the party, whereas other politicians were concerned about growing inequality and the rise of urban poverty. A critical element of ESEA spoke directly to the problem of financial inequity that Conant and other observers had noted. Title 1 of the act provided federal dollars to schools with significant numbers of students from poverty backgrounds. This proved a sizable benefit to many central-city school districts, as it provided a source of income apart from local property tax revenues, which had been depressed by White flight and the movement of business out of the cities (Ravitch, 1983; Silver & Silver, 1991).

Title 1 of ESEA addressed the problem of inequality, implicitly acknowledging the importance of equity in educational resources. It also established a general pattern for school funding. In the later 1960s and 1970s, many state legislatures adopted similar financial formulas for providing state aid to urban public schools. Although these new sources of funding did not completely erase the differences in support between city and suburban schools, they eventually came to narrow the spending gap by as much as half. Even if there continued to be significant disparities between urban and suburban schools, in that case, federal and state laws made the differences considerably less severe than they might have been. This was a major step in the development of liberal social policy in the postwar era. It helped to restore the principle that public education ought to be equal everywhere, critical if the American credo of equal opportunity was ever truly to be realized (Hummel & Nagle, 1973; Silver & Silver, 1991).

Title 1, however, was just the beginning: There were still other educational initiatives begun under the Johnson administration's War on Poverty. Perhaps the best known was Head Start, a federally funded preschool program aimed at boosting the achievement of children from poor families. Conceived as a broad social welfare intervention, Head Start was intended to help children overcome the developmental disadvantages they may have faced in areas with many social problems. It also was designed as a source of support for poor families. The program started with a great deal of fanfare and grew quickly to serve more than half a million children in its first year. Critics noted that Head Start often did not provide much educational content, focusing instead on social, medical, and psychological services that families in high-poverty areas may have needed. The President, they charged, had launched the program too fast, hoping to boost support for his antipoverty initiatives. Head Start proved popular from the very beginning, however, and eventually began to employ certified teachers to staff its various centers and classrooms. By the 1970s more than a million children were enrolled in the program each year, and assessments showed that it provided a significant boost to achievement in the early grades, although long-term effects were harder to document. Like Title 1, Head Start represented a historically new approach to addressing inequality in education: providing compensatory programs and funding to make the impact of schooling more equitable (Vinovskis, 1999; Zigler & Muenchow, 1992).

Despite widespread support for Head Start and similar initiatives in urban communities, such programs also became a source of controversy. In the wake of the civil rights movement, public sensitivities to questions of race and inequality were running especially high. Critics objected to the very term *compensatory*, arguing that it implied that the clients of these programs were somehow deficient or deviant. Social scientists also came under fire for using the term *culturally deprived* to describe the poor and minority residents of the inner city, who typically were the recipients of these services. The very notion of cultural deprivation seemed to suggest that these people lacked certain values and productive habits, and that they needed to imitate the conventions of the White middle class. Not surprisingly, such suggestions proved offensive to many inner-city residents, especially activists who had struggled proudly against racism and discrimination. In addition to this, new scholarship challenged the deprivation perspective, demonstrating the resourcefulness and resiliency of different types of city dwellers. By the 1980s the terms *culturally deprived* and *compensatory* had generally fallen out of use, and social scientists eventually turned to the concepts of social and cultural capital to account for differences in the educational backgrounds of various groups. Meanwhile, federal and state programs providing urban schools with additional resources for their impoverished students became larger and more important (Ravitch, 1983; Schram, 1995; Tucker, 1994).

Regardless of how these programs were described, however, it was clear that they were intended to do more than simply equalize school funding levels. They also were supposed to offset inequities in the social and cultural backgrounds of different groups of students. When it came to achievement, after all, the playing field of life was not always level. As seen in the previous chapter, an entire generation of African Americans had been denied the opportunity of attending high school just when secondary education was becoming widely available in American history. Coming from the South, with its long and violent experience of discrimination and educational inequity, Blacks were at a disadvantage compared to most Whites, at least as regarded formal schooling. In this respect, Head Start and similar policy initiatives were born of recognition that poor families lacked educative resources that more affluent parents were able to provide to children. These included prior educational experiences, but also certain informal educational factors, ranging from books and magazines to music lessons and summer camps. When sociologist James Coleman completed a massive federal government survey of student achievement in 1966, he found that family background factors were more important determinants of academic outcomes in children than school funding. This was a very controversial discovery, but it was upheld in countless additional studies. This eventually led Coleman, along with others, to develop and articulate the concept of social capital. To understand why some children were successful in school and others were not, it was necessary to look outside of the schools, to the social and economic environments in which children acquired their formative experiences (Coleman, 1990; Lagemann, 2000).

As indicated earlier, theories of social and cultural capital were formulated to capture these very dimensions of life. Although these ideas did not seem to render judgments about the people's way of living, they certainly suggested that various socially valued abilities and behavior are more readily evident in some communities than in others. This was close to the concept of deprivation, but it also was different. Given agreement about the existence of such productive attributes, it was possible to see the task of schools as compensating individuals who lacked social and cultural capital by enabling them to acquire these abilities and to learn the requisite forms of behavior. In other words, schooling would provide poor children with information and skills that their families and communities could not. It was possible, in that case, to preserve the basic purpose of compensatory education without declaring particular communities culturally inadequate or deviant. The schools were simply a way to learn about the larger world, and to acquire the attributes necessary for success in life. And this is what students in city schools wanted, as much as anyone else. Given their backgrounds, and their families' historic lack of formal education, some children simply needed more schooling than others to achieve these ends. Even though academic theories of social and cultural capital took longer to articulate such a perspective, this view became a cornerstone of liberal government social policy in the 1960s and 1970s (Coleman, 1990; Schram, 1995; Ravitch, 1983).

Lyndon Johnson's War on Poverty was relatively short-lived, but its imprint extended far beyond his departure from the presidency in 1969. In the 1970s and 1980s the compensatory logic of Title 1 and Head Start was extended to many other educational programs, including an array of job-training initiatives intended to help the poor find stable sources of employment. One example was the Comprehensive Employment Training Act (or CETA), passed in the mid-1970s. CETA was designed to train the unemployed for new jobs as the occupational structure of the economy changed. It provided stipends for individuals from poor backgrounds, and emphasized the importance of developing skills through various forms of vocational and basic academic education. Passed in response to changes in the economy, this measure and others like it represented yet another step in the new federal strategy of providing education as a means of helping people break out of poverty (Franklin & Ripley, 1984).

A parallel but somewhat different initiative in this period revolved around special education. As noted in the previous chapter, special classes for blind, deaf, and "slow" children had been established in many American schools earlier in the century. In the postwar period, as the school population expanded and enrollment through the high school years became a societal norm, and as new ways of classifying learning problems were discovered, enrollments in these classes mushroomed. Between 1948 and 1968 the number of special education students increased from less than 400,000 to more than 2 million, and the population continued to grow in the years that followed. In the early 1960s new research had led to the development of the concept of *learning disabilities,* contributing to a growing body of professional knowledge to inform the field. At the same time, educators and parent groups began to push for broader support of special education and for integration of special-needs students with the rest of the school population. In the late 1960s a series of court cases challenged the principle of separate classes for special education students, employing basically the same logic that had informed the *Brown* decision. The plaintiffs in these instances held that separate education was unequal, and that students in such classes suffered a stigma that was difficult to overcome. Although these challenges did not result in a landmark Supreme Court decision regarding special education, they did contribute to a growing movement to bring special education into the mainstream (Safford & Safford, 1996).

The field of special education continued to grow in the closing decades of the century. In 1975 the Education for All Handicapped Children Act was passed by Congress and signed into law by President Gerald Ford. With this measure, the federal government required school districts to provide special education students with free and appropriate schooling in the least restrictive environment possible (Winzer, 1993). The idea of compensatory education, backed by federal authority, now extended to children with learning disabilities and other special needs. By the early 1990s the number of children in federally mandated special education programs exceeded 12% of the population of the public schools, nearly half of them labeled "learning disabled." The goal of special education was to provide the extra training and resources necessary to help these students keep up with the other children in the schools. This was redemptive schooling of a different kind, requiring a massive investment of financial resources and professional expertise, but it also reflected the national preoccupation with using schools to achieve greater levels of social and economic equity (Carrier, 1986).

Perhaps the most ambitious program of compensatory education measures, however, was directed at the issue of gender. Inspired by the civil rights movement of the 1950s and 1960s, feminist activists began to criticize the treatment of women in schools during the late 1960s and early 1970s. Although girls had exhibited high levels of academic achievement since the latter part of the 19th century, these critics felt that schools reinforced sex discrimination in many other areas of life. They noted many problems: textbooks that perpetuated invidious gender stereotypes, counselors who urged students toward sex-typed courses and career options, curricular differentiation with boys excelling in math and science and girls in humanities, teachers who favored boys over girls in class discussions, and school athletic programs that heavily favored male sports and often glorified the accomplishments of boys who participated. They also pointed out that the administration of schools was dominated by men, a situation that subtly taught students that males should occupy positions of authority. Reflecting these concerns, the National Organization for Women (NOW) included a provision in its 1967 women's bill of rights calling for "equal and unsegregated education."

Continued agitation and lobbying around these questions eventually led to passage 5 years later of Title IX as an amendment to federal education legislation. A rather simple provision, Title IX declared that "no person ... shall, on the basis of sex, be excluded from participation in, be denied the benefits of, or be subjected to discrimination under any education program or activity receiving federal financial assistance." Because federal aid to schools had become widespread, it was a measure with potential teeth. It took several years for regulations governing the implementation of the legislation to be articulated, as Republican opponents created obstacles to them, but by the late 1970s activists were able to use Title IX to challenge sex discrimination in education across the country (Tyack & Hansot, 1990).

The problem of sexism in the schools turned out to be troublesome and difficult to remedy. Title IX could be considered as compensatory in the sense of correcting past inequities, but its impact was mixed. There continued to be battles over Title IX regulations in Congress, but many states had adopted similar provisions by the 1980s. School districts eventually began to respond, especially in the area of women's athletics. The 1970s witnessed a fivefold increase in female participation in competitive sports. By the end of the decade, more than a third of all high school athletes nationally were girls, although there was a great deal of variation across states and districts. This, of course, directly affected only a small portion of the student body, even though it held significant symbolic value. There were halting advances in additional areas too. Textbooks were revised to feature fewer stereotypes, and the number of women administrators slowly increased. Other aspects of the educational system proved more difficult to change, however. Curricular differentiation was naggingly persistent despite efforts to boost female enrollments in math and science. Vocational education classes remained highly segregated by gender, even though the number of girls in technical courses more than doubled. Powerful norms continued to govern the behavior of teachers and students in schools and classrooms, making it difficult to change historic patterns of gender-linked behavior and communication patterns. Research showed teachers continuing to call more on the boys, and many girls still did not want to challenge conventions for fear of being unpopular. In the case of gender, consequently, compensatory education proved to be a frustrating and elusive goal, although a number of important advances were made (Sadker & Sadker, 1994; Tyack & Hansot, 1990). Even with the best of intentions, it turned out to be very difficult to legislate certain changes in the schools, especially if large groups of students and educators were ambivalent about altering the status quo.

In spite of such dilemmas, the effect of all these programs was a virtual sea change in American education. By the end of the 1970s compensatory education programming of one kind or another had become nearly a cradle-to-grave enterprise, extending from the very young (Head Start) to the adult population (job training), and to children excluded by gender or special needs. It represented a view of education as a mechanism for reducing inequality—defined in myriad ways—that had become firmly entrenched as a vital element of social policy. A substantial research and evaluation enterprise was established by the federal government to monitor these programs, and to address a host of other educational questions. As a matter of course, schooling had become a way of overcoming all kinds of social problems. A seemingly indispensable feature of the American political landscape in the late 20th century, it had become virtually inviolable. Then, as never before, education of one sort or another was seen as profoundly influencing an individual's social standing. As such, it was too important to be left simply to the local authorities, especially the overburdened school bureaucracies of the nation's large urban areas (Lagemann, 2000; Silver & Silver, 1991).

POLITICAL CONTROVERSIES OVER EDUCATION AS SOCIAL POLICY

Federal measures to provide compensatory education of one form or another enjoyed a high degree of public support, as they seemed to extend the benefits of schooling to new groups in the population at relatively little social cost. But they also engendered political opposition, and were depicted as intrusive, liberal elements of social policy. The same was true of the role of federal courts in school desegregation, the other major point of government intervention in the educational system. As noted earlier, the Swan case in 1971 established a critical precedent for the use of busing to desegregate public schools. In the years that followed, desegregation plans requiring some form or another of bussing for students attending segregated schools were implemented in scores of cities, most of them by order of federal or state authorities. These decisions followed the reasoning of the 1954 *Brown* decision in holding that separate schools represented a singular harm to students, and that school districts had a moral and educational duty to actively resist segregation in any form. This view was abetted by Coleman's 1966 survey, which found that integrated schooling produced high achievement levels, particularly in minority students. With this, equality in education became linked firmly to the idea of desegregation, and bussing became the primary mode of achieving this goal (Orfield et al., 1996; Wilkerson, 1979).

Millions of school children were affected by the busing plans established in the 1970s, most of which moved students from one area of a city to another to achieve levels of integration established by the courts. In many instances, this approach to ending inequity was met with anger and conflict, as parents, most of them White, protested the end of "neighborhood schools." In certain cities, such as Boston, these battles turned violent and confrontational (Lukas, 1985). Politicians, especially the Republicans, seized on these sentiments, blasting federal intervention in schooling as unnecessary and intrusive. Others defended it but found themselves fighting a losing battle in the realm of public opinion. The logic of arguments that had been made in 1954 dictated solutions of the kind being implemented in the 1970s. But local groups of citizens, especially in the North and West, had not imagined that the *Brown* decision applied to their own communities, and they began to question the wisdom of the judiciary. The logic of the desegregation movement was clear-cut. If indeed education was a critical determinant of an individual's future, and access to it was a right guaranteed by the state, then some measure of equality in its provision had to be ensured. For opponents of segregation, this was true even if it meant disrupting the lives of millions of families and pitting neighbors against one another in the conflicts that ensued. For others, the bussing controversy became a growing source of irritation and anger, one that would ultimately help to usher in a new era in American politics (Hochschild, 1985; Stolee, 1993; Wolters, 1984).

A parallel controversy arose in connection with yet another federal initiative in this era: a policy stance widely known as *affirmative action*. This idea employed the compensatory logic of desegregation and the programs just described but applied it to the politically sensitive arenas of higher education and employment. Basically, the principles of affirmative action held that groups that had been the objects of discrimination in the past should be permitted first consideration for opportunities in the present and future. This was deemed a necessary step to overcome the accumulated weight of past exclusions, and to permit members of these groups to develop the human and cultural capital that historically had been denied them. In the realm of education, affirmative action policies affected students in higher education, particularly with regard to entrance to professional and graduate programs, although they also influenced hiring practices in schools and universities. These initiatives concerned both gender and race, but it was the latter question that proved most controversial.

In the mid-1970s a White medical school applicant named Allan Bakke sued the University of California, arguing that he had been denied admission in favor of less qualified minority students. In 1978 the U.S. Supreme Court ruled that the school's admissions policies had established rigid racial categories or quotas that were deemed discriminatory and therefore unconstitutional. On the other hand, the Supreme Court also ruled that universities could use race or other background characteristics as one criteria—among many—in making admission decisions. While the *Bakke* case did not fully resolve the legality of affirmative action policies, it did become a focal point for public debate of the issue, and in this way fanned the flames of dissension over race and inequality in American life. Recent research suggests that the *Bakke* case and the attending furor has exerted little long-term influence on admission practices, but the question of race and higher education continues to be a turbulent issue today. New court challenges to affirmative action in university entrance decisions have been launched in recent years and may soon reach the Supreme Court (Gruhl & Welch, 1990; Wilkerson, 1979).

By the end of the 1970s, the political storm that had gathered over desegregation and affirmative action helped to establish a conservative tenor in debates about education. These concerns became a part of the anti–big-government movement that propelled Ronald Reagan into office in 1980. A degree of public cynicism about other measures also appeared, particularly job training programs, as many of them seemed to do little to boost employment, especially among the chronically poor. CETA, for instance, had come under sharp attack on these grounds. These issues were linked in the minds of many to the broad Reagan campaign against antipoverty programs and welfare and his goal of shifting responsibility for such services to the states. Vowing to end federal involvement in education as a part of his program to reduce the size of government bureaucracy, Reagan proposed to close the U.S. Department of Education, or at least remove it as a cabinet position. This was a promise that he was never able to fulfill, however. The federal role in education had simply grown too large, and the government's commitment to using schools to address issues of social inequity had become too thoroughly entrenched as a matter of policy and public expectations. Urban communities, civil rights groups, teachers unions, and other special interests lobbied heavily against curtailment of various federal education programs. Hundreds of millions of dollars were at stake in these decisions, representing thousands of jobs and services to millions of students. A new politics of education had emerged at the national level, with various forms of schooling representing a partial transfer of wealth from the upper and middle classes to the urban poor. This made it very difficult to change federal education policies that had been started under Lyndon Johnson (Haynes, 1991).

The Reagan years provided a clear demonstration of just how firmly entrenched the idea of compensatory programming in education had become as a matter of American social policy. Had Reagan decided arbitrarily to end the various programs established in the 1960s and 1970s, especially such popular ones as Head Start or Title 1, the political fallout would have been enormous. Indeed, if other aspects of Reagan's conservative program were to be realized, such as massive reductions in welfare budgets and a big tax cut for the wealthy, he could hardly afford the political cost of attacking education as well.

In addition to this, conservative opposition to education measures was not as strong as it was to other social programs. Mainstream public opinion had long been more sympathetic to expenditures for education than for welfare payments, reflecting a traditional American belief in the power of self-improvement. If the federal government was going to tax the wealthy to help the poor, providing compensatory education was a politically palatable way to do it. What was more, there also was growing evidence of these policies having made a difference. After lagging for most of the 20th century, rates of Black graduation from high school began to catch up to those for Whites in the 1970s and 1980s, eventually reaching near equivalency. Black college enrollments also climbed dramatically, ultimately amounting to about two thirds of the White attendance rate. Although important differences in academic achievement continued to exist, these trends helped to establish a growing Black middle class, including a number of people who entered the major professions with high-status university credentials (Jencks, 1998). This was a significant development in itself, but the role of education in the process helped to highlight the importance of federal policies designed to attack problems of discrimination and inequity. These circumstances helped to make the major federal education programs relatively secure politically, even in an age of retrenchment (Farley, 1997; Levitan, Johnston, & Taggart, 1975; Stockman, 1986).

Perhaps even more significant, conventional wisdom had come to hold schooling as very important for the country as a whole. Americans of nearly every social strata believed that education was a vital national interest, necessary for competing on a global scale with such rising economic powers as the Japanese and Europeans. This was a position even the most ardent Reaganite could hardly take issue with. It was perhaps best expressed in a 1983 report issued by a special federal commission, *A Nation at Risk*. Noting problems of declining achievement in American schools, the report called for a massive reform of education, focusing on higher standards of performance. *A Nation at Risk* also served to deflect attacks on the Department of Education, but its overall impact was momentous. National polls showed a widespread public concern that education was slipping in quality, and that this was linked to American economic strength. In short, schooling had simply become too important a part of the nation's social and economic life for the federal government not to play a leading role in formulating policy questions. This invariably also meant government funding for key elements of the educational system. It became a political imperative that leaders of both parties could not ignore, yet another dimension of the human capital revolution. Not only was schooling indispensable as an agent of economic growth and individual earning power, it also was a critical instrument of social policy. As the significance assigned to education by the public increased, its political importance grew as well (Ginsberg & Plank, 1995).

At the time Reagan's successor, George H. Bush, was elected in the late 1980s, public schooling in the United States had changed significantly since the 1950s. The role of the schools had broadened to include attacking social inequities, providing a variety of social services, and promoting national economic development. Once concerned primarily with providing instruction in a variety of subjects, the schools had become vital instruments of social policy. Federal funding for education registered in the billions of dollars, with programs ranging from Head Start to special education funds to Pell grants for needy college students. State governments added billions more. Public support for these initiatives was so strong that Bush campaigned by describing himself as the "education president," even though he eventually found himself hobbled by budgetary woes and could propose little meaningful change in school policies. It was the dawn of a new era in the history of American education, the cresting of the human capital revolution, and a time when schooling was becoming a principal national concern (Greene, 2000).

HIGH SCHOOLS AND THE YOUTH CULTURE

At the same time that American culture became more divided along racial and urban/suburban lines, and was increasingly preoccupied with education, it also became split along generational lines. As suggested in the earlier discussion of *Rebel Without a Cause*, the postwar period saw the development of a national youth culture, much larger and more pervasive than the collegiate culture that began to flourish in the 1920s. One of the keys to this development was the rise of the high school as a truly mass institution at the start of this period (Angus & Mirel, 1999; Haubrich, 1993).

As the size of high schools grew after 1950, they ultimately included larger numbers of the total teenage population. This meant that a broad cross section of adolescents was brought together in one institution for the first time in history. This was a part of the comprehensive vision dating from the Kingsley Commission, the idea of a secondary institution that brought youth from various social classes and groups together. Educators believed that the high school should be a universal American tradition, even though they did not feel everyone should study the same subjects. Statistical evidence points to the success of these arguments. As the number of adolescents grew in the 1950s and 1960s, high school enrollments climbed dramatically. This was a consequence of both the postwar baby boom and improved rates of high school attendance (West, 1996). By the end of the 1950s, more than 80% of American teenagers attended high school, making it practically a universal experience for the first time in American history (Angus & Mirel, 1999). This had a number of important consequences.

One effect of the high school's growth was the fact that adolescents as a social group were segregated from the rest of society for a significant amount of time each week, through most of the year, in institutions where they constituted the vast majority of the populace. Because of age grading, and the differentiated structure of most high schools, they did not even have systematic contact with youth in different age groups, such as young adults over 18 or 19. This contributed to the development of what James Coleman described as the "adolescent society," a set of social relations with its own behavioral norms and cultural artifacts. From the very start it was a phenomenon rooted largely in the American high school (Coleman, 1961, 1965). This was an important component of what many observers of American life at the time began to refer to as the "youth culture" (Cohen, 1997).

The institution of schooling, in that case, was a critical component of the development of this distinctive aspect of modern American civilization. Coleman argued that the social world of high school adolescence was defined by status groups associated with different sorts of school activities. In general, he found that athletics played an especially important role in the social life of high school students, especially boys. Academic performance was less important, although it may have gained significance as students progressed through school (Coleman, 1961). Other studies examined the influence of the larger youth culture, mostly existing outside the schools, which was commercially directed by record companies, the radio, television and print media, and a host of other enterprises. Adolescents had preferred distinctive forms of music for several decades, and dancing had been popular with the rise of dating as a distinctive teenage activity in the 1920s and 1930s (Palladino, 1996). But in the 1950s and 1960s, these aspects of the youth subculture assumed larger proportions.

In the 1950s new forms of teenage entertainment came into being, with the rapid rise of rock-and-roll music as a popular idiom. New dances came into play also, and teenagers became enamored of a variety of distinctive forms of consumption. Fast cars, cigarette smoking and alcohol, and the hint of sexual promiscuity came to represent the new youth culture and to distinguish it from the clean-cut images of youth from earlier decades. Despite attempts at censorship, these images were spread through the media, including radio, the movies, and the increasingly ubiquitous television. It is doubtful that any more than a minority of teens actually engaged in such activities routinely, but even for those who did not, the idea of rebellion against adult mores exerted a powerful appeal (Gilbert, 1986). This was an impulse that would exert even greater influence in the decades to follow.

If music and movies were important features of youth culture, clothing may have been equally significant. High school students in earlier decades often had dressed like miniature adults, with boys wearing coats and ties and girls dresses or skirts. As the number of students in school increased, these standards of dress began to be considered outmoded. As one study of students in Milwaukee found, by the late 1950s high school students there had shed coats, ties, and dresses in favor of slacks, shirts, and sweaters (Haubrich, 1993). In the 1960s high school dress codes became a subject of student protests and were eliminated in schools across the country. By the 1970s jeans and T-shirts were the norm in many schools, even among younger faculty members, and adolescent tastes were becoming a major force in the world of adult fashion (Grant, 1988; Palladino, 1996).

At about the same time there was a dramatic shift in sexual mores, with a corresponding change in teenage behavior. Rates of nonmarital sex among teenagers had increased significantly by the early 1970s, jumping from less than 20% to more than a third in less than a decade. This prompted a movement to make sex education a major element of the secondary curriculum, but even this moderate response helped to fuel national anxieties about teenage sexuality, and no coherent national response could be agreed on. By the latter part of the 1980s a clear majority of teens reportedly had engaged in one form or another of significant consensual sexual activity. This represented a sharp break from the past, as recently as the 1950s. At the same time, the number of single-parent households increased dramatically and teen pregnancy became a primary concern of national policymakers. By the 1990s nearly a quarter of all children were born to single mothers, the majority of them teenagers. At the close of the 20th century, traditional forms of family life had been dramatically altered by these changes, with only about half of American households representing the nuclear family that had predominated in earlier times. Sexuality had become a prominent feature of popular culture, and a central aspect of the rapidly evolving high school-based adolescent society (Chilman, 1978; Esman, 1990; Palladino, 1996, Vinovskis, 1995). It remains a critical educational and social issue.

It is important to recognize the role of the school as a vehicle for these developments. These trends in youth culture coincided with the movement to consolidate and expand high schools across the country, plans that educators had endorsed enthusiastically in the 1950s and 1960s. The average size of public high schools more than doubled between 1950 and 1970, and these figures understate the size of high schools most students attended in these years (due to the large number of small rural districts with combined elementary–secondary schools). Ernest Boyer, writing in the early 1980s, put the number of high schools at about 16,000, which made the average enrollment at that point nearly 900 (Boyer 1983). *High School and Beyond* data collected in the 1970s and 1980s indicate that the typical public high school at that time had some 875 students, and more than 40% had above 900 (Bryk, Lee, & Holland, 1993). It was the latter schools, of course, that enrolled the majority of the nation's high school students, and continue to do so today. These larger high schools have historically been concentrated in urban areas, but many suburban districts also established massive secondary schools as their teenage populations expanded rapidly in the postwar years. For metropolitan youth, the institutional norm became a large, differentiated public high school.

Research suggested that the development of bigger high schools, with greater numbers of students and psychological distance between adolescents and adults, may have promoted the development of this school-based youth culture. Barker and Gump (1964), in their analysis of high school size in the 1960s, found that greater numbers of students were excluded from school activities in larger schools, a condition that contributed to more widespread alienation from the institution and its goals. More recent research has associated a loss of adult control in big schools and a reduction in the degree of personalism in contact between students and adults. A number of studies have argued that greater school size inhibits student learning, especially when it makes it difficult for adolescents and adults to communicate meaningfully (Bracy, 1998; Haller, 1992). This point was made emphatically by scholars comparing private—particularly Catholic—and public high schools. These authors reported that school size was a significant factor in accounting for the superior academic performance and school climate of private institutions (Bryk et al., 1993; Coleman, Hoffer, & Kilgore, 1982). Bigger, it turned out, was not always better.

These developments were enhanced by a general movement to expand students' rights in high schools across the country. In 1969 the U.S. Supreme Court handed down a decision in the case *Tinker v. Des Moines Independent School District*, wherein it ruled that a suspension of two students for wearing black armbands to protest the Vietnam War represented a violation of their First Amendment rights (Zirkel, 1999). *Tinker* set off a wave of litigation that soon broadened the definition of self-expression to include everything from dress to hairstyles to displays of affection on school premises. Although not all of these challenges to conventional authority were successful, educators found themselves on the defensive, forced to justify traditional rules, policies, and practices that had existed for generations. The new legal standard became one of requiring an educational rationale for policies governing the behavior of students, and many school districts chose to minimize such measures rather than risk additional protests and potential litigation (Olson, 1972). Developments such as these helped to usher in a new era of permissiveness in the nation's high schools.

This set of problems was complicated by changes in the culture of schools during the 1960s and 1970s. There was a resurgence of interest in the ideas of progressive education and curricular experimentation at this time, and a movement to radically alter disciplinary practices. Many schools attempted to make courses more relevant to the interests of students, dropping core requirements in mathematics, history, and the sciences in favor of new experiential learning approaches or interdisciplinary units. In the same spirit, student conduct codes were changed—sometimes in response to student protests—to allow greater freedom, especially with regard to dress and deportment. These shifts in the degree of adult supervision exercised by the schools only added even greater momentum to the development of an independent youth culture, in all of its colorful variants. In some big, impersonal high schools, the infrequency of contact between teens and adults eventually led to youth subcultures that appeared to militate actively against the academic purposes of the institution. In such instances, the schools may have lost control of student socialization altogether, and merely provided a place for teens to meet and plan their own events and activities (Grant, 1988).

This seems to have been especially true in major cities, and in schools with large minority student populations (Lee & Smith, 1997), but it also has been evident in suburban institutions. Sociologist Pamela Bettis (1996) has described the lack of efficacy experienced by urban youth in large schools. Another social scientist, Signythia Fordham (1996), has suggested that large all-Black high schools engender a student culture of resistance to academic achievement. The English scholar Paul Willis (1977) has observed a parallel subculture among working-class youth in Great Britain. In her perceptive analysis of student cultures in a suburban setting, *Jocks and Burnouts*, Penelope Eckert (1989) found a high level of disengagement among working-class youth, for whom the school had come to represent a point of negative reference. The development of overt student cultures of "resistance" in such settings was observed to have been fostered by the very size of the schools. Indeed, Eckert reported that opposition appeared to be less as the size of the school decreased. There is considerable evidence, on the other hand, that smaller schools—again, especially Catholic schools that foster a clear sense of community—have enjoyed greater success with urban students (Greely, 1982). Educators' insistence on the need for larger schools may thus have contributed to some of the most difficult problems faced by American secondary institutions in recent decades. This was yet another irony of the call for larger comprehensive high schools.

As Coleman and other observers have noted, youth culture often took the immediate community and its values as a point of departure. This accounted for a heavy value placed on athletics in most high schools

(Coleman, 1961). But with the social and economic differentiation of the metropolitan landscape, this has resulted in a variegated adolescent culture, or—alternatively—a set of youth subcultures (Coleman, 1965). By the 1980s this could be seen nationally in the highly fragmented forms of youth identity that existed in the popular media (Giroux, 1996). If these assorted elements of adolescent society performed a major role in the socialization that occurred in the large, differentiated metropolitan high schools during the latter part of the 20th century, what has happened to the conventional vision of the high school as an agent of democratic socialization? In the large and impersonal secondary institutions of metropolitan America today, most socialization for teens is conducted by different networks of peers. Particularly in the larger schools, adolescent society reigns supreme. This may be yet another aspect of how the comprehensive high school ideal, handed down from an earlier time, has contributed to challenges facing secondary education as the nation begins a new century.

CASE: WOODSTOCK NATION

Late in the summer of 1969 over a half-million young people gathered near Woodstock, New York, just an hour north of New York City, to hear a remarkable variety of musical performers brought together for a three-day festival. The turnout far exceeded even the most optimistic projections, as many of those who came had learned about the event through word of mouth and did not even buy tickets. The festival organizers struggled with the logistics of providing food, toilet facilities, and medical service to the massive crowd, but all observers remarked on the peaceful demeanor of the gathering and the extraordinary spirit of brotherhood and sharing that prevailed. Plagued by rain and the absence of shelter and basic services, the event was marked by sentiments of opposition to the U.S. military campaign in Vietnam, and a winking consent to the use of hallucinogenic drugs, sexual freedom, and unbridled nonconformity. For many, the Woodstock experience came to represent a moment when the values and distinctive cultural tastes of American youth achieved their most singular form of expression. Going well beyond the high school world of the adolescent society that Coleman and others described, Woodstock seemed to demonstrate that young people could reject the norms of the larger society and establish their own social and political identities. It was, in the words of Theodore Roszak, a key element in the making of a counterculture (Gitlin, 1987; Roszak, 1969).

As noted earlier, a striking increase in fertility during the 15 years following World War II produced a historically large cohort of Americans who shared the experience of growing up in the 1950s and 1960s. Numbering nearly 50 million, these "baby boomers" came of age during a time of great prosperity. Theirs was the first generation of Americans to realize near universal high school attendance, and they participated in the various forms of adolescent socialization then taking form across the country. Unlike previous cohorts of youth, they had a common set of social and cultural reference points, ranging from music to an unequivocal sense of national identity. They also shared a healthy suspicion of the older generation (Patterson, 1996).

When the baby-boom students graduated from high school, they moved on to college in record numbers. Although American postsecondary institutions enrolled just 2 million students in 1946, by 1970 the numbers had quadrupled to more than 8 million. There had been an early increase due to the GI Bill, which provided tuition benefits to veterans, but that group of students had largely left by the mid-1950s. The major source of these new students was the relatively affluent baby-boom generation, as many as a third of whom enrolled in postsecondary institutions. The number of colleges and universities did not increase nearly as much, but the average size of their campuses grew dramatically. By the end of the 1960s it was not uncommon for large state institutions, which grew most rapidly at this time, to enroll tens of thousands of students. Under these circumstances, the universities dropped any pretense of governing the daily living habits of their students, even those residing on campus. Apart from a limited number of basic rules, students were left largely to their own devices outside of class. This created a fertile field for the development of alternative lifestyles and cultural practices. It also opened the door to widespread sexual freedom. It was a new age on American campuses, and record numbers of youth were determined to go to college. By the early 1970s many of the nation's postsecondary institutions were veritable hotbeds of radical sentiments of one sort or another (Heineman, 1993; Roszak, 1969).

The baby-boom phenomenon started its decline in the 1970s, and fertility levels began to dip substantially, but the nation's schools and colleges already were nearly bursting with students. It was the largest cohort of youth in American history, and its members had experienced life in institutional settings where they constituted a vast majority. It was little wonder, in that case, that they began to question the adult world that demanded their obedience and conformity. Given their numbers, and collective buying capacity, the postwar youth generation wielded great social and economic power. Whether it was intended or not, their influence was pervasive, and it ultimately changed the face of American life (Owram, 1996).

It would be wrong to suggest, of course, that the entire baby-boom generation was represented by the people who attended the Woodstock festival. Like any historically large group, the postwar generation included individuals of all kinds, including many who identified strongly with traditional values and American nationalism. But a significant portion of the baby boomers grew to become quite suspicious of established authority figures and institutions, especially mainstream politicians, the police, and the military. Two major historical events account for much of this sentiment: the civil rights movement and the war in Vietnam. Both of

these rather prolonged episodes blatantly seemed to contradict the pro-
fessed ideals of American civilization, albeit in different ways. As noted
earlier, the civil rights movement confronted racism and discrimination in
a dramatic and often confrontational manner. It revealed the inconsistency between traditional principles of equality and freedom and the reality of cruel oppression and injustice. Thousands of college students
volunteered to participate in civil rights campaigns, and witnessed firsthand the brutal response of reactionary racists in the South and elsewhere. Millions of others followed these struggles in the press and on
television, wondering just how the standards of democracy they had
learned in school could be reconciled with the events unfolding before
their eyes. This was an important lesson in the realities of American politics, and it impressed many of them profoundly (Halberstam, 1998).

The Vietnam War represented a different kind of learning experience,
one that proved considerably more divisive among both American youth
and the nation as a whole. The war began as an operation to support the
flagging pro-West regime in South Vietnam, a process that led to
full-scale U.S. military involvement by the late 1960s. The armed services had relied on a modest draft from the beginning of the conflict, one
that permitted college students to defer their service while attending
school. This, of course, proved a substantial boon to enrollments, and at
the same time focused the draft on those too poor or academically un-
prepared to make it to college. Some saw the injustice in this early on,
but many youth did not become concerned about the war until it threatened to affect their own lives directly. When the Nixon administration began to dramatically escalate the war in the late 1960s and early 1970s,
and changed the draft to a lottery without exemptions, antiwar protests
surged in magnitude. Even though Nixon succeeded in polarizing public
opinion about the war, drawing heavily on lingering cold-war sentiments,
the ensuing national debate helped to radicalize millions more youth who
had grown up believing the United States a defender of democracy. The
war's widely publicized atrocities, the corruption and cruelty of the South
Vietnamese regime, and the fact that no formal declaration of hostilities
was ever made all contributed to a growing impression that U.S. involvement in the conflict was ill advised or just plain wrong. To many it appeared as yet another instance of traditional authority figures
manipulating the levers of power simply to maintain the status quo
(Gitlin, 1987; Ravitch, 1983).

The historical experience of the civil rights struggles and the antiwar
movement contributed to a rising level of skepticism among many youth
about adult institutions and their values. Protests against university
complicity in war-related research, and about curricular reform issues,
rocked the campuses. Berkeley (California), Madison (Wisconsin), Ann
Arbor (Michigan), and other large academic centers became the sites of
immense struggles between students and college administrators. In
1970 the announcement of U.S. bombing in Cambodia led to massive
protests and to the killing of four students by the Ohio National Guard at

Kent State University. This sense of moral outrage that this engendered was compounded by the release of the so-called "Pentagon Papers" just a short time later, revealing the manipulative plots that lay behind the Nixon administration and its war effort. The Watergate scandal and Richard Nixon's dramatic fall from power in 1974 were the final blows, along with the sudden collapse of the South Vietnamese government shortly afterward. Public confidence in the government and other traditional institutions was at a low ebb, particularly among the young. "Never trust anyone over 30" became a popular slogan among high school and college-aged youth. The experiences of the previous decade had taught them to be inherently suspicious of existing social and economic arrangements. A strong "antiestablishment" ethic had taken hold of many in the baby-boom generation by this time, and before long its influence was quite pervasive. This too became a critical part of the counterculture (Heineman, 1993; Roof, 1993).

The very size of the baby-boom generation magnified the effects of these developments and gave them added cultural force. American youth represented a massive market for alternative music, clothing, and other cultural artifacts, and in each of these realms its tastes set new standards and fashion sensibilities. Alternative tastes in food, footwear, jewelry, and a host of other forms of expression flourished. Rock music had entered the mainstream by the 1970s, and garments made of such casual cotton fabrics as denim, gingham, and chambray were ubiquitous. In the words of sociologist Fred Davis, antifashion became the new mainstream taste in clothing, as the antiformalism of the young grew to be a dominant force in the apparel industry. T-shirts and jeans became signature fashion articles, eventually drawing the attention of name designers. Organic crops also became popular, prompting new companies to enter the industry in order to serve the expanding market for alternative products. In these and countless other ways, the postwar generation changed the shape of popular culture (Davis, 1992; Jones, 1980; Russell, 1982).

Their impact on politics was equally palpable. The left-of-center presidential campaigns of Eugene McCarthy (1968) and George McGovern (1972) were fueled by the antiestablishment opinions of the baby boomers, as was much of the most virulent opposition to Nixon and his policies. After Nixon's demise, politicians ignored baby-boomer concerns at their peril, and the election of the slightly offbeat and unconventional Jimmy Carter as president in 1976 was partly a reflection of their influence, as was the rejection of traditionalist Gerald Ford. By the 1980s, however, the political momentum of the postwar generation had become fragmented. Without a clear moral cause such as civil rights or an unjust war, its energy was divided between a spectrum of smaller movements: antiracism, feminism, gay rights, and the concerns of other special interests. This eventually allowed the conservative revolution led by Ronald Reagan to prevail, attacking many of the social values the postwar generation had fought to uphold (Owram, 1996).

In the end, it appears, the Woodstock nation asserted its will with considerable authority, but it also became part of a changing set of American traditions. Because of their prevalence, the baby boomers, especially as they entered early adulthood, eventually found themselves in the mainstream of a shifting national culture. This came as something of a shock to many, but it too was partly a function of numbers. The postwar generation was large enough to impose many of its tastes on the country and, indeed, the world. Given its size and economic power, advertisers catered to the preferences of this group and its often nontraditional and diverse tastes. But the shift to a new cultural mainstream also was a relatively simple matter of age. No generation can remain radical indefinitely. Inevitably, even the most revolutionary ideas can become conventional wisdom. Consequently, members of the baby-boom generation ultimately became less enamored of change, and started looking for sources of stability in their lives. As the oft-cited cartoon character Pogo once said, "We have seen the enemy and they are us!" At the same time that they aged, the boomers began to grow somewhat more cautious, especially as they started having children of their own. With this it was left to the next generation to discover the vitality and ferment of the Woodstock nation—and as the continuing popularity of the music, movies, and other artifacts of that age has suggested, some have.

The experience of the baby-boom generation represented a particular process of learning, one conducted on a grand historical scale. As already noted, its members were products of the schools, the first generation of Americans to attend high schools and colleges in very large numbers. While there, they developed a distinctive set of social relationships, values, and customs that became collectively known as the "youth culture" of the time. This eventually became a vast and variegated social landscape in itself, embracing a wide range of different subcultures, but it was bound together in a pervasive distrust of traditional sources of authority and the mores of adult society. Eventually, the youth culture, in all of its variety, entered the mainstream, establishing itself as a new norm or tradition, and impressing its values and customs on the rest of American culture. Partly a creation of the schools, many elements of the Woodstock nation have become integrated into the dominant pattern of education today. And perhaps it is against this new set of "traditional" cultural forms that the next generations of students will find themselves rebelling.

SCHOOLS, YOUTH, AND THE CHANGING ECONOMY

Yet another critical element of the postwar period was the changing American economy, and the importance of a well-trained workforce. Despite the proclivities of baby boomers for alternative lifestyles, the human capital revolution continued to gain momentum. Perhaps the most important manifestation of this was the shifting role of education in the labor market. Ever-higher levels of formal schooling became an expectation of American employers, and this was reflected in the monetary returns paid to individuals with different kinds of educational credentials. As the economy evolved from one based on manufacturing to one dominated by services and technological development, the significance of education increased quickly. It was the dawning of a new era, a time when brute strength and common-sense know-how no longer were sufficient to secure a good job. Suddenly, thinking and analytical skills were considered important, and schooling was the most reliable way of cultivating and documenting such abilities (Murnane & Levy, 1996).

Early in the 20th century most American youth started to work before age 20, even if only on a part-time basis (Kett, 1977). Employment rates for high school-aged youth contracted dramatically in the 1930s, however, as a consequence of the Great Depression. This ended during the Second World War, as demand for labor skyrocketed. By the postwar period the job market for youth had been restored somewhat, but patterns of high school enrollment established during the depression also returned. The fact that more youth enrolled in high school meant that fewer took jobs than in earlier times, and it was more difficult to acquire work experience in such fields as manufacturing and office work (Angus & Mirel, 1999). Consequently, the transition from school to work became a little more complicated than it had been in the past.

The nation's economy also changed profoundly in the decades following the Second World War. In the immediate postwar period, industrial jobs were plentiful, and it was the prospect of employment in the booming factories of the great Northern cities that drew African Americans out of the South in the 1950s. Despite minor periodic downturns, the urban industrial economy was flush during the 1950s, but it already showed signs of change in the following decade (Teaford, 1990). By the mid-1960s some observers already were warning that the demand for unskilled labor would be limited in the future, although even these projections underestimated the rate of long-term change (Harrison, 1972; Havighurst, 1966). No one, however, anticipated the shifting relationship of education and employment that came to characterize the closing decades of the century.

As noted earlier, of course, the rapid growth of American secondary education was premised on the principle of differentiation: the notion that high school youth were destined to enter a variety of different occupational fields on graduation. This was in large part a legacy of the Progressive Era and of the social efficiency rationale for the vocational education movement. The Cardinal Principles held that the high school should be preparation for life, and vocational education advocates argued that there were many different roads that students may take in their working careers.

This was certainly true in the 1920s, when a fraction of the high school-aged population attended school, even in the cities (Krug, 1972). And it continued to hold in the immediate postwar period. Industrial employment remained quite robust, and even if many high school graduates did not take jobs as manual laborers, the rationale for vocational training was still rather clear (Coleman, 1965). As the urban economy changed, however, the relevance of vocational training weakened. Before long, vocational education became supplanted with a variety of other curricular options, particularly a somewhat watered down academic curriculum called the "general course." Youth taking this plan of study were not being prepared for any particular future employment; nor were they trained for additional schooling. Instead, they simply were given a broad, unfocused education, one intended to prepare them for life. Some historians have referred to this as "warehousing," or simply keeping youth out of the labor force and off the streets (Angus & Mirel, 1999; Sedlak et al., 1986).

Changing curricular patterns were partly a response to shifts in the economy. Even if most jobs did not change in the short term, the labor market was evolving rapidly and demanding new skills of entry-level workers. Literacy requirements in the workplace were rising, especially in the 1960s and 1970s, at about the same time that the academic quality of urban high schools began to be questioned (Ginzberg, 1975; Levine & Zipp, 1993). This was a major element of the crisis of urban education that emerged in the 1970s and 1980s. And it was linked to the rising national interest in education reflected in the publication of *A Nation at Risk* in the early 1980s. In many cities employers expressed concern about the poor quality of inner-city high schools and the difficulties they faced in finding capable workers. Such questions became more commonplace in the latter 1980s, as employment opportunities in downtown offices expanded rapidly in connection with the burgeoning banking, financial services, and insurance industries (Levine & Trachtman, 1988). It was the dawn of a new era.

These changes were related to a set of larger shifts in the American economy that have received much attention in recent years. During the 1950s more than a quarter of all U.S. workers were employed in manufacturing. When employees in industry were added to other sectors of the economy requiring similar skills, over 40% of the labor force could be classified as "blue collar," both skilled and unskilled. Another 35% were clerical workers, most of them employed in urban offices. On the other hand, managerial and professional employment accounted for less than a quarter of the nation's overall employment (Levy, 1987; Long, 1958). Given this, it appeared quite reasonable for Conant and others to surmise that the majority of American youth would not require education beyond the secondary level. For these students, vocational or commercial training would be considered most appropriate. Only a minority of the "brightest" youth were thought to need preparation for postsecondary education, perhaps 20% at the most (Conant, 1959, 1961).

The basic occupational structure of the American labor force changed slowly through the 1960s, with a gradual shift away from employment in manufacturing and toward greater numbers of workers in the "service sector." In 1970 more than a quarter of the nation's workers were employed in manufacturing, and the number of positions requiring higher education had changed relatively little. But the years that followed witnessed a dramatic transformation that continues to unfold today. Beginning in the 1970s, and accelerating in the decades afterward, the number of manufacturing jobs began to plummet (Levy, 1987). Nationwide, the proportion of the labor force employed in manufacturing fell from about a quarter to 18% between 1970 and 1990, and it continued to drop thereafter (Murphy & Welch, 1993). The impact of this was evident first in the cities, as noted earlier, but eventually it affected all areas of the country. Economists speculate that it was due both to technological change and to the movement of jobs to other countries (Abramovitz & David, 1996). Whatever the causes, it was a set of changes that came to have important implications for schools. The number of jobs for which relatively little formal education was necessary had started to sharply contract (Grubb, 1995).

Jobs in manufacturing were replaced by positions in offices, and by growth in management and technical and professional employment. This was slow to develop, but beginning in the 1980s a shift toward jobs requiring progressively higher levels of education had become evident (Cohn & Hughes, 1994; Murphy & Welch, 1989). This was reflected in wage rates for workers with different levels of education. At the start of the 1970s the hourly earnings for employees with less than a high school education and those for college graduates were about $7 apart, and high school graduates earned only about $1.50 more per hour than nongraduates. Because of the large cohort of college graduates produced in the 1960s and 1970s, the advantage of college actually shrank appreciably in the 1970s, and in 1979 only about $6 separated the hourly wages of high school dropouts and college graduates. But soon afterward the gap began to widen, and by the mid-1990s college graduates earned nearly $10 more per hour than high school noncompleters, and $7 per hour more than high school graduates (Datazone, 1999). In other words, the labor market began to pay even bigger returns to students who went to college.

This appears to have occurred because of two trends. First, dollar returns to college education increased slightly across the 1980s and 1990s, roughly 7%. At the same time, however, the wages of high school dropouts fell by more than a quarter, and those of high school graduates declined by about 8%. The impact on high school dropouts was particularly dramatic (Stern et al., 1989). Thus, by the 1990s, the earnings premium for attending college was greater than at any time in the postwar period. This, not surprisingly, helped to spur a corresponding jump in college enrollments.

Beginning in the mid-1980s, ever-larger numbers of American high school graduates entered college. In the late 1970s less than half of high school seniors continued on to college; by the late 1990s the figure approached 70% (Murphy & Welch, 1993). These figures reflect, of course, careful decisions on the part of students, given the decline of employment opportunities for workers lacking higher education and given the growing wage differentials. By 1990 it was calculated that a college degree, on average, was worth half a million dollars more than a high school diploma in lifetime earnings. Figures such as these helped to make the idea of attending college attractive to a much broader range of American youth than had been the case just two decades earlier (Hunt, 1995).

A dramatic rise in female labor force participation in the 1970s and 1980s also contributed to this general trend. Among the most rapidly growing areas of female employment were the professions, and other jobs requiring some measure of higher education. This was partly the consequence of the women's movement of the 1960s and 1970s, an offshoot of the civil rights movement that itself became a major force in American life. It also reflected the self-conscious effort of young women to challenge the existing sexual division of labor. These tendencies may have been augmented by the sex-equity reforms achieved in the 1970s and 1980s under the auspices of Title IX, discussed earlier. As a result of these changes in outlook, female enrollments in college also climbed sharply, particularly in the 1980s and 1990s. This was the case despite a lower responsiveness in female enrollments to wage dividends for college (Averett & Burton, 1996; Geiger, 1993). By the final decade of the century, women substantially outnumbered men among undergraduates for the first time in American history. This development contributed to the rapid rise in high school graduates continuing on to college in the 1990s; indeed, the rate of college entry among women was about 10% greater than among men.

Across the country, educational expectations were rising in the late 20th century. In an analysis of White high school graduates in 1960 and 1980, Marlis Buchmann found that students' expectations of the highest degree they would earn changed significantly between these two cohorts. Altogether, the number expecting to simply end their education at high school fell from more than a quarter to just 18%, almost a 30% drop. At the same time, those expecting to earn graduate or advanced professional degrees increased from about 12 to over 21% (Buchman, 1989). More youth at the latter date planned to graduate from college than to simply end their education at high school. These trends would only accelerate in the years to follow.

Such changes in students' educational plans can be interpreted as a rational response to the changing job market. As Buchmann and other observers noted, the earning power of high school diplomas faded in the 1980s, at the same time that returns to college education began to increase significantly. This was partly due to shifts in the occupational structure, especially the decline in manufacturing employment. But it was also due to the growing preference of employers to hire workers—especially beginning employees—with higher levels of education (Carnevale & Desrochers, 1997). In a thoughtful analysis of federal statistics, Kevin Murphy and Finis Welch have pointed out that employment of workers with college education increased in all industrial sectors in the 1980s, contributing to a broad rising demand for higher levels of educational attainment. These changes helped to fuel a continuing expansion of higher education through the late 1980s and early 1990s, despite a drop in the number of high school graduates as the baby boomers aged (Murphy & Welch, 1993). By the middle of the 1990s, consequently, a large majority of high school graduates across the country were continuing on to some form or another of higher education.

The changing economy also helped to underscore the importance of educational differences between inner-city and suburban communities. Although the latter kept pace with the new expectations of the economy, the former fell farther behind (Harrison, 1972; Sexton & Nickel, 1992). For inner-city neighborhoods, and the students who live in them, the prospect of vocational education providing a means of economic development had faded. This was evident as early as the late 1970s, and was reported by Earnest Boyer in 1983 (Boyer, 1983). In the 1980s and 1990s it was reflected somewhat in the improved rates of college enrollment for African Americans, but postsecondary participation rates for Hispanic students has lagged behind the advance of other groups in the past two decades. As the new service economy has continued to develop, these patterns of educational differentiation posed a significant problem. It has been linked to a widening income gap separating workers with higher-education credentials from those who lack them (Bishop, 1989; Katz, 2000).

All of these changes reflect the impact of the human capital revolution. The emphasis in the closing decades of the 20th century, as never before in recent history, was on academic skills. This was evident in the behavior of employers (Sexton & Nickel, 1992; Stern et al., 1989; Wilson, 1995) The growing educational mismatch between the expectations of downtown employers and the preparation of city high school students was a major impetus behind urban school reform campaigns of the 1980s and 1990s. In Chicago it led to Mayor Richard M. Daley assuming control of the public schools and instituting a series of changes aimed at restoring public confidence in the system, chiefly by focusing on test scores (Shipps, 1998; Wong

& Moulton, 1998). Leaders in other cities have undertaken similar interventions, even though it is not clear that long-term gains in academic achievement will result from such a reform strategy. The fates of hundreds of thousands of poor and minority central-city youths hang in the balance. In the meantime, urban children often lack the social and cultural capital to compete for higher education opportunities. Families living in poverty are concentrated in the larger cities, as are single-parent households and children from minority ethnic and racial groups. These are all factors associated with lower levels of academic achievement, and city schools may well require additional resources to help their students to succeed scholastically (Alexander, Entwisle, & Olson, 1997; Rury, 1993).

James Conant and other proponents of the comprehensive high school believed that the allocation of students to various types of curricula would correspond to the demand for various skills in the labor market. The historical development of the economy and corresponding changes in high school enrollments have proven this view to be correct in certain respects. The picture that has emerged in the last 15 years of the century, however, is quite different from the one educators envisioned in the late 1950s. The changing occupational structure, with the resulting demand for stronger educational credentials, shifted the ways that students make their educational plans. Today, more than ever, the emphasis is on getting into college and on using one's education to find a secure niche in the rapidly evolving world of employment. Academic skills carry a premium, and educators at all levels of the school system are struggling with the challenge of improving achievement. As the nation's interest in schooling has grown, the stakes of success and failure in the schools have gone way up. For better or worse, the development of the economy is driving the educational system in new directions. Finding ways to address the social and economic needs of the 21st century will constitute the next major challenge for American education.

EDUCATION AND SOCIAL CHANGE IN THE POSTWAR ERA

There can be little question that American society has changed profoundly since the 1940s and 1950s. As seen earlier, shifts in ideology, government policies, the social and demographic organization of cities, and in the economy all have contributed to the ways that Americans live their daily lives and relate to one another. In the course of these changes, education has become an increasingly important aspect of the national culture. Today, as never before, where one goes to school—with what is learned there—carries profound implications for the likelihood of success in the future.

A number of historical developments converged in the decades following the Second World War to shape the relationship of education and social change. First, ideological currents in the immediate postwar period helped to set a new tone for social change in the years to follow. The 1954 *Brown* decision marked a historic shift in American thinking about questions of race and social equity. At the same time, however, racial segregation and the movement of Southern Blacks to Northern cities divided urban and suburban school districts, creating sharp disparities in educational resource allocation and curricular orientation. Although educators dating back to Horace Mann had imagined the school as an instrument of democratic socialization, by the 1970s it had evolved into an agency of racial isolation and alienation. Rather than bringing students from the nation's principal social/ethnic groups together, in many respects the schools helped to highlight their differences in a new era of social and cultural segregation.

At the same time, however, schools became instruments of federal social policy, intended to help alleviate the very problems they had come to reflect. Education grew to be thought of as a form of compensation for social and cultural inequities, and a way of helping individuals to pull themselves into the mainstream of society. Schools also have been considered sources of economic development, and in this respect they have become a vital aspect of national policy. Expenditures on education have increased steadily as a result. In addition to this, the interest of federal and state governments in schooling has escalated in recent decades. The age when education was purely a local concern has long passed. Now education is considered a tool to promote certain types of social change. Whether it has been successful in that regard, on the other hand, is an open question.

Meanwhile, there have been difficult problems linked to the schools, just because they have become such a prevalent feature of modern life. One is the development of a pervasive youth culture, often working at cross-purposes to the institutions that play host to it. Educators' insistence on the importance of large schools in the 1950s and 1960s may have helped to compromise adult authority in the face of the growing influence of the youth culture. The relaxation of rules and changing standards of conduct helped make the schools into centers of an elaborate social world for adolescent youth, diverting energy and enthusiasm away from academic interests. Even if educational leaders were not proponents of many of these reforms in student life, the campaign for larger schools helped to set the stage for other developments in the evolution of a school-based "adolescent society" in the postwar period. As noted in discussing the Woodstock nation, this came to have wide ramifications in postwar America. The impact of this generation of young people on all facets of American history at this time was palpable.

Finally, changes in the economy altered the very premise of a differentiated curriculum for the nation's schools and colleges. Observers like

Conant already had noted the heavily academic orientation of some high schools in the 1960s. In the 1980s this tendency became even more pronounced, as ever larger numbers of high school graduates prepared to enter college of one sort or another. The rationale for vocational secondary education became weaker as the manufacturing sector of the economy stagnated or even disappeared, as it had in many larger cities by the 1980s. By the last decade of the century, schools across the country were attempting to offer stronger academic programs to all students. In the face of significant change in the economy, and the rapidly rising value of academic skills, the academic curriculum was no longer considered suitable for only the most gifted students. The old comprehensive school ideal inherited from the Progressive Era has acquired an increasingly academic demeanor in the face of these changes. This represented a significant shift in the purposes of schooling

But some things have been lost too. At the end of the 20th century few observers bother to discuss the high school as an instrument for bringing students from different backgrounds together. The common school ideal, espoused by Horace Mann, rarely has been invoked in this new age of higher standards and economic predominance. Smaller schools are now being urged to give adults greater authority and diminish the influence of the youth culture, in all of its varied manifestations, and the differentiated curriculum is giving way to a greater interest in academic preparation. These developments have been driven in large part by changes in the economy and public perceptions about the importance of education, especially at the postsecondary level. But concern with children learning about democracy from the schools, acquiring an appreciation for diversity of backgrounds and viewpoints, and the process of democratic decision-making appears to have faded from view. Government subsidies are focused increasingly on boosting achievement, but the other purposes of schools—articulated by Dewey and his many students and colleagues—seem to receive little attention today. And nearly 50 years after the *Brown* decision, as suburbanization has polarized most large urban areas into Black and White enclaves, the federal government has largely abandoned the aggressive pursuit of desegregation. Given this, it appears that the age of the public school as an instrument of social policy may have reached a limit. It might be time for members of the public to begin questioning some of the current directions of American schools, and to ask policymakers about how education can effectively address new patterns of inequity now becoming manifest in different parts of the country.

Epilogue

At the stroke of midnight, January 1, 2000, celebrations around the world marked the beginning of a new millennium. Despite quibbles about the precise timing of this epochal moment—purists argued that it should be observed a year later—there was little disagreement about its significance. As television images reflected a heightened sense of global awareness in the wake of these festivities, feelings of amity and optimism ran especially high. Among the themes touched on in innumerable public discussions about the new millennium was the importance of education. If people were to live in peace and prosperity, and humankind were to move forward, schooling of one sort or another was seen as critical. As never before, education had become an expression of hope for the future.

Historians often are reluctant to write about their own times. Many claim that it is difficult to gain a sense of perspective, to put events in order, and to identify probable lines of influence from one development to another. It is with some trepidation, then, that one undertakes to chronicle the last decade or so in the history of American education. It was a time of great development in all sectors of the nation's school system, a series of events that has led directly to its present set of circumstances. Given that it is still largely under way, finding words to characterize this dynamic period is a difficult and hazardous task. Still, there are certain trends that one can discuss. These major developments provide an outline of the age, and offer a historical frame for comprehending the development of schools today.

At the same time, it is also true that all of the various forces discussed in the preceding six chapters continue to play a role, one way or another, in the development of American education. The weight of history is not carried lightly. National polls show that Americans continue to believe in the principle of free and universal public education, both as an instrument of assimilation and a way of promoting national unity, and as a means of economic advancement, personal and collective. Race, gender, and social class still produce invidious distinctions within the schools, and across the larger society that sustains them. Despite the growing role of the federal government in education, schooling remains a highly localized affair, and differences in the provision and quality of instruction from one place to another, sometimes in close proximity to one another, can be quite dramatic. And finally there is the economy. As seen earlier, education has been linked in various ways to economic activity since the very first schools, but in the past several decades the influence of the labor market has been especially striking. To understand American schools today, one must consider the collective impact of all these elements and decide which of them are most significant at this particular time.

Among the major developments of the 1990s, few events in education have been as important as the so-called *standards movement,* a part of what has become known as *systemic reform* undertaken by state governments at the urging of national political figures. The basic idea behind these developments was that the curricula of the schools ought to be "aligned" with systems of assessment, so that reliable estimates could be made of what children were learning and of how well the schools were performing their instructional mission. Marshall Smith, an education scholar and undersecretary of education in the Clinton administration, is often credited with originating this idea, but by the late 1990s the impact of systemic reform could be felt across the country. By that time, most of the states had identified learning standards in the major subject areas for each grade level. These were goals and objectives that teachers were expected to aim for in classroom practice; in practical terms they often amounted to a state-mandated curricular framework. More importantly, however, the states then followed by instituting standardized tests to assess the effects of these measures. Although the tests varied a great deal in their sophistication and degree of difficulty, the effect was to produce a new atmosphere of accountability and recrimination in public education, wherein schools and teachers were increasingly judged on the basis of their students' performances. With these developments, public concern with education, already historically significant, began to reach even higher levels (Smith & Scoll, 1995; Vinovskis, 1996).

In some cases the emphasis on testing was taken to new extremes. In Chicago, for instance, Mayor Richard M. Daley announced in the late 1990s that public school children in certain grades would be required to achieve a predetermined score on the Iowa Test of Basic Skills (ITBS), a nationally normed achievement test, before they could proceed to the next grade level. Among the children tested each year were eighth graders, so that a passing score was needed for promotion into high school. As one might imagine, this placed enormous pressure on teachers and students to succeed, but progress was slow and uneven. One problem was that the ITBS was not designed to assess how much children had learned from a particular curriculum. Instead, it compared their overall achievement against that of a national sample of students in the same grade. This meant that the children in Chicago's public schools, with the vast majority from poor, minority households, were being asked to perform at the same levels in reading and math as students from affluent and traditionally mainstream backgrounds. Not surprisingly, children from more prosperous neighborhoods in the city tended to perform better on these exams than students from poverty households. Historically, differences in social and cultural capital appear to have accounted for great disparities in the school performance of children from different backgrounds, and this has continued to be true into the 21st century. On top of this, the public schools in Chicago suffered by comparison to those elsewhere. They had greater numbers of students from poor or otherwise disadvantaged backgrounds, many Chicago teachers taught without full credentials, and class sizes were large. Consequently, the challenge of raising scores on this sort of test was enormous. Only through massive investment in extra instructional time, summer school, and special sessions were advances made possible. Still, thousands of school children suffered through mind-numbing test preparation exercises that probably contributed little to their overall education. For those who did not succeed, some of them good students who simply did not test well, there was the humiliation of failing a grade and falling behind one's peers. It was a policy that engendered considerable controversy but it also has received a great deal of public support (Bryk et al., 1998).

Assessment policies like those employed in Chicago became known as *high-stakes testing,* and became an increasingly popular feature of American schooling as the 20th century drew to a close. President Bill Clinton touted Chicago as a model for the nation to follow in combating "social promotion," and his successor in the White House, George W. Bush, campaigned on an education platform that focused on increasing the amount of testing required of American school children. Unlike his father, the younger Bush appears to have made education a high priority in his administration, and he has proposed significant increases in federal spending on schools. But he also contributed to a growing national obsession with standardized testing to measure the results of schooling. Just where these tendencies will take the nation's schools is hard to predict (Rury, 1999a).

In many respects it is possible to see the rush to institute new regimes of standard assessments in American education as a corollary of the human capital revolution, and a correspondingly narrow way of viewing the function of schools. The point of systemic reform, after all, was to make schooling more productive in terms of specific curricula, and most of the attention of the testers was focused on mathematics, science, and reading. These, of course, were the subject areas most frequently linked to the new service and professional sectors of the economy and to the higher demand for advanced educational credentials. Standardized tests simply were a form of technology well suited to the task of identifying individuals who had developed these abilities, and schools that successfully imparted them. Making schools accountable for producing more such skilled individuals was thus a strategy for strengthening the national capacity for economic growth and at the same time improving the productivity and earning power of individual Americans. In other words, education is seen as just another factor of production, subject to measurement and improvement like sources of energy, new machinery, raw material, and waste management.

Ultimately, historians may look back at this era in the history of education as testimony to the power of the human capital revolution as it approached its logical apogee. If education is to be viewed primarily as an economic resource, after all, it makes perfect sense to use tests to ensure that schools turn out uniformly and optimally acceptable products. There also are international manifestations of this way of viewing schools, as evidenced by the high level of public interest in the Third International Mathematics and Science Study (TMSS), a comparison of performance on a single standardized test given to samples of students in more than 30 countries. The relatively poor performance of Americans in this assessment exercise became a point of national concern, and no doubt fueled interest in intensified testing policies in the United States. But the ideology of the human capital revolution, framing schools in narrowly economic terms, probably would have produced the same result, even if perhaps a little less expeditiously. For the moment, the other purposes of schools appear to have been made subsidiary to their economic function, at least as regards national policy. Just when and how this era will eventually change, of course, is beyond the ken of a historian.

But what about the question of education and social change? How are these two facets of modern life related, and how has their interaction shifted throughout history? This, of course, is the question posed at the beginning of this book. Given the many historical events discussed in the preceding chapters, perhaps it is now possible to offer some answers.

As suggested in the book's opening chapter, the interrelationship of education and social change is quite complex. Clearly, the schools and educational practices observed throughout history have been shaped by larger social forces, just as have other social institutions and practices. Many of the major processes of social transformation discussed earlier were economic: the search for labor in the New World, the rise of the factory system, the onset of full-scale industrialization, and the human capital revolution. Each of these events bore significant implications for education, and led to changes in the schools. The factory system provided models for creating more orderly and uniform schools; industrialization helped inspire the social efficiency movement, the celebration of differentiation, and the rise of testing during the Progressive Era. The human capital revolution has focused attention on the economic value of education and on the role of schooling in national development. In each of these instances, the institution of schooling responded to social change dictated by the process of economic expansion and development. Given this historical record, there can be little doubt that the shifting economy has exerted a powerful influence over the schools.

But social change is not simply economic. As suggested in chapter 1, ideology has been an important component of the shifting relations between major social and political groups in American history, and this too has affected the schools. Ideology has been informed by underlying economic relationships, but it also has been shaped by religion, the development of science, and a host of other influences. Racist and sexist ideology has operated historically to limit the educational opportunities available to African Americans and women. Other minority groups suffered similar patterns of discrimination in the schools as a consequence of beliefs that held all non-White or non-Protestant students to be inferior in motivation or ability. As noted in chapter 6, these attitudes were slow to change, despite breakthroughs such as the 1954 *Brown* decision and the rise of the civil rights movement. In certain respects, women have achieved greater progress in the continuing struggle against the ideological forces of restriction and exclusion, but sexism continues to exert a powerful influence in the schools today. In these respects, and perhaps in countless others, it is possible to say that ideology has been a major element of social change that has served to shape the course of American education throughout history.

At the same time, families have changed. As observed in earlier discussions of childhood experiences, at different points in American history, patterns of socialization—rearing the young—and relationships between family members have evolved significantly. Families became smaller over the course of American history, demographic episodes like the baby boom notwithstanding, and this has contributed toward greater intimacy and affection in household relations. It also has meant that parents have even greater resources to devote to the education of their children, and this has played a role in the growth of schooling, especially postsecondary enrollment in the postwar period. In this regard, the baby boomers and the generations that followed them have been among the most privileged children in history. On the other hand, the number of single-parent households also has increased dramatically, especially in the nation's larger cities during the past several decades. These families typically have fewer resources, both psychological and financial, to contribute to their children's education. Students from poor single-parent households pose a great challenge to the schools today.

Finally, there is yet another element of social change, one that can perhaps best be described simply as community. As noted in chapter 3, it was the cohesiveness of early rural settlements that accounted for much of the success of the 19th-century common schools. Families knew one another, and a sense of shared values and goals in life served to reinforce the role of the school in imparting academic skills, social norms, and culturally sanctioned knowledge. This process reflected the influence of social capital, the stock of relationships and resources that children in these settings could draw upon to succeed in acquiring relevant values, skills, and knowledge. As noted earlier, the level of social capital in these settings probably was quite high. And then came urbanization. This too was a corollary of economic growth, but it exerted a particular type of influence on social relations and the schools. The rapid growth of cities in the 19th and early 20th century altered familiar patterns of social interaction among Americans. With people continually on the move, it became more difficult to know and trust one's neighbors, and shared values were not always evident. As a result, the stock of social capital available to children in such circumstances was diminished. They had fewer relationships and social resources to draw on as they struggled with the demands of school and learning enough to meet the demands of the future. Schools and other institutions struggled to help fill this void, providing a growing range of services and resources to help students succeed, and to create a sense of community in the midst of seemingly constant urban change. With the development of massive, complicated metropolitan regions in the latter part of the 20th century, however, the challenges of creating a sense of community that spanned the divisions of race, ethnicity, and social class became even greater. The scale and complexity of modern life had made it increasingly difficult to establish the sense of shared values and goals that had once held communities together. Education, as a consequence, became a source of public concern, and schools found the task of imparting essential skills and knowledge a formidable one. Today the challenge of establishing a sense of community to support the nation's schools continues to be an important problem facing American democracy.

Social change, then, has clearly influenced the schools. Society has become more complicated, and as a result the demands that it has placed on the educational system have grown. But what about the reverse question? How have the schools affected society? Here too there are definite patterns that history reveals to the attentive observer. Education has clearly influenced the direction of social change, in both dramatic and rather subtle ways.

It has become a central tenet of American civilization that schooling is a vehicle of social betterment. In the past, education was considered a way of improving the moral condition of the common folk and contributing to the greater stability of the social order. This was seen in the case of the New York Manumission Society in chapter 2, and their compatriots in the New York Public School Society in chapters 3 and 4. It also was depicted as a means of self-improvement for individuals, and as an instrument of social mobility for the talented and industrious members of society who are dissatisfied with their lot in life. As noted earlier, schooling became a powerful instrument of social mobility for the offspring of European immigrants to the United States, albeit in varying degrees. Education thus contributed to social change by simply making society better and by providing alternative pathways to success for those individuals and groups who were able to utilize it toward such purposes. However incremental, this too was a part of social change.

Perhaps more significant was the role of education in providing groups and individuals a means of challenging dominant forms of ideology and the social norms and practices that accompanied them. This was explored in chapter 4, which contrasted the experiences of women and African Americans in the latter part of the 19th century. Following the Civil War, Blacks eagerly embraced schooling as a way to escape the degradation and ignorance of slavery, only to see their hopes frustrated by the resurrection of white supremacy following Reconstruction. Dramatic advances in literacy among African Americans were made, despite the meager support that Southern states extended to Black schools. By and large, however, schooling was not a means to social advancement for the nation's Black population in this era, despite the success of a few individuals such as W. E. B. DuBois. For White women, on the other hand, schooling was a potent—if delimited—instrument of social improvement. Young women flocked to the newly established public high schools in the decades following the Civil War, soon outnumbering the young men by as much as two to one. Relatively high levels of formal education helped women to move into such new occupations as clerical employment and social work, along with the expanding fields of nursing and teaching. Female labor-force participation grew significantly, partly because of the growing numbers of educated women entering offices, classrooms, and hospitals across the country. Old barriers erected in the name of sexism were falling, and even if new ones were being erected, it was clear that American women would continue to march forward in the quest for yet new opportunities in the future.

The lessons to be drawn from these historical experiences are manifold. On the one hand they demonstrate both the power and limitations of education as a means of ameliorating the effects of ideology. One might say that the schools were strong enough to overcome certain aspects of sexist ideology, but not so powerful that they could fully resist the forces of racism in the 19th century. It was not until the following century that the educational system became a means of confronting and defeating racism, as demonstrated in the NAACP campaign to end segregated and unequal schooling. Then the results were quite dramatic, even though it eventually took decades for meaningful changes to occur in many school systems. And in most of metropolitan America today the quest for desegregated and equal education remains a source of frustration for activists still seeking social justice and equity. Even when the schools have successfully challenged the dominant ideology, the process of change is often slow and halting, and new barriers often appear to have been erected just beyond the point where old obstacles had been cleared away. Still, recent advances in Black education have been significant, and the development of a sizable Black middle class of university-trained professionals is an important historical achievement. It is a step in the right direction and a foundation on which further progress can be made.

The history of the schools working to change society also is marked by well-intended failures and unplanned cases of success. The many progressive experiments at using the schools to help build community and to impart stronger social values do not appear to have exerted much lasting effect. One by one, the major centers of these reforms—Gary was among the most prominent—reverted to traditional models of school organization and instructional practice. Dewey's call to make the school into an agency of democratic values and practices, it appears, had relatively little effect on the larger social order. This certainly does not mean that his ideas were wrong, just that the power of schools as social institutions to affect such changes is limited. On the other hand, the very existence of high schools and colleges in the decades following World War II, coupled with rapidly rising enrollments in these institutions, helped to foster the rise of a pervasive youth culture in the United States, an event that continues to shape the nation's culture in ways that could hardly have been foreseen some 50 years ago. This was an unintended consequence of the growth of modern school systems, but it nonetheless came to exert a powerful influence on the nation's social and cultural development. As places where large numbers of children, adolescents, and young adults meet together on a daily basis—a vast portion of the nation's population—schools have become incubators of unplanned social change. It is difficult to predict just what new influences will emerge from this aspect of the nation's educational system in the future.

Then there is the human capital revolution. Simply put, education has become a major source of economic productivity in the 20th century, particularly during the years following the Second World War. Economic historians have found that a high school education added significantly to the earnings of both men and women early in the 20th century, and more recently economists have determined that the relative income of college graduates is at an all-time high. This certainly was good for the individuals possessing these educational credentials, but it also meant that the U.S. economy could enjoy the benefits of their enhanced skills and productivity as well. Enrollments in American schools surged upward across the 20th century, first in the high schools and after the Second World War in the nation's colleges and universities. This represented an enormous investment in resources, but it helped to fuel a postwar period of general economic prosperity that has continued to the present. At the same time, education came to be seen as a means of ameliorating social and economic inequality. As a matter of social policy, education and training programs have been designed to combat poverty and unemployment. Government assistance programs have been devised to address inequities in educational funding, and the growing share of federal and state involvement in the nation's school system has focused on creating greater equality of opportunity. Education has thus become both a source of economic development and an instrument of social policy. This is a dramatic change from the start of the century, and perhaps a suggestion of its future importance as an agent of societal transformation.

Over the course of American history, it is clearly evident that society has changed the schools, at the same time that the schools have exerted a telling influence on the shape of social change. The major social forces that have affected the schools—industrialization, urbanization, ideological change—were deeply rooted in the American historical experience. Most of these forces originated in the 18th or 19th century, and they helped to give shape to the foundational elements of the nation's educational system. It seems to be only more recently, as the schools became an ever larger factor in American life, that they have started to exert a telling influence themselves. Enrolling the vast majority of American youth from ages 5 until 18 and beyond, today they embrace more than 80 million people. This alone would seem to represent a capacity for social change unparalleled in American history, and already it is possible to see evidence of the power of schooling to influence the direction of social and economic development. If there is a general historical trend, it is that schooling has become an ever-more significant factor in American life, and a potential force in the process of social change. This development alone would seem to cast a bright light on the prospects for education exerting a potent influence on the future course of American history.

References

Abramovitz, M., & David, P. A. (1996). Technological change and the rise of intangible investments: The U.S. economy's growth-path in the twentieth century. In *OECD documents, Employment and growth in the knowledge-based economy* (pp. 35–60). Paris: Organization for Economic Cooperation and Development.

Abrams, P. (1982). *Historical sociology*. Ithaca, NY: Cornell University Press.

Adams, D. W. (1995). *Education for extinction: American Indians and the boarding school experience, 1875–1928*. Lawrence: University Press of Kansas.

Aghion, P., & Williamson, J. G. (1998). *Growth, inequality, and globalization: Theory, history, and policy*. New York: Cambridge University Press.

Alexander, K., Entwisle, D., & Olson, L. S. (1997). *Children, schools, and inequality*. Boulder, CO: Westview Press.

Anderson, A. B., & Pickering, G. W. (1986). *Confronting the color line: The Broken promise of the civil rights movement in Chicago*. Athens: University of Georgia Press.

Anderson, E., & Moss, A. A., Jr. (1999). *Dangerous donations: Northern philanthropy and Southern Black education, 1902–1930*. Columbia: University of Missouri Press.

Anderson, J. D. (1988). *The education of Blacks in the South, 1860–1935*. Chapel Hill: University of North Carolina Press.

Angus, D., & Mirel, J. (1999). *The failed promise of American high school, 1890–1995*. New York: Teachers College Press.

Archdeacon, T. J. (1983). *Becoming American: An ethnic history*. New York: Free Press.

Ashton, T. S. (1948). *The industrial revolution, 1760–1830*. New York: Oxford University Press.

Averett, S. L. & Burton, M. I. (1996). College attendance and the college wage premium: Differences by gender. *Economics of Education Review, 15*(1), 37–49.

Axtell, J. (1974). *The school upon a hill: Education and society in colonial New England*. New Haven, CT: Yale University Press.

Axtell, J. (1985). *The invasion within: The contest of cultures in Colonial North America*. New York: Oxford University Press.

Ayers, E. L. (1992). *The promise of the new South: Life after reconstruction*. New York: Oxford University Press.

Babson, S. (1999). *The unfinished struggle: Turning points in American labor, 1877–present*. Lanham, MD: Rowman & Littlefield.

Bailyn, B. (1960). *Education in the forming of American society: Needs and opportunities for study*. New York: Random House.

Bailyn, B. (1967)/ *The ideological origins of the American Revolution*. Cambridge, MA: Belknap Press of Harvard University Press.

Bannister, R. C. (1979). *Social Darwinism: Science and myth in Anglo-American social thought*. Philadelphia: Temple University Press.

Barker, R. G., & Gump, P. V. (1964). *Big school small school*. Stanford, CA: Stanford University Press.

Barton, J. J. (1975). *Peasants and strangers: Italians, Rumanians, and Slovaks in an American city, 1890–1950*. Cambridge, MA: Harvard University Press.

Beadie, N. (1999). From student markets to credential markets: the creation of the regents examination system in New York state, 1864–1890. *History of Education Quarterly, 39*(1), 1–30.

Becker, G. S. (1964). *Human capital; A theoretical and empirical analysis, with special reference to education*. New York: National Bureau of Economic Research; distributed by Columbia University Press.

Berkhofer, R. F. (1965). *Salvation and the savage; An analysis of Protestant missions and American Indian response, 1787–1862*. Lexington: University of Kentucky Press.

Bernard, R. M., & Vinovskis, M. A. (1977). The female school teacher in ante-bellum Massachusetts. *Journal of Social History, 10*(3), 332–345.

Bettis, P. J. (1996). Urban students, liminality, and the postindustrial context. *Sociology of Education, 69*(2), 105–125.

Binder, F. M. (1974). *The age of the common school: 1830–1865*. New York: Wiley.

Binder, F. M., & Reimers, D. M. (1995). *All the nations under heaven: An ethnic and racial history of New York City*. New York: Columbia University Press.

Bishop, J. (1989). Occupational training in high school: When does it pay off? *Economics of Education Review, 8*(1), 1–15.

Blackwelder, J. K. (1997). *Now hiring: The feminization of work in the United States, 1900–1995*. College Station: Texas A & M University Press.

Blassingame, J. W. (1972). *The slave community: Plantation life in the ante-bellum South*. New York: Oxford University Press.

Bledstein, B. (1976). *The culture of professionalism: The middle class and the development of higher education in America*. New York: Norton.

Blount, J. M. (1998). *Destined to rule the schools: Women and the superintendency, 1873–1995*. Albany: State University of New York Press.

Blumin, S. M. (1976). *The urban threshold: Growth and change in a nineteenth-century American community*. Chicago: University of Chicago Press.

Bond, H. M. (1966). *The education of the Negro in the American social order*. New York: Octagon Books.

Bourdieu, P., & Coleman, J. S. (1991). *Social theory for a changing society*. Boulder, CO: Westview Press.

Bowles, S., & Gintis, H. (1976). *Schooling in capitalist America: Educational reform and the contradictions of economic life*. New York : Basic Books.

Boyer, E. L. (1983). *High school: A report on secondary education in America*. New York: Harper & Row.

Boyer, P. S. (1978). *Urban masses and moral order in America, 1820–1920*. Cambridge, MA: Harvard University Press.

Bracy, G. E. (1998). An optimal size for high schools? Research. *Phi Delta Kappan, 79*(5), 406.

Brint, S., & Karabel, J. (1989). *The diverted dream: Community colleges and the promise of educational opportunity in America, 1900–1985*. New York: Oxford University Press.

Brown, E. E. (1902). *The making of our middle schools: An account of the development of secondary education in the United States*. New York: Longmans, Green.

Brown, J. A. (1992). *The definition of a profession: The authority of metaphor in the history of intelligence testing, 1890–1930*. Princeton, NJ: Princeton University Press.

Brown, R. D. (1989). *Knowledge is power: The diffusion of information in early America, 1700–1865*. New York: Oxford University Press.

Brown, R. D. (1996). *The strength of a people: The idea of an informed citizenry in America, 1650–1870*. Chapel Hill: University of North Carolina Press.

Brownlee, W. E. (1979). *Dynamics of ascent: A history of the American economy*. New York: Knopf.

Bryk, A., Lee, V. E., & Holland, P. B. (1993). *Catholic schools and the common good*. Cambridge, MA: Harvard University Press.

Bryk, A., Sebring, S., Bender, P., Kerbow, D., Rollow, S., & Easton, J. Q. (1998). *Charting Chicago school reform: Democratic localism as a lever for change*. Boulder, CO: Westview Press.

Buchman, M. (1989). *The script of life in modern society: Entry into adulthood in a changing world*. Chicago: University of Chicago Press.

Bullock, H. A. (1967). *A history of Negro education in the South: From 1619 to the present*. Cambridge, MA: Harvard University Press.

Bulmer, M. (1984). *The Chicago School of Sociology: Institutionalization, diversity, and the rise of sociological research*. Chicago: University of Chicago Press.

Burke, C. B. (1982). *American collegiate populations*. New York: New York University Press.

Bushman, R. L. (1967). *From Puritan to Yankee: Character and the social order in Connecticut, 1690–1765*. Cambridge, MA: Harvard University Press.

Butchart, R. E. (1980). *Northern schools, Southern Blacks, and Reconstruction: Freedmen's education, 1862–1875*. Westport, CT: Greenwood Press.

Butler, J. (2000). *Becoming American: The revolution before 1776*. Cambridge, MA: Harvard University Press.

Calam, J. (1971). *Parsons and pedagogues: The S.P.G. adventure in American education*. New York: Columbia University Press.

Callahan, R. (1962). *Education and the cult of efficiency: A study of the social forces that have shaped the administration of the public schools*. Chicago: University of Chicago Press.

Carnevale, A. P., & Desrochers, D. M. (1997). The role of the community college in the new economy: Spotlight on education. *Community College Journal, 67*(5), 26–33.

Carrier, J. G. (1986). *Learning disability: Social class and the construction of inequality in American education*. New York: Greenwood.

Chafe, W. H. (1986). *The unfinished journey: America since World War II*. New York: Oxford University Press.

Chilman, C. S. (1978). *Adolescent sexuality in a changing American society: Social and psychological perspectives*. Washington, DC: Government Printing Office.

Chudacoff, H. P. (1975). *The evolution of American urban society*. Englewood Cliffs, NJ: Prentice Hall.

Clarke, E. H. (1873). *Sex in education: Or, a fair chance for the girls*. Boston: J. R. Osgood and Company.

Clinton, C. (1984). *The other Civil War: American women in the nineteenth century*. New York: Hill & Wang.

Cochran, T. C. (1981). *Frontiers of change: Early industrialism in America*. New York: Oxford University Press.

Cohen, P. C. (1982). *A calculating people: The spread of numeracy in early America*. Chicago: University of Chicago Press.

Cohen, R. D. (1990). *Children of the mill: Schooling and society in Gary, Indiana, 1906–1960.* Bloomington: Indiana University Press.

Cohen, R. D. (1997). The delinquents: Censorship and youth culture in recent U.S. history. *History of Education Quarterly, 37*(3), 251–270.

Cohen, R. D., & Mohl, R. A. (1979). *The paradox of progressive education: The Gary plan and urban schooling.* Port Washington, NY: Kennikat.

Cohn, E., & Hughes, W. W. (1994). A benefit-cost analysis of investment in college education in the United States, 1969–1985. *Economics of Education Review, 13*(2), 109–23.

Coleman, J. (1961). *The adolescent society: The social life of the teenager and its impact on education.* New York: Basic Books.

Coleman, J. (1965). *Adolescents and the schools.* New York: Basic Books.

Coleman, J. S. (1988). Social capital in the creation of human capital. *American Journal of Sociology, 94*(S), 94–121.

Coleman, J. S. (1990). *Foundations of social theory.* Cambridge: MA: Belknap Press of Harvard University.

Coleman, J., Hoffer, T., & Kilgore, S. (1982). *High school achievement: Public, Catholic and private schools compared.* New York: Basic Books.

Coleman, M. C. (1993). *American Indian children at school, 1850–1930.* Jackson: University Press of Mississippi.

Conant, J. B. (1959). *The American high school today: A first report to interested citizens.* New York: McGraw-Hill.

Conant, J. B. (1961). *Slums and suburbs: A commentary on schools in metropolitan areas.* New York: McGraw-Hill.

Cook, R. (1998). *Sweet land of liberty? The African-American struggle for civil rights in the twentieth century.* New York: Longman.

Cowan, R. S. (1997). *A social history of American technology.* New York: Oxford University Press.

Cravens, H. (1993). *Before Head Start: The Iowa Station and America's children.* Chapel Hill: University of North Carolina Press.

Cremin, L. A. (1951). *The American common school: An historic conception.* New York: Bureau of Publications, Teachers College, Columbia University.

Cremin, L. A. (1961). *The transformation of the school: Progressivism in American education, 1876–1957.* New York: Knopf.

Cremin, L. A. (1970). *American education: The colonial experience, 1607–1783.* New York: Harper & Row.

Cremin, L. A. (1980). *American education: The national experience, 1783–1876.* New York: Harper & Row.

Crunden, R. M. (1982). *Ministers of reform: The Progressives' achievement in American civilization, 1889–1920.* New York: Basic Books.

Cuban, L. (1984). *How teachers taught: Constancy and change in American classrooms, 1890–1880.* New York: Longman.

Curry, L. P. (1981). *The free Black in urban America, 1800–1850: The shadow of the dream.* Chicago: University of Chicago Press

Curti, M. E. (1959). *The social ideas of American educators, with new chapter on the last twenty-five years.* Totowa, NJ: Littlefield, Adams.

Dalzell, R. F. (1987). *Enterprising elite: The Boston Associates and the world they made.* Cambridge, MA: Harvard University Press.

Datazone, The. (1999). *Average real hourly wages of all workers by education, 1973–1997.* http://epinet.org/datazone/wagebyed_all.html

Davies, M. W. (1982). *Woman's place is at the typewriter: Office work and office workers, 1870–1930*. Philadelphia: Temple University Press.

Davis, F. (1992). *Fashion, culture and identity*. Chicago: University of Chicago Press.

Dawley, A. (1976). *Class and community: The industrial revolution in Lynn*. Cambridge, MA: Harvard University Press.

Degler, C. N. (1980). *At odds: Women and the family in America from the Revolution to the present*. New York: Oxford University Press.

Demos, J. (1970). *A little commonwealth: Family life in Plymouth Colony*. London: Oxford University Press.

Demos, J. (1986). *Past, present, and personal: The family and the life course in American history*. New York: Oxford University Press.

Dewey, J. (1938). *Experience and education*. New York: Macmillan.

Dewey, J., & Dewey, E. (1915). *Schools of to-morrow*. New York: E. P. Dutton & Co.

DiMaggio, P. (1982). Cultural capital and school success: The impact of status culture participation on the grades of U.S. high school students. *American Sociological Review, 47*(2), 189–201.

Doherty, T. (1988). *Teenagers and teenpics: The juvenilization of American movies in the 1950s*. Boston: Unwin Hyman.

Donato, R. (1997). *The other struggle for equal schools: Mexican Americans during the civil rights era*. Albany: State University of New York Press.

Douglas, A. (1977). *The feminization of American culture*. New York: Knopf.

Drost, W. (1967). *David Snedden and education for efficiency*. Madison: University of Wisconsin Press.

Dublin, T. (1979). *Women at work: The transformation of work and community in Lowell, Massachusetts, 1826–1860*. New York: Columbia University Press.

DuBois, W. E. B. (1935). *Black reconstruction: An essay toward a history of the part which black folk played in the attempt to reconstruct democracy in America, 1860–1880*. New York: Harcourt, Brace and Company.

Dykhuizen, G. (1973). *The life and mind of John Dewey*. Carbondale: Southern Illinois University Press.

Eckert, P. (1989). *Jocks and burnouts: Social categories and identity in the high school*. New York: Teachers College Press.

Eddy, E. D. (1957). *Colleges for our land and time: The land-grant idea in American education*. New York: Harper.

Engelhardt, T. (1995). *The end of victory culture: Cold war America and the disillusioning of a generation*. New York: Basic Books.

Eskew, G. T. (1997). *But for Birmingham: The local and national movements in the civil rights struggle*. Chapel Hill: University of North Carolina Press.

Esman, A. H. (1990). *Adolescence and culture*. New York: Columbia University Press.

Faler, P. G. (1981). *Mechanics and manufacturers in the early industrial revolution: Lynn, Massachusetts, 1800–1860*. Albany: State University of New York Press.

Farley, R. (1997). Racial trends and differences in the United States 30 years after the Civil Rights decade. *Social Science Research, 26*(3), 235–262.

Fass, P. S. (1977). *The damned and the beautiful: American youth in the 1920s*. New York: Oxford University Press.

Finkelstein, B. (1989). *Governing the young: Teacher behavior in popular primary schools in nineteenth-century United States*. New York: Falmer Press.

Fischer, D. H. (1989). *Albion's seed: Four British folkways in America*. New York: Oxford University Press.

Fisher, B. M. (1967). *Industrial education: American ideals and institutions*. Madison: University of Wisconsin Press.

Fishlow, A. (1966a). The American common school revival: Fact or fancy? In H. Rosovsky (Ed.), *Industrialization in Two Systems* (pp. 40–67). New York: Wiley.

Fishlow, A. (1966b). Level of nineteenth century investment in education. *Journal of Economic History, 26*, 418–436.

Fliegelman, J. (1982). *Prodigals and pilgrims: The American revolution against patriarchal authority, 1750–1800*. New York: Cambridge University Press.

Foner, E. (1988). *Reconstruction: America's unfinished revolution, 1863–1877*. New York: Harper & Row.

Foner, E., & Mahoney, O. (1995). *America's reconstruction: People and politics after the Civil War*. New York: HarperCollins.

Fordham, S. (1996). *Blacked out: Dilemmas of race, identity and success at Capitol High*. Chicago: University of Chicago Press.

Fox, K. (1985). *Metropolitan America: Urban life and urban policy in the United States, 1940–1980*. New Brunswick, NJ: Rutgers University Press.

Franklin, B. M. (1994). *From "backwardness" to "at-risk": Childhood learning difficulties and the contradictions of school reform*. Albany: State University of New York.

Franklin, G. A., & Ripley, R. B. (1984). *CETA: Politics and policy, 1973–1982*. Knoxville: University of Tennessee Press.

Franklin, J. H. (1961). *Reconstruction: After the Civil War*. Chicago: University of Chicago Press.

Franklin, V. P. (1979). *The education of Black Philadelphia: The social and educational history of a minority community, 1900–1950*. Philadelphia: University of Pennsylvania Press.

Fredrickson, G. M. (1971). *The Black image in the white mind; The debate on Afro-American character and destiny: 1817–1914*. New York: Harper & Row.

Fuchs, E., & Havighurst, R. (1972). *To live on this earth*. Garden City, NY: Doubleday.

Fuller, W. E. (1982). *The old country school: The story of rural education in the Middle West*. Chicago: University of Chicago Press.

Gabaccia, D. (1994). *From the other side: Women, gender, and immigrant life in the U.S., 1820–1990*. Bloomington: Indiana University Press.

Geiger, R. L. (1986). *To advance knowledge: The growth of American research universities, 1900–1940*. New York: Oxford University Press.

Geiger, R. L. (1993). *Research and relevant knowledge: American research universities since World War II*. New York: Oxford University Press.

Gilbert, J. B. (1986). *A cycle of outrage: America's response to the juvenile delinquent of the 1950s*. New York: Oxford University Press.

Gilmore-Lehne, W. J. (1989). *Reading becomes a necessity of life: Material and cultural life in rural New England, 1780–1835*. Knoxville: University of Tennessee Press.

Ginsberg, R., & Plank, D. N. (Eds.). (1995). *Commissions, reports, reforms, and educational policy*. Westport, CT: Praeger.

Ginzberg, E. (1975). *The manpower connection: Education and work*. Cambridge, MA: Harvard University Press.

Giroux, H. (1996). *Fugitive cultures: Race, violence and youth*. New York: Routledge.

Gitlin, T. (1987). *The sixties: Years of hope, days of rage*. New York: Bantam.

Gleason, P. (1992). *Speaking of diversity: Language and ethnicity in twentieth-century America*. Baltimore, MD: Johns Hopkins University Press.

Goldin, C. (1990). *Understanding the gender gap: An economic history of American women*. New York: Oxford University Press.

Goldin, C. (1998). America's graduation from high school: The evolution and spread of secondary schooling in the twentieth century. *Journal of Economic History, 58*(2), 345–374.

Goldin, C. (2001). The human capital century and American leadership: Virtues of the past. *Journal of Economic History, 61* (June), 263–292.

Goldin, C., & Katz, L. F. (1999a). Human capital and social capital: The rise of secondary schooling in America, 1910–1940. *Journal of Interdisciplinary History, 29*(4), 683–723.

Goldin, C., & Katz, L. F. (1999b). The shaping of higher education: The formative years in the United States, 1890 to 1940. *Journal of Economic Perspectives, 13*(1), 37–62.

Goldin, C., & Katz, L. F. (2000). Education and income in the early twentieth century: Evidence from the prairies. *Journal of Economic History, 60*(3), 782–818.

Goldman, E. E. (1952). *Rendezvous with destiny: A history of modern American reform*. New York, Knopf.

Goldsmith, W. W., & Blakely, E. J. (1992). *Separate societies: Poverty and inequality in U.S. cities*. Philadelphia: Temple University Press.

Goodwyn, L. (1978). *The populist moment: A short history of the agrarian revolt in America*. New York: Oxford University Press.

Gordon, L. D. (1990). *Gender and higher education in the Progressive Era*. New Haven, CT: Yale University Press.

Gould, S. J. (1981). *The mismeasure of man*. New York: Norton.

Graff, H. J. (1995). *Conflicting paths: Growing up in America*. Cambridge, MA: Harvard University Press.

Graham, P. A. (1967). *Progressive education from Arcady to academe: A history of the Progressive Education Association, 1919–1955*. New York: Teachers College Press.

Graham, P. A. (1974). *Community and class in American education, 1865–1918*. New York: Wiley.

Grant, G. (1988). *The world we created at Hamilton High*. Cambridge, MA: Harvard University Press.

Greeley, A. (1982). *Catholic schools and minority students*. New Brunswick, NJ: Transaction Books.

Greene, J. P. (1988). *Pursuits of happiness: The social development of early modern British colonies and the formation of American culture*. Chapel Hill: University of North Carolina Press.

Greene, J. R. (2000). *The presidency of George Bush*. Lawrence: University Press of Kansas.

Greven, P. J. (1977). *The Protestant temperament: Patterns of child-rearing, religious experience, and the self in early America*. New York: Knopf.

Grubb, N. (1995). Postsecondary education and the sub-baccalaureate labor market: Corrections and extensions. *Economics of Education Review, 14*(3), 285–299.

Gruhl, J., & Welch, S. (1990). The impact of the *Bakke* decision on Black and Hispanic enrollment in medical and law schools. *Social Science Quarterly, 71*(3), 458–473.

Gulliford, A. (1991). *America's country schools*, 2nd ed. Washington, DC: Preservation Press.

Halberstam, D. (1998). *The children*. New York: Random House.

Haller, E. J. (1992). High school size and student indiscipline: Another aspect of the school consolidation issue? *Educational Evaluation and Policy Analysis, 14*(2), 145–156.

Hampel, R. L. (1986). *The last little citadel: American high schools since 1940.* Boston: Houghton Mifflin.

Harlan, L. R. (1958). *Separate and unequal.* Chapel Hill: University of North Corolina Press.

Harlan, L. R. (1972). *Booker T. Washington; The making of a Black leader, 1856–1901.* New York: Oxford University Press.

Harlan, L. R. (1983). *Booker T. Washington: The wizard of Tuskegee, 1901–1915.* New York: Oxford University Press.

Harris, B. J. (1978). *Beyond her sphere: Women and the professions in American History.* Westport, CT: Greenwood Press.

Harrison, B. (1972). *Education, training and the urban ghetto.* Baltimore, MD: Johns Hopkins University Press.

Harzig, C. (Ed.). (1997). *Peasant maids—City women: From the European country-side to urban America.* Ithaca, NY: Cornell University Press.

Haubrich, P. (1993). Student life in Milwaukee high schools, 1920–1985. In J. L. Rury & F. A. Cassell (Eds.), *Seeds of crisis: Public schooling in Milwaukee since 1920* (pp. 193–228). Madison: University of Wisconsin Press.

Havighurst, R. (1964). *The public schools of Chicago: A survey for the Board of Education of the City of Chicago.* Chicago: Board of Education of the City of Chicago.

Havighurst, R. (1966). *Education in metropolitan areas.* Boston: Allyn and Bacon.

Hawes, J. M., & Hiner, N. R. (1985). *American childhood: A research guide and handbook.* Westport, CT: Greenwood Press.

Hawkins, H. (1972). *Between Harvard and America: The educational leadership of Charles W. Eliot.* New York: Oxford University Press.

Hawkins, H. (1962). *Booker T. Washington and his critics: Black leadership in crisis.* Lexington, MA: Heath.

Hawkins, M. (1997). *Social Darwinism in European and American thought, 1860–1945: Nature as model and nature as threat.* New York: Cambridge University Press.

Hawley, A. H. (1950). *Human ecology: A theory of community structure.* New York: Ronald Press.

Haynes, J. (1991). *Sleepwalking through history: America in the Reagan years.* New York: Norton.

Hays, S. P. (1964). The politics of reform in municipal government in the Progressive Era. *Pacific Northwest Quarterly, 55*(4), 157–169.

Hays, S. P. (1995). *The response to industrialism, 1885–1914.* Chicago: University of Chicago Press.

Heimert, A. (1966). *Religion and the American mind, from the Great Awakening to the Revolution.* Cambridge, MA: Harvard University Press.

Heineman, K. J. (1993). *Campus wars: The peace movement at American state universities in the Vietnam Era.* New York: New York University Press.

Henretta, J. A. (1973). *The evolution of American society, 1700–1815: An interdisciplinary analysis.* Lexington, MA: Heath.

Henriksen, L. L. (1988). *Anzia Yezierska: A writer's life.* New Brunswick, NJ: Rutgers University Press.

Herbst, J. (1989). *And sadly teach: Teacher education and professionalization in American culture.* Madison: University of Wisconsin Press.

Herbst, J. (1996). *The once and future school: Three hundred and fifty years of American secondary education*. New York: Routledge.

Hershberg, T. (Ed.). (1981). *Philadelphia: Work, space, family, and group experience in the nineteenth century. Essays toward an interdisciplinary history of the city*. New York: Oxford University Press.

Higgs, R. (1971). *The transformation of the American economy, 1865–1914: An essay in interpretation*. New York: John Wiley and Sons.

Higgs, R. (1977). *Competition and coercion: Blacks in the American economy*. New York: Cambridge University Press.

Hiner, N. R. (1979). *Cotton Mather and his children*. In B. Finkelstein (Ed.), *Regulated children/liberated children: Education in psychohistorical perspective* (pp. 24–43). New York: Psychohistory Press.

Hochschild, J. (1985). *The new American dilemma: Liberal democracy and school desegregation*. New Haven, CT: Yale University Press.

Hofstadter, R. (1955a). *Academic freedom in the age of the college*. New York: Columbia University Press.

Hofstadter, R. (1955b). *The age of reform: From Bryan to F. D. R.* New York: Knopf.

Hofstadter, R. (1963). *Anti-intellectualism in American life*. New York: Vintage.

Hofstadter, R. (1971). *America at 1750: A social portrait*. New York, Knopf.

Hogan, D. (1985). *Class and reform: School and society in Chicago, 1880–1930.* Philadelphia: University of Pennsylvania Press

Hogan, D. (1989). The market revolution and disciplinary power: Joseph Lancaster and the psychology of the early classroom system. *History of Education Quarterly, 29*(3), 381–417.

Hogan, D. (1990). Modes of discipline: Affective individualism and pedagogical reform in New England, 1820–1850. *American Journal of Education, 99*(1), 1–56.

Hogan, D. (1992) Examinations, merit, and morals: the market revolution and disciplinary power in philadelphia's public schools, 1838–1868. *Historical Studies in Education, 4*(1), 31–78.

Hogan, D. (1996) "To better our condition": Educational credentialing and "the silent compulsion of economic relations" in the United States, 1830 to the present. *History of Education Quarterly, 36*(3), 243–270.

Horowitz, H. I.. (1987). *Campus life: Undergraduate cultures from the end of the eighteenth century to the present.* New York: Knopf.

Horsman, R. (1981). *Race and manifest destiny: The origins of American racial Anglo-Saxonism*. Cambridge, MA: Harvard University Press.

Hoxie, F. E. (1984). *A final promise: The campaign to assimilate the Indians, 1880–1920*. Lincoln: University of Nebraska Press.

Hummel, R. C., & Nagle, J. M. (1973). *Urban education: Problems and prospects*. New York: Oxford University Press.

Hunt, E. (1995). *Will we be smart enough? A cognitive analysis of the coming workforce*. New York: Russell Sage Foundation.

Ignatiev, N. (1995). *How the Irish became White*. New York: Routledge.

Jackson, K. (1985). *The crabgrass frontier: The suburbanization of the United States*. New York: Oxford University Press.

Jacobson, M. F. (1998). *Whiteness of a different color: European immigrants and the alchemy of race*. Cambridge, MA: Harvard University Press.

Jencks, C. (1998). The Black–White test score gap: An introduction. In C. Jencks and M. Phillips (Eds.), *The Black–White test score gap* (pp. 1–9). Washington, DC: Brookings Institution.

Jonçich, G. M. (1968). *The sane positivist: A biography of Edward L. Thorndike.* Middletown, CT: Wesleyan University Press.

Jones, L. Y. (1980). *Great expectations: America and the baby boom generation.* New York: Coward, McCann & Geoghegan.

Kaestle, C. F. (1973a). *The evolution of an urban school system: New York City, 1750–1850.* Cambridge, MA: Harvard University Press.

Kaestle, C. F. (1973b). *Joseph Lancaster and the monitorial school movement: A documentary history.* New York: Teachers College Press.

Kaestle, C. F. (1983). *Pillars of the republic: Common schools and American society, 1780–1860.* New York: Hill and Wang.

Kaestle, C. F. (2001). Federal aid to education since World War II: Purposes and politics. In J. Jennings (Ed.), *The future of the federal role in elementary and secondary education* (pp. 13–35). Washington, DC: Center on Education Policy.

Kaestle, C. F., & Vinovskis, M. (1980). *Education and social change in nineteenth-century Massachusetts.* New York: Cambridge University Press.

Kalmijn, M., & Kraaykamp, G. (1996). Race, cultural capital, and schooling: An analysis of trends in the United States. *Sociology of Education, 69*(1), 22–34.

Kantor, H. A. (1988). *Learning to earn: School, work, and vocational reform in California, 1880–1930.* Madison: University of Wisconsin Press.

Kantor, H., & Brenzel, B. (1993). Urban education and the "Truly Disadvantaged": The historical roots of the contemporary crisis, 1945–1990. In M. B. Katz (Ed.), *The underclass debate: Views from history* (pp. 366–401). Princeton, NJ: Princeton University Press.

Kantor, H., & Lowe, R. (1995). Class, race, and the emergence of federal education policy: From the New Deal to the Great Society. *Educational Researcher, 24*(3), 4–11.

Karier, C. J. (1972). Liberalism and the quest for orderly change. *History of Education Quarterly 12*(1), 57–80.

Karier, C. J. (1979). The quest for orderly change: Some reflections. *History of Education Quarterly, 19*(2), 159–177.

Kasson, J. F. (1999). *Civilizing the machine: Technology and republican values in America, 1776–1900.* New York: Hill and Wang.

Katz, L. (2000). Technological change, computerization, and the wage structure. In E. Brynjolfsson & B. Kahin (Eds.), *Understanding the digital economy* (pp. 219–243). Cambridge, MA: MIT Press.

Katz, M. B. (1968). *The irony of early school reform: Educational innovation in mid-nineteenth century Massachusetts.* Cambridge, MA: Harvard University Press.

Katz, M. B. (1971). *Class, bureaucracy, and schools: The illusion of educational change in America.* New York: Praeger.

Katzman, M. T. (1971). *The political economy of urban schools.* Cambridge, MA: Harvard University Press.

Katznelson, I., & Weir, M. (1985). *Schooling for all: Class, race, and the decline of the democratic ideal.* New York: Basic Books.

Kenny, K. (2000). *The American Irish: A history.* New York: Longman.

Kerber, L. K. (1980). *Women of the Republic: Intellect and ideology in Revolutionary America.* Chapel Hill: University of North Carolina Press.

Kessler-Harris, A. (1982). *Out to work: A history of wage-earning women in the United States.* New York: Oxford University Press.

Kessner, T. (1977). *The golden door: Italian and Jewish immigrant mobility in New York City, 1880–1915.* New York: Oxford University Press.

Kett, J. (1977). *Rites of passage: A history of youth and adolescence in America*. New York: Harper.

King, R. H. (!996). *Civil rights and the idea of freedom*. Athens: University of Georgia Press.

Kleppner, P. (1984). *Chicago divided: The making of a Black mayor*. DeKalb: Northern Illinois University Press.

Kliebard, H. M. (1986). *The struggle for the American curriculum, 1893–1958*. Boston: Routledge & Kegan Paul.

Kliebard, H. M. (1999). *Schooled to work: Vocationalism and the American curriculum, 1876–1946*. New York: Teachers College Press.

Klinkner, P. A., & Smith, R. M. (1999). *The unsteady march: The rise and decline of racial equality in America*. Chicago: University of Chicago Press.

Kluckhohn, C. (1949). *Mirror for man: The relation of the anthropology to modern life*. New York: McGraw-Hill.

Kluger, R. (1976). *Simple justice: The history of Brown v. Board of Education and Black America's struggle for equality*. New York: Knopf.

Kozol, J. (1991). *Savage inequalities: Children in America's schools*. New York: Crown.

Krug, E. A. (1964). *The shaping of the American high school, 1880–1920*. New York: Harper & Row

Krug, E. A. (1972). *The American high school, 1920–1940*. Madison: University of Wisconsin Press.

Kuper, A. (2000). *Culture: The anthropologists' account*. Cambridge, MA: Harvard University Press.

Labaree, D. F. (1988). *The making of an American high school: The credentials market and the Central High School of Philadelphia, 1838–1939*. New Haven, CT: Yale University Press.

Lagemann, E. C. (1979). *A generation of women: Education in the lives of progressive reformers*. Cambridge, MA: Harvard University Press.

Lagemann, E. C. (Ed.). (1985). *Jane Addams on education*. New York: Teachers College Press.

Lagemann, E. C. (2000). *An elusive science: The troubling history of educational research*. Chicago: University of Chicago Press.

Lamont, M., & Lareau, A. (1988). Cultural capital: Allusions, gaps and glissandos in recent theoretical developments. *Sociological Theory, 6*, 153–168.

Landes, D. S. (1969). *Unbound Prometheus: Technological change and industrial development*. New York: Cambridge University Press.

Landes, D. S. (1998). *The wealth and poverty of nations: Why some are so rich and some so poor?* New York: W. W. Norton.

Lannie, V. P. (1968). *Public money and parochial education: Bishop Hughes, Governor Seward, and the New York school controversy*. Cleveland: Press of Case Western Reserve University.

Lannie, V. P. (Ed.). (1974). *Henry Barnard, American educator*. New York: Teachers College Press.

Lareau, A., & Horvat, E. M. (1999). Moments of social inclusion and exclusion: Race, class, and cultural capital in family–school relationships. *Sociology of Education, 72*(1), 37–53.

Larkin, J. (1988). *The reshaping of everyday life, 1790–1840*. New York: Harper & Row.

Lasch, C. (1991). *The true and only heaven: Progress and its critics*. New York: Norton.

Laslett, P. (1965). *The world we have lost*. New York: Scribner.

Laurie, B. (1997). *Artisans into workers: labor in nineteenth-century America.* Urbana: University of Illinois Press.

Lee, V., & Smith, J. (1997). High school size: Which works best and for whom? *Educational Evaluation and Policy Analysis, 19*(3), 205–227.

Leloudis, J. L. (1996). *Schooling the New South: Pedagogy, self, and society in North Carolina, 1880–1920.* Chapel Hill: University of North Carolina Press.

Lemann, N. (1991). *The Promised Land: The great Black migration and how it changed America.* New York: Knopf.

Lemann, N. (1999). *The big test: The secret history of the American meritocracy.* New York: Farrar, Straus and Giroux.

Levine, D. O. (1986). *The American college and the culture of aspiration, 1915–1940.* Ithaca, NY: Cornell University Press.

Levine, M., & Trachtman, R. (1988). *American business and the public schools: Case studies of corporate involvement in public education.* New York: Teachers College Press.

Levine, M., & Zipp, J. F. (1993). A city at risk: The changing social and economic context of public schooling in Milwaukee. In J. L. Rury & F. A. Cassell (Eds.), *Seeds of crisis: Public schooling in Milwaukee since 1920* (pp. 42–73). Madison: University of Wisconsin Press.

Levitan, S. A., Johnston, W. B., & Taggart, R. (1975). *Still a dream: The changing status of Blacks since 1960.* Cambridge, MA: Harvard University Press.

Levy, F. (1987). *Dollars and dreams: The changing American income distribution.* New York: Russell Sage Foundation.

Lewis, D. L. (1993). *W. E. B. Du Bois: Biography of a race, 1868–1919.* New York: Holt.

Litwack, L. F. (1961). *North of slavery: The Negro in the free States, 1790–1860.* Chicago: University of Chicago Press.

Lipset, S. M. (1979). *The first new nation: The United States in historical and comparative perspective.* New York: Norton.

Lockridge, K. A. (1974). *Literacy in colonial New England: An enquiry into the social context of literacy in the early modern West.* New York: Norton.

Long, C. D. (1958). *The labor force under changing income and employment.* Princeton, NJ: Princeton University Press.

Lucas, C. J. (1994). *American higher education: A history.* New York: St. Martin's.

Lukas, J. A. (1985). *Common ground: A turbulent decade in the lives of three American families.* New York: Alfred A. Knopf.

Luker, R. E. (1991). *The social gospel in Black and White: American racial reform, 1885–1912.* Chapel Hill: University of North Carolina Press.

Main, J. T. (1965). *The social structure of revolutionary America.* Princeton, NJ: Princeton University Press.

Margo, R. A. (1990). *Race and schooling in the South, 1880–1950: An economic history.* Chicago: University of Chicago Press.

Markowitz, R. J. (1993). *My daughter, the teacher: Jewish teachers in the New York City schools.* New Brunswick, NJ: Rutgers University Press.

Marsden, G. M. (1994). *The soul of the American university: From Protestant establishment to established nonbelief.* New York: Oxford University Press.

Massey, D., & Denton, N. (1993). *American apartheid: Segregation and the making of the underclass.* Cambridge, MA: Harvard University Press.

May, E. R. (1964). *The Progressive Era: 1901–1917.* New York: Time, Inc.

McCluskey, N. G. (1958). *Public schools and moral education: The influence of Horace Mann, William Torrey Harris, and John Dewey.* New York: Columbia University Press.

McLoughlin, W. G. (1985). Evangelical child rearing in the age of Jackson: Francis Wayland's views on when and how to subdue the wilfulness of children. In N. R. Hyner & J. M. Hawes (Eds.), *Growing up in America: Children in historical perspective* (pp. 87–108). Urbana: University of Illinois Press. (Original work published 1975.)

Meier, A. (1963). *Negro thought in America, 1880–1915: Racial ideologies in the age of Booker T. Washington.* Ann Arbor: University of Michigan Press.

Messerli, J. (1972). *Horace Mann: A biography.* New York: Alfred A. Knopf.

Meyer, J. W., Tyack, D., Nagel, J., & Gordon, A. (1979). Public education as nation-building in America: Enrollments and bureaucratization in the American states, 1870–1930. *American Journal of Sociology, 85*(3), 591–613.

Miller, P. (1956). *Errand into the wilderness.* Cambridge, MA: Belknap Press of Harvard University Press.

Miller, P. (1959). *Orthodoxy in Massachusetts, 1630–1650* (with a new preface by the author). Boston: Beacon Press.

Minton, H. L. (1988). *Lewis M. Terman: Pioneer in psychological testing.* New York: New York University Press.

Mintz, S., & Kellogg, S. (1988). *Domestic revolutions: A social history of American family life.* New York: Free Press.

Mirel, J. (1993). *The rise and fall of an urban school system: Detroit, 1907–81.* Ann Arbor: University of Michigan Press.

Modell, J. (1989). *Into one's own: From youth to adulthood in the United States, 1920–1975.* Berkeley: University of California Press.

Mohl, R. A. (1971). *Poverty in New York, 1783–1825.* New York: Oxford University Press.

Mohraz, J. J. (1979). *The separate problem: Case studies of Black education in the North, 1900–1930.* Westport, CT: Greenwood Press.

Monkkonen, E. (1988). *America becomes urban: The development of U.S. cities and towns, 1790–1980.* Berkeley: University of California Press.

Moore, J. R. (1979). *The post-Darwinian controversies: A study of the Protestant struggle to come to terms with Darwin in Great Britain and America, 1870–1900.* Cambridge, England: Cambridge University Press.

Mora, M. T. (1997). Attendance, schooling quality, and the demand for education of Mexican Americans, African Americans, and Non-Hispanic Whites. *Economics of Education Review, 16*(4), 407–418.

Moran, G. F., & Vinovskis, M. (1992). *Religion, family, and the life course: Explorations in the social history of early America.* Ann Arbor: University of Michigan Press.

Morgan, E. S. (1966). *The Puritan family; Religion & domestic relations in seventeenth-century New England.* New York: Harper & Row.

Morgan, E. S (1975). *American slavery, American freedom: The ordeal of colonial Virginia.* New York: Norton.

Morris, R. C. (1981). *Reading, 'riting, and reconstruction: The education of freedmen in the South, 1861–1870.* Chicago: University of Chicago Press.

Moss, A. A., Jr. (1981). *The American Negro Academy: Voice of the talented tenth.* Baton Rouge: Louisiana State University Press.

Murnane, R. J., & Levy, F. (1996). *Teaching the new basic skills: Principles for educating children to thrive in a changing economy.* New York: Free Press.

Murphy, K. M., & Welch, F. (1989). Wage premiums for college graduates: Recent growth and possible explanations. *Educational Researcher, 18*(4), 17–26.

Murphy, K. M., & Welch, F. (1993). Industrial change and the importance of skill. In S. Danziger & P. Gottschalk (Eds.), *Uneven tides: Rising inequality in America* (pp. 101–132). New York: Russell Sage Foundation.

Myrdal, G. (1944). *An American dilemma: The Negro problem and modern democracy*. New York: Harper & Bros.

Nasaw, D. (1979). *Schooled to order: A social history of public schooling in the United States*. New York: Oxford University Press.

Nash, G. B. (2000). *Red, white, and Black: The peoples of early North America*. Upper Saddle River, NJ: Prentice Hall. (Original work published 1974.)

Nash, M. A. (2001). "Cultivating the powers of human beings": Gendered perspectives on curricula and pedagogy in academies of the new republic. *History of Education Quarterly, 41*(2), 239–249.

Nevins, A. (1938). *The gateway to history*. New York: D. C. Heath.

Norton, M. B. (1980). *Liberty's daughters: The Revolutionary experience of American women, 1750–1800*. Boston: Little, Brown.

Olson, R. K. (1972). Tinker and the administrator. *School & Society 100,*(2339), 86–89.

Omi, M., & Winant, H. (1994). *Racial formation in the United States: From the 1960s to the 1980s*. New York: Routledge & Kegan Paul.

Orfield, G. (1978). *Must we bus? Segregated schools and national policy*. Washington, DC: Brookings Institution.

Orfield, G. (1983). *Public school desegregation in the United States, 1968–1980*. Washington, DC: Joint Center for Political Studies.

Orfield, G., Eaton, S., & the Harvard Project on School Desegregation. (1996). *Dismantling desegregation: The quiet reversal of Brown v. Board of Education*. New York: New Press.

Owram, D. (1996). *Born at the right time: A history of the baby-boom generation*. Toronto: University of Toronto Press.

Palen, J. J. (1997). *The urban world*. New York: McGraw-Hill.

Palladino, G. (1996). *Teenagers: An American history*. New York: Basic Books.

Parkerson, D., & Parkerson, J. A. (1998). *The emergence of the common school in the U.S. countryside*. Lewiston, NY: Edwin Mellen.

Patterson, J. T. (1996). *Grand expectations: The United States, 1945–1974*. New York: Oxford University Press.

Perkinson, H. (1968). *The imperfect panacea: American faith in education, 1865–1965*. New York: Random House.

Perlmann, J. (1988). *Ethnic differences: Schooling and social structure among the Irish, Italians, Jews, and Blacks in an American city, 1880–1935*. New York: Cambridge University Press.

Perlmann, J., & Margo, R. (2001). *Women's work? American teachers, 1750–1920*. Chicago: University of Chicago Press.

Peterson, P. E. (1985). *The politics of school reform, 1870–1940*. Chicago: University of Chicago Press.

Polenberg, R. (1980). *One nation divisible: Class, race, and ethnicity in the United States since 1938*. New York: Viking.

Pollard, S. (1965). *The genesis of modern management: A study of the industrial revolution in Great Britain*. Cambridge, MA: Harvard University Press.

Portes, A. (1998). Social capital: Its origins and applications in modern sociology. In J. Hagan & K. S. Cook (Eds.), *Annual review of sociology* (Vol. 24, pp. 1–24). Palo Alto, CA: Annual Reviews.

Powers, J. B. (1992). *The "girl question" in education: Vocational education for young women in the Progressive Era*. New York: Falmer Press.

Pred, A. R. (1966). *The spatial dynamics of U.S. urban-industrial growth, 1800–1914*. Cambridge, MA: MIT Press.

Prucha, F. P. (1976). *American Indian policy in crisis: Christian reformers and the Indian, 1865–1900*. Norman: University of Oklahoma Press.

Rabb, T., & Rotberg, R. (Eds.). (1981). *Industrialization and urbanization: Studies in interdisciplinary history*. Princeton, NJ: Princeton University Press.

Rabb, T., & Rotberg, R. (Eds.). (1982). *The new history, the 1980s and beyond: Studies in interdisciplinary history*. Princeton, NJ: Princeton University Press.

Ravitch, D. (1974). *The great school wars: 1805–1973. A history of the public schools as a battlefield of social change*. New York: Basic Books.

Ravitch, D. (1978). *The revisionists revised: A critique of the radical attack on the schools*. New York: Basic Books.

Ravitch, D. (1983). *The troubled crusade: American education, 1945–1980*. New York: Basic Books.

Ravitch, D. (2000). *Left back: A century of failed school reforms*. New York: Simon & Schuster.

Reese, W J (1986). *Power and the promise of school reform: Grassroots movements during the Progressive Era*. Boston: Routledge & Kegan Paul.

Reese, W. J. (1995). *The origins of the American high school*. New Haven, CT: Yale University Press.

Reese, W. J. (2001). The origins of progressive education. *History of Education Quarterly, 41*(1), 1–24.

Reiss, A. J. (Ed.). (1964). *Louis Wirth on cities and social life: Selected papers*. Chicago: University of Chicago Press

Rendall, J. (1985). *The origins of modern feminism*. London: Macmillan.

Reuben, J. A. (1996). *The making of the modern university: Intellectual transformation and the marginalization of morality*. Chicago: University of Chicago Press.

Rodgers, D. T. (1978). *The work ethic in industrial America, 1850–1920*. Chicago: University of Chicago Press.

Rodgers, D. T. (1998). *Atlantic crossings: Social politics in a progressive age*. Cambridge, MA: Belknap Press of Harvard University Press.

Roof, W. C. (1993). *A generation of seekers: The spiritual journeys of the baby boom generation*. New York: HarperCollins.

Roscigno, V. J., Ainsworth, D., & Race, J. W. (1999). Cultural capital, and educational resources: Persistent inequalities and achievement returns. *Sociology of Education, 72*(3), 158–178.

Rosenberg, R. (1982). *Beyond separate spheres: Intellectual roots of modern feminism*. New Haven, CT: Yale University Press.

Roszak, T. (1969). *The making of a counter culture: reflections on the technocratic society and its youthful opposition*. Garden City, NY: Doubleday.

Roszak, T. (1994). *The cult of information: A neo-Luddite treatise on high tech, artificial intelligence, and the true art of thinking*. Berkeley: University of California Press.

Rotberg, R. I. (Ed.). (2001). *Patterns of social capital: Stability and change in historical perspective*. New York: Cambridge University Press.

Rotella, E. J. (1981). *From home to office: U.S. women at work, 1870–1930*. Ann Arbor, MI: University Microfilms International.

Rothman, S. M. (1978). *Woman's proper place: A history of changing ideals and practices, 1870 to the present*. New York: Basic Books.

Rousmaniere, K. (1997). *City teachers: Teaching and school reform in historical perspective*. New York: Teachers College Press.

Rudolph, F. (1962). *The American college and university, a history*. New York: Knopf.

Rudolph, F. (1965). *Essays on education in the early republic; Benjamin Rush, Noah Webster, Robert Coram, Simeon Doggett, Samuel Harrison Smith, Amable-Louis-Rose de Lafitte du Courteil, Samuel Knox*. Cambridge, MA: Belknap Press of Harvard University Press.

Rudolph, F. (1978). *Curriculum: A history of the American undergraduate course of study since 1636*. San Francisco: Jossey-Bass.

Rumberger, R., & Willms, J. D. (1992). The impact of racial and ethnic segregation on the achievement gap in California high schools. *Educational Evaluation and Policy Analysis, 14*(4), 377–396.

Rury, J. (1983, September). The New York African Free School, 1825–1835: Conflict over community control. 44:3. *PHYLON*, pp. 187–198.

Rury, J. (1985, September). Philanthropy, self help and social control: The New York Manumission Society and free Blacks, 1785–1810. 46:3. *PHYLON*, 231–241.

Rury, J. L. (1988a, Summer). Imagining Gender in educational history: Themes from the lives of colonial women. *Educational Foundations*, pp. 45–60.

Rury, J. (1988b, Spring) The variable school year: Measuring differences in the length of American school terms in 1900. *Journal of Research and Development in Education*, pp. 29–36.

Rury, J. (1989). Who became teachers: The social characteristics of teachers in American history. In D. Warren (Ed.), *American teachers: Histories of a profession at work* (pp. 9–48). Macmillan and AERA.

Rury, J. L. (1991). *Education and women's work: Female schooling and the division of labor in urban America, 1870–1930*. Albany: State University of New York Press.

Rury, J. L. (1993). The changing social context of urban education: A national perspective. In J. L. Rury & Frank A. Cassel (Eds.), *Seeds of crisis: Public schooling in Milwaukee since 1920* (pp. 10–41). Madison: University of Wisconsin Press.

Rury, J. L. (1999a). Historians and policy making. *American Journal of Education, 107*(4), 321–327

Rury, J. (1999b). Race, space and the politics of Chicago's public schools: Benjamin Willis and the tragedy of urban education. *History of Education Quarterly, 39*, 2.

Rury, J., & Harper, G. (1986). The trouble with coeducation: Mann and women at Antioch, 1853–1860. *History of Education Quarterly, 26*(4), 481–502.

Russell, L. B. (1982). *The baby boom generation and the economy*. Washington, DC: Brookings Institution Press.

Russett, C. E. (1976). *Darwin in America: The intellectual response, 1865–1912*. San Francisco: W. H. Freeman.

Rutman, D. B. (Ed.). (1970). *The Great Awakening: Event and exegesis*. New York: Wiley.

Rutman, D. B. (1977). *American Puritanism*. New York: Norton.

Ryan, A. (1995). *John Dewey and the high tide of American liberalism*. New York: Norton.

Sadker, M., & Sadker, D. (1994). *Failing at fairness: How America's schools cheat girls*. New York: C. Scribner's Sons.

Safford, P. L., & Safford, E. J. (1996). *A history of childhood and disability*. New York: Teachers College Press.

Sanders, J. W. (1977). *The education of an urban minority: Catholics in Chicago, 1833–1965.* New York: Oxford University Press.

Schnore, L. F. (1965). *The urban scene: Human ecology and demography.* New York: Free Press.

Schnore, L. F. (Ed.). (1974). *The new urban history: Quantitative explorations by American historians.* Princeton, NJ: Princeton University Press.

Schram, S. F. (1995). *Words of welfare: The poverty of social science and the social science of poverty.* Minneapolis: University of Minnesota Press.

Schultz, S. K. (1973). *The culture factory: Boston public schools, 1789–1860.* New York: Oxford University Press.

Scott, A. F. (1978). What, then, is the American: This new woman? *Journal of American History, 65*(3), 679–703

Scott, A. F. (1979). The ever widening circle: The diffusion of feminist values from the Troy Female Seminary, 1822–1872. *History of Education Quarterly, 19*(1), 3–25.

Sedlak, M., Pullian, D., & Wheeler, C. (1986). *Selling students short: Classroom bargains and academic reform in the American high school.* New York: Teachers College Press.

Selden, S. (1999). *Inheriting shame: The story of eugenics and racism in America.* New York: Teachers College Press.

Sellers, C. (1991). *The market revolution: Jacksonian America, 1815–1846.* New York: Oxford University Press.

Semel, S., & Sadovnick, A. (Eds.). (1999). *"Schools of tomorrow," schools of today: What happened to progressive education.* New York: P. Lang.

Sexton, E., & Nickel, J. F. (1992). The effects of school location on the earnings of Black and White youths. *Economics of Education Review, 11*(1), 11–18.

Sharpless, J. B. (1977). *City growth in the United States, England and Wales, 1820–861: The effects of location, size and economic structure on inter-urban variations in demographic growth.* New York: Arno Press.

Shipps, D. (1998). Corporate influences on Chicago school reform. In C. Stone (Ed.), *Changing urban education* (pp. 161–183). Lawrence: University Press of Kansas.

Silver, H., & Silver, P. (1991). *An educational war on poverty: American and British policy-making, 1960–1980.* New York: Cambridge University Press.

Silverman, K. (1984). *The life and times of Cotton Mather.* New York: Harper & Row.

Sitkoff, H. (1978). *A new deal for Blacks: The emergence of civil rights as a national issue.* New York: Oxford University Press.

Sitkoff, H. (1993). *The struggle for Black equality, 1954–1992.* New York: Hill and Wang.

Sklar, K. K. (1973). *Catharine Beecher: A study in American domesticity.* New Haven, CT: Yale University Press.

Sklar, K. K. (1993). The schooling of girls and changing community values in Massachusetts towns, 1750–1820. *History of Education Quarterly, 33*(4), 511–542.

Sklar, K. K. (1995). *Florence Kelley and the nation's work: The rise of women's political culture, 1830–1900.* New Haven, CT: Yale University Press.

Skocpol, T. (Ed.). (1984). *Vision and method in historical sociology.* New York: Cambridge University Press.

Smith, D. B. (1980). *Inside the great house: Planter life in eighteenth century Chesapeake society.* Ithaca, NY: Cornell University Press.

Smith, D. (1991). *The rise of historical sociology.* Philadelphia: Temple University Press.

Smith, M. S., & Scoll, B. W. (1995). The Clinton human capital agenda. *Teachers College Record, 96*(3), 389–404.

Solomon, B. M. (1985). *In the company of educated women: A history of women and higher education in America*. New Haven, CT: Yale University Press.

Solomon, L. C. (1970). Estimates of the costs of schooling in 1880 and 1890. *Explorations in Economic History. 2nd Ser., 7*(4), 531–581.

Soltow, L., & Steven, E. (1981). *The rise of literacy and the common school in the United States: A socioeconomic analysis to 1870*. Chicago: University of Chicago Press.

Spindler, G. D. (1963). *Education and culture: Anthropological approaches*. New York: Holt, Rinehart and Winston.

Spring, J. H. (1976). *The sorting machine: National educational policy since 1945*. New York: McKay.

Stern, D., et al. (1989). Labor market experience of teenagers with and without high school diplomas. *Economics of Education Review, 8*(3), 233–246.

Stockman, D. A. (1986). *The triumph of politics: Why the Reagan revolution failed*. New York: Harper & Row.

Stolee, M. (1993). The Milwaukee desgregation case. In J. L. Rury & F. A. Cassell (Eds.), *Seeds of crisis: Public schooling in Milwaukee since 1920. Madison: University of Wisconsin Press*.

Stone, C. N. (1998). Introduction. In C. Stone (Ed.), *Changing urban education*. Lawrence: University Press of Kansas.

Stowell, D. O. (1999). *Streets, railroads, and the great strike of 1877*. Chicago: University of Chicago Press.

Szasz, M. (1974). *Education and the American Indian: The road to self-determination, 1928–1973*. Albuquerque: University of New Mexico Press.

Szasz, M. C. (1977). Federal boarding schools and the Indian child: 1920–1960. *South Dakota History, 7*(4), 371–384.

Szasz, M. C. (1988). *Indian education in the American colonies, 1607–1783*. Albuquerque: University of New Mexico Press.

Takaki, R. T. (1979). *Iron cages: Race and culture in 19th-century America*. New York: Oxford University Press.

Tanner, L. N. (1997). *Dewey's laboratory school: Lessons for today*. New York: Teachers College Press.

Taylor, G. R. (1968). *The transportation revolution, 1815–1860*. New York: Harper.

Teaford, J. C. (1990). *Rough road to rennaisance: Urban revitalization in America, 1940–1985*. Baltimore, MD: Johns Hopkins University Press.

Thernstrom, S. (1964). *Poverty and progress: Social mobility in a nineteenth century city*. Cambridge, MA: Harvard University Press.

Thernstrom, S. (1973). *The other Bostonians: Poverty and progress in the American metropolis, 1860–1970*. Cambridge, MA: Harvard University Press.

Trent, J. W., Jr. (1994). *Inventing the feeble mind: A history of mental retardation in the United States*. Berkeley: University of California Press.

Tuchman, B. W. (1978). *A distant mirror: The calamitous 14th century*. New York: Knopf.

Tucker, W. H. (1994). *The science and politics of racial research*. Urbana: University of Illinois Press.

Tyack, D. B. (1967). *George Ticknor and the Boston Brahmins*. Cambridge, MA: Harvard University Press.

Tyack, D. (1974). *The one best system: A history of American urban education*. Cambridge, MA: Harvard University Press.

Tyack, D. B. (1978). The spread of public schooling in Victorian America: In search of a reinterpretation. *History of Education [Great Britain], 7*(3), 173–182.

Tyack, D. B., & Cuban, L. (1995). *Tinkering toward utopia: A century of public school reform.* Cambridge, MA: Harvard University Press.

Tyack, D. B., & Hansot, E. (1982). *Managers of virtue: Public school leadership in America, 1820–1980.* New York: Basic Books.

Tyack, D. B., & Hansot, E. (1990). *Learning together: A history of coeducation in American schools.* New Haven, CT: Yale University Press.

Tyack, D. B., James, T., & Benavot, A. (1987). *Law and the shaping of public education, 1785–1954.* Madison: University of Wisconsin Press.

Tyler, A. F. (1962). *Freedom's ferment: Phases of American social history to 1860.* New York: Harper & Row.

Veysey, L. R. (1965). *The emergence of the American university.* Chicago: University of Chicago Press.

Vinovskis, M. A. (1970). Horace Mann on the economic productivity of education. *New England Quarterly, 43*(4), 550–571.

Vinovskis, M. A. (1972). Trends in Massachusetts education, 1826–1860. *History of Education Quarterly, 12*(4), 501–529.

Vinovskis, M. (Ed.). (1979). *Studies in American historical demography.* New York: Academic Press.

Vinovskis, M. A. (1995). *Education, society, and economic opportunity: A historical perspective on persistent issues.* New Haven, CT: Yale University Press.

Vinovskis, M. A. (1996). An analysis of the concept and uses of systemic educational reform. *American Educational Research Journal, 33*(1), 53–85.

Vinovskis, M. (1999). *History and educational policymaking.* New Haven, CT: Yale University Press.

Vinovskis, M. A., & Bernard, R. M. (1978). Beyond Catharine Beecher: Female education in the antebellum period. *Signs, 3*(4), 856–869.

Vinyard, J. E. M. (1976). *The Irish on the urban frontier: Nineteenth century Detroit, 1850–1880.* New York: Arno Press.

Violas, P. C. (1978). *The training of the urban working class: A history of twentieth-century American education.* Chicago: Rand McNally.

von Waltershausen, A. S. (1999). *The workers' movement in the United States, 1879–1885.* Cambridge: Cambridge University Press.

Ward, D. (1975). *Cities and immigrants; A geography of change in nineteenth-century America.* New York: Oxford University Press.

Warren, D. R. (1974). *To enforce education: A history of the founding years of the United States Office of Education.* Detroit: Wayne State University Press.

Webber, T. L. (1978). *Deep like the Rivers: Education in the slave quarter community, 1831–1865.* New York: Norton.

Weber, M. (1930). *The Protestant ethic and the spirit of capitalism* (T. Parsons, Trans., with foreword by R. H. Tawney). New York: Scribner.

Wells, A. S., & Crain. R. L. (1997). *Stepping over the color line: African American students in White suburban schools.* New Haven, CT: Yale University Press.

Welter, B. (1966). The cult of true womanhood: 1820–1860. *American Quarterly, 18*(2), 151–174.

Welter, R. (1962). *Popular education and democratic thought in America.* New York: Columbia University Press.

Werum, R. (1997). Sectionalism and racial politics: Federal vocational policies and programs in the predesegregation South. *Social Science History, 21*(3), 399–453.

West, E. (1996). *Growing up in twentieth-century America: A history and reference guide.* Westport, CT: Greenwood Press.

Westbrook, R. B. (1991). *John Dewey and American democracy.* Ithaca, NY: Cornell University Press

Westbrook, R. B. (1994). On the private life of a public philosopher: John Dewey in love. *Teachers College Record, 96*(2), 183–197.

Wiebe, R. H. (1967). *The search for order, 1877–1920.* New York: Hill and Wang.

Wilkerson, J. H. (1979). *From Brown to Bakke: The Supreme Court and school integration.* New York: Oxford University Press.

Williamson, J. (1984). *The crucible of race: Black-White relations in the American South since emancipation.* New York: Oxford University Press.

Willis, P. (1977). *Learning to labor.* New York: Routledge.

Wilson, W. J. (1987). *The truly disadvantaged: The inner city, the underclass, and public policy.* Chicago: University of Chicago Press.

Wilson, W. J. (1995). *When work disappears: The world of the new urban poor.* New York: Alfred A. Knopf.

Winzer, M. A. (1993). *The history of special education: From isolation to integration.* Washington, DC: Gallaudet University Press.

Wise, A. E. (1968). *Rich schools, poor schools: The promise of equal educational opportunity.* Chicago: University of Chicago Press.

Wishy, B. W. (1967). *The child and the Republic: The dawn of modern American child nurture.* Philadelphia: University of Pennsylvania Press.

Wolters, R. (1984). *The burden of Brown: Thirty years of school desegregation.* Knoxville: University of Tennessee Press.

Wong, K., & Moulton, M. (1998). Governance Report Cards: Accountability in the Chicago Public School System. *Education and Urban Society, 30*(4), 459–478.

Wood, P. H. (1974). *Black majority; Negroes in colonial South Carolina from 1670 through the Stono Rebellion.* New York: Knopf.

Woodward, C. V. (1974). *The strange career of Jim Crow,* 3rd rev. ed. New York: Oxford University Press.

Woody, T. (1923). *Quaker education in the colony and state of New Jersey.* Philadelphia: University of Pennsylvania.

Woody, T. (1929). *A history of women's education in the United States.* New York: Science Press.

Yezierska, A. (1925). *Bread givers: A struggle between a father of the old world and a daughter of the new.* Garden City, NY: Doubleday, Page.

Zelizer, V. A. (1985). *Pricing the priceless child: The changing social value of children.* New York: Basic Books.

Zhou, M., & Bankston, C. L. III. (1994). Social capital and the adaptation of the second generation: The case of Vietnamese youth in New Orleans. *International Migration Review, 28*(4), 821–845.

Zigler, E., & Muenchow, S. (1992). *Head Start: The Inside story of America's most successful educational experiment.* New York: Basic Books.

Zilversmit, A. (1967). *The first emancipation: The abolition of slavery in the North.* Chicago: University of Chicago Press.

Zilversmit, A. (1993). *Changing schools: Progressive education theory and practice, 1930–1960.* Chicago: University of Chicago Press.

Zirkel, P. A. (1999). The 30th anniversary of "Tinker." *Phi Delta Kappan, 81*(1), 34–40, 58.

Zschoche, S. (1989). Dr. Clarke revisited: Science, true womanhood, and female collegiate education. *History of Education Quarterly, 29*(4), 545–569.

Zunz, O. (1982). *The changing face of inequality: Urbanization, industrial development, and immigrants in Detroit, 1880–1920.* Chicago: University of Chicago Press.

Index